Spaces of Justice

This collection is inspired by the transdisciplinary possibilities posed by the connections between space and justice. Drawing on a variety of theoretical influences that include Henri Lefebvre, Gilles Deleuze and Felix Guattari, Doreen Massey, Gillian Rose, Walter Benjamin, Elias Canetti, Antonio Negri and Yan Thomas, the contributors to this book conduct a series of jurisprudential, aesthetic and political inquiries into 'just' modes of occupying space, and the ways in which space comes under the signs of law and justice. Bringing together leading critical legal scholars with theorists and practitioners from other disciplines within the humanities, *Spaces of Justice* investigates unexplored associations between law and architectural theory, the visual arts, geography and cultural studies. The book contributes to the ongoing destabilisation of the boundaries between law and the broader humanities and will be of considerable interest to scholars and students with an interest in the normative dimensions of law's 'spatial turn'.

Chris Butler and **Edward Mussawir** are lecturers at the Griffith Law School, Australia. Chris researches in the areas of social theory, critical approaches to state power and urban political ecology. His book *Henri Lefebvre: Spatial Politics, Everyday Life and the Right to the City* (2012) is published by Routledge. Edward's research focuses on various themes in jurisprudence including jurisdiction, judgment and the work of Gilles Deleuze. He is the author of *Jurisdiction in Deleuze: The Expression and Representation of Law* (2011).

Space, Materiality and the Normative
Series Editors: Andreas Philippopoulos-Mihalopoulos and Christian Borch

Space, Materiality and the Normative presents new ways of thinking about the connections between space and materiality from a normative perspective. At the interface of law, social theory, politics, architecture, geography and urban studies, the series is concerned with addressing the use, regulation and experience of space and materiality, broadly understood, and in particular with exploring their links and the challenges they raise for law, politics and normativity.

Books in this series:

Spatial Justice: Body, Lawscape, Atmosphere
Andreas Philippopoulos-Mihalopoulos

Urban Commons: Rethinking the City
Christian Borch and Martin Kornberger

Animals, Biopolitics, Law: Lively Legalities
Irus Braverman

A Jurisprudence of Movement: Common Law, Walking, Unsettling Place
Olivia Barr

Spacing Law and Politics: The Constitution and Representation of the Juridical
Leif Dahlberg

Forthcoming:

Placing International Law: Authority, Jurisdiction, Technique
Fleur Johns, Shaun McVeigh, Sundhya Pahuja, Thomas Skouteris and Robert Wai

Spaces of Justice

Peripheries, passages, appropriations

Edited by Chris Butler and
Edward Mussawir

LONDON AND NEW YORK

First published 2017
by Routledge
2 Park Square, Milton Park, Abingdon, Oxon, OX14 4RN

and by Routledge
711 Third Avenue, New York, NY 10017

First issued in paperback 2018

Routledge is an imprint of the Taylor & Francis Group, an informa business

© 2017 Chris Butler and Edward Mussawir

The right of Chris Butler and Edward Mussawir to be identified as editors of this work has been asserted by them in accordance with sections 77 and 78 of the Copyright, Designs and Patents Act 1988.

All rights reserved. No part of this book may be reprinted or reproduced or utilised in any form or by any electronic, mechanical, or other means, now known or hereafter invented, including photocopying and recording, or in any information storage or retrieval system, without permission in writing from the publishers.

Trademark notice: Product or corporate names may be trademarks or registered trademarks, and are used only for identification and explanation without intent to infringe.

British Library Cataloguing in Publication Data
A catalogue record for this book is available from the British Library

Library of Congress Cataloging-in-Publication Data
A catalog record for this book has been requested

ISBN 13: 978-1-138-33346-8 (pbk)
ISBN 13: 978-1-138-95521-9 (hbk)

Typeset in Baskerville by
Servis Filmsetting Ltd, Stockport, Cheshire

 Printed in the United Kingdom by Henry Ling Limited

Contents

Contributors	vii
Acknowledgements	ix
Assembling spaces of justice	1
CHRIS BUTLER AND EDWARD MUSSAWIR	

PART I
Peripheries

1	**Spatial justice in a world of violence**	21
	ANDREAS PHILIPPOPOULOS-MIHALOPOULOS	
2	**Justice 'from room to room': toward a concept of procedural space in Kafka's *The Trial* and the fictional work of Western jurisprudence**	37
	EDWARD MUSSAWIR	
3	**Artists and gentrification: is that warehouse conversion my fault?**	54
	ZANNY BEGG	

PART II
Passages

4	**Mourning place**	73
	OLIVIA BARR	
5	**Walking with the dead: coronial law and spatial justice in the necropolis**	94
	MARC TRABSKY	

vi Contents

PART III
Appropriations

6 **Space, politics, justice**   113
CHRIS BUTLER

7 **Immersing, comprehending and reappropriating:**
Milan, unreformed, in the alternative architectures
of Ugo La Pietra   132
ALEXANDRA BROWN

8 **This agitated veil: a spatial justice of the crowd?**   150
ILLAN RUA WALL

Index   166

Contributors

Olivia Barr is a Senior Lecturer at Melbourne Law School. Olivia writes at the intersections of jurisprudence, geography and history and is currently curious about questions of movement, lawful place, roads of the South and the creation and conduct of the laws of friendship. Her book *A Jurisprudence of Movement: Common Law, Walking, Unsettling Place* (2016) is published by Routledge.

Zanny Begg is a cross-disciplinary artist, writer and curator and a Lecturer in the Faculty of Art and Design at the University of New South Wales. Zanny was the director of Tin Sheds Gallery at the University of Sydney from 2010 to 2014, where she curated *Baadlands: An Atlas of Experimental Cartography* (2013) and *Emergen/City* (2013). Her recent exhibitions include *The List*, Campbeltown Arts Centre (2014), *Things Fall Apart*, Artspace Sydney (2012) and *Emeraldtown, Gary Indiana*, Artspace, Sydney (2010). Zanny's writing has appeared in *Art and Text, ChtoDelat?, Law Text Culture* and *Overland*.

Alexandra Brown is a Postdoctoral Research Associate in the Faculty of Architecture, Design and Planning at the University of Sydney. She is a registered architect and holds a Ph.D. in architectural history and theory. Her research concerns the history and theory of architecture and radicality, particularly within Italy during the 1960s and 1970s. She has published in *Cultural Studies Review* and *Lucida* and has also written for *Architecture Australia*.

Chris Butler is a Lecturer at the Griffith Law School, Australia. He researches in the areas of social theory, critical approaches to state power and urban political ecology, and he is currently writing on the politics and aesthetics of inhabitance. Chris's work has appeared in *Law Text Culture, Social and Legal Studies* and *Law and Critique*, and his book *Henri Lefebvre: Spatial Politics, Everyday Life and the Right to the City* (2012) is published by Routledge.

Edward Mussawir is a Lecturer at the Griffith Law School, Australia. His work has focused on questions of jurisdiction and jurisprudence, particularly in the philosophy of Gilles Deleuze. Ed is the author of *Jurisdiction in Deleuze: The Expression and Representation of Law* (Routledge, 2011) and co-editor of *Law and the Question of the Animal: A Critical Jurisprudence* (Routledge, 2013). He is currently

viii Contributors

researching the idea of the 'person' in Western law and the work of French jurist Yan Thomas.

Andreas Philippopoulos-Mihalopoulos is Professor of Law and Theory, and Director of the Westminster Law and Theory Lab at the University of Westminster. Andreas has published widely in the fields of critical legal theory, autopoiesis, philosophy, architecture, geography, art and object-oriented ontology. His books include *Absent Environments: Theorising Environmental Law and the City* (Routledge-Cavendish, 2007); *Niklas Luhmann: Law, Justice, Society* (Routledge, 2010) and *Spatial Justice: Body, Lawscape, Atmosphere* (Routledge, 2015).

Marc Trabsky is a Lecturer in the School of Law at La Trobe University, Australia. He researches in the areas of legal theory, history and aesthetics and has written on topics such as law and the dead, coronial law and forensic medicine and the relationship between law and technology. Marc's work has been published in *Griffith Law Review*, *Australian Feminist Law Journal* and the *International Journal of Law in Context*.

Illan rua Wall is an Associate Professor in the School of Law at the University of Warwick. He is on the editorial board of *Law and Critique* and he is an editor of the blog www.criticallegalthinking.com. Illan's current research focuses on the relations between law, disorder and constituent power and his publications include *Human Rights and Constituent Power: Without Model or Warranty* (Routledge, 2011) and *New Critical Legal Thinking: Law and the Political* (with Costas Douzinas and Matthew Stone) (Birkbeck Law Press, 2012).

Acknowledgements

Chris and Ed would like to express our appreciation to Olivia Barr, Zanny Begg, Anne Bottomley, Andreas Philippopoulos-Mihalopoulos, Lee Stickells, Amelia Thorpe, Marc Trabsky and Illan Wall for making the original symposium at Minjerribah (which launched this project) such a fantastic two days of ideas and debate. We are very grateful to Madonna Adcock, Carol Ballard and Julia Barker for their truly top-notch administrative and logistical support in the preparation of that event. We would also like to thank each of the contributors to this collection for their spirit of collaboration and their preparedness to prioritise completion of their chapters in the face of many other competing demands. Thanks are also due to Brad Sherman, who first encouraged us to think about this project, and to the Griffith Law School's Socio-Legal Research Centre for providing the funding that enabled it to happen. Laura Muir, Colin Perrin and Lucy Buchan at Routledge have been extremely patient and good-humoured in their wait for the final manuscript, and without their encouragement, assistance and expertise this book would not have been possible. Many thanks to Linda Starke for retrieving that old negative of Brown Lake circa 1988.

Chris is deeply grateful to Paulette, Sagine and Hayes for all their love and support, and their tolerance of his absent-mindedness and distraction in the months leading up to the submission of this collection. Ed's part would also not have been possible without the boundless encouragement of Marika, Clemmie and Freddie for him to keep working on these 'letters'.

Assembling spaces of justice

Chris Butler and Edward Mussawir

Introducing *Spaces of Justice*

This book has its origins in a symposium we convened in December 2013 which aimed to explore the transdisciplinary possibilities of thinking about the spatial dimensions of justice. Offering a unique set of perspectives on the contours and interstices of law's 'spatial turn', the essays collected here offer a series of ontological, historical, aesthetic, jurisprudential and political inquiries into just modes of inhabitance and the deeper conceptual connections between space, justice and juridical relations.

The *Spaces of Justice* symposium was held on the island of Minjerribah, situated in Moreton Bay off the coast of Brisbane.[1] More commonly referred to by its colonial name of 'Stradbroke Island', this is a place where the contradictions between the injustices of colonisation and the possibilities of justice have been starkly visible, right from the establishment of Moreton Bay as a prison camp in 1824. Today, Minjerribah is most prominent in the local imagination as a secluded residential refuge, providing opportunities for escape, leisure and ludic pleasures. But the island's status as a popular site for beach holidays, fishing excursions and camping glosses over the complexity of its place within the history and geography of southeast Queensland, and largely ignores the continuing ownership of this land by the Nunukul and Gorenpul peoples (Peacock 2001). It would be impossible to adequately introduce this book without first acknowledging something of the history of the continuing struggles for justice over the site where our symposium was held.

The history and present reality of colonisation on Minjerribah provides many examples of how First Peoples' struggles for justice are inextricably bound to both disputes – about land ownership, the distribution of resources, participation in decision-making, and the recognition of cultural identity and practices – and to counter-hegemonic demands which challenge the dominance of institutional processes for settling questions of autonomy and self-management. The colonial

---

1 This event was made possible through the financial support from the Griffith Law School's Socio-Legal Research Centre.

2 Assembling spaces of justice

occupation of the island began in late 1824 with military and convict labour involvement in the sounding of the channel connecting Moreton Bay to the South Pacific Ocean. Throughout the 1820s the scale of this European presence on Minjerribah progressively increased, and while early contact was largely peaceful, by the late 1820s there was a steady rise in conflicts over instances of 'territorial encroachment' and sexual violence (Evans 1992, 29; 2008). This culminated in a series of skirmishes and brutal reprisals in the Moreton Bay penal area throughout 1831 and 1832, which saw the military authorities dispatch troops to summarily punish the Nunukul and the Nughi people (Evans 1992, 30).[2]

As in other parts of Australia throughout the nineteenth century, the people of Minjerribah suffered terrible rates of mortality from the introduction of diseases such as smallpox, consumption, influenza and syphilis (Evans 2008, 20). Communities on the island were also subject to the injustices that followed the progressive dispossession of traditional lands and the implementation of state policies that led to the destruction of traditional family structures and widespread institutionalisation of individuals. Despite these impacts of colonisation, the Nunukul and Gorenpul have maintained a continuous occupation and cultural connection to the land and waters of Minjerribah, which was recognised in 2011 by a Federal Court determination of native title rights and interests (*Delaney v Qld* [2011]). In the years following this determination, several Indigenous Land Use Agreements have been settled and opportunities have increased for traditional owners to become more deeply involved in decision-making about social planning and land-use development on the island.

But of course, a native title determination is never a resolution of First Peoples' struggles for self-determination. In recent years there have been significant disputes over conflicting spatial use values for the lands and waters of Minjerribah. One prominent example has been the successful campaign against the Queensland State Government's attempts to extend sand mining leases and reverse a previous commitment to establish a national park over 80 per cent of the island (North Stradbroke Island Protection and Sustainability Act 2011).[3] The history of these nodes of conflict on Minjerribah reveals both the unfinished character of struggles for justice and the inevitably spatial character of the aspirations which generate them. Reflections on the ways in which space is constituted by these contradictory relations were a central concern of the presentations and discussions that took place at the *Spaces of Justice* symposium. In order to explore a broad range of perspectives on the relationships between space, justice and legality, our aim was to assemble scholars with interests in the fields of law, history, critical social theory, the visual arts and architecture. While this book provides merely a record of the papers that were presented at the symposium, it also aims to reveal the fortunate

---

2 The Nughi people are the traditional owners of Moorgumpin or Moreton Island.

3 During a late-night sitting of the Queensland Parliament on 25 May 2016, the Queensland Government successfully amended legislation to restore the originally agreed timetable for the phasing out of sand mining by 2019.

mix of ideas that came together at that event and, perhaps more indirectly, retains for the reader some traces of the island itself.

A brief history of spatial justice

It would appear to be an uncontroversial assertion that the question of justice haunts the humanities and social sciences. Whether we are discussing definitional concerns, institutional design, implementation mechanisms or the distribution of resources and services, theories of justice seem to be ubiquitous. This is just as true in the spatial disciplines such as human geography and urban planning as in other areas of the humanities and social sciences. Historically, the search for the spatial 'location' of justice within the city itself can be traced back at least as far as Plato's *Republic*, where he presents justice as deriving from social harmony and the proper positioning of the individual within the *polis* (Plato 1987; Mendieta 2001, 82). However, it is not surprising that the significant body of work which has addressed the spatial consequences of justice does not dwell on these classical influences, but is primarily concerned with addressing the inequalities and *injustices* that characterise contemporary urban life. One prominent example of this approach to the concept of 'spatial justice' is the recent research programme which explores the idea of the 'just city' (Fainstein 2010; Marcuse et al. 2009).

Overwhelmingly, this scholarship tends to operate within the paradigm of distributive justice and consequently, in one way or another, much of this literature pivots around the work of John Rawls as the chief proponent of the dominant philosophical approach to justice within contemporary liberal democracies. Rawls famously outlines his theory of justice as promoting the functioning of a 'well-ordered society', by ensuring equality in access to political liberties and allowing inequality only where it provides greatest benefits to the least-advantaged (Rawls 1999). He embeds these principles in a reworked version of the social contract in order to articulate a version of justice which is oriented towards fairness in the distribution of resources. Despite its influence in bolstering the strength of a liberal distributive paradigm in contemporary theories of justice, it is also true that, from the outset, Rawls's idea of justice as fairness has been the subject of extensive criticism. An early emblematic example of these critical responses can be seen in Robert Paul Wolff's Marxist critique of Rawls's failure to interrogate existing institutional arrangements, and his ambivalence towards the role of relations of production, in favour of emphasising patterns of distribution. For Wolff, *A Theory of Justice* is ultimately unable to account for the structural injustices intrinsic to capitalist social relations and effectively operates as a justification for the institutional status quo within liberal democracies (Wolff 1977, 202–207).

Within critical geography, a work which demonstrates both the centrality of Rawls's approach and the urge to hold his work at some distance is David Harvey's *Social Justice and the City* (Harvey 1973). This book set the scene for the wave of Anglophone Marxist geography that followed during the 1970s and 1980s, by rejecting the empiricist orthodoxy of geographical inquiry, and focusing

4 Assembling spaces of justice

instead on the structuring role played by circuits of capital accumulation in processes of urbanisation.[4] The impact of *Social Justice and the City* on the development of an historical-geographical materialist method for urban studies has tended to obscure the book's place as a central reference point for subsequent writing on the concept of spatial justice. In challenging the utility of *A Theory of Justice* for addressing manifestations of urban injustice, Harvey charts the shift in his own intellectual development, from a primarily Rawlsian 'predisposition to regard social justice as a matter of eternal justice and morality to regard it as something contingent upon the social processes operating in society as a whole' (Harvey 1973, 15).

This realisation prompted Harvey to introduce the notion of 'territorial social justice' as a way of acknowledging the geographical dimensions of a 'just' distribution of resources within the city. Framed around the satisfaction of tests of 'need', 'contribution to the common good' and 'merit' in the distribution of resources, Harvey identifies the necessary conditions for the expression of territorial social justice in the design of institutional mechanisms for the distribution of resources, in order that they enhance the prospects of those within the most disadvantaged territory (Harvey 1973, 116–117). In developing this concept, Harvey criticises Rawls's theory of justice, in similar terms to Wolff, for its inability to adequately recognise the role of production in generating unjust forms of distribution. While this is a distinct difference between Harvey and Rawls, in *Social Justice and the City* Harvey never thoroughly develops an alternative, Marxist account of justice and, as a consequence, the formulation of spatial justice that emerges from this book is tightly focused on distribution within a given territory. Similarly, much of the work that followed in its wake remained claustrophobically caught within the parameters of Rawls's social liberalism and a Kantian ethical framework, an approach which Gordon Pirie describes as the pursuit of 'social justice in space' (Pirie 1983, 471).[5]

It wasn't until Harvey returned to these questions in *Justice, Nature and the Geography of Difference* that the intellectual debate over spatial justice began to noticeably shift again (Harvey 1996). In this work, Harvey draws on Iris Marion Young's direct challenge to the Rawlsian distributive paradigm, by arguing for the importance of reckoning with 'two social conditions that define injustice: oppression, the institutional constraint on self-development, and domination, the institutional constraint on self-determination' (Young 1990, 37). Understanding the sources of injustice in these terms allows Young to present justice as an

---

4 Harvey's own intellectual journey from liberalism to Marxism can be best charted through a comparison of the methodology underlying his first book *Explanation in Geography* with the approach adopted in *The Limits to Capital* (Harvey 1969; 1982).

5 See also Smith 1994. For further explorations of the geographical dimensions of social and distributional justice see the essays collected in Merrifield and Swyngedouw 1999 and Marcuse 2009. Unfortunately it is beyond the scope of this introduction to delve fully into the intricacies of arguments over the capacity of Marxist theory to adequately embrace a theory of justice. Some of the most important contributors to these early debates include Buchanan 1982; Douzinas and Warrington 1986; Geras 1985; Hunt 1985; and Lukes 1985.

'enabling' concept, which not only encompasses questions of distribution, but also acknowledges:

> the institutional conditions necessary for the development and exercise of individual capacities and collective communication and cooperation . . . [including] . . . decisionmaking procedures, division of labour, and culture.
>
> (Young 1990, 39)

Taking account of the various 'faces of oppression' and forms of social domination leads Young to make the case for a 'radical democratic pluralism' which is driven by a politics of difference (Young 1990, 168).

Harvey takes some inspiration from Young's approach to justice and identifies the possibility of building a bridge between her account and Marxist geography's concerns with just forms of urban development and emancipatory forms of political struggle. However, he is characteristically wary of embracing particularity and difference at the expense of remaining aware of the continuing importance of universalising tendencies such as capital accumulation and collective struggles in determining the possibilities for social justice in the city (Harvey 1992; 1996, 348–350). A warmer welcome for the sort of pluralistic politics of difference that Young emphasises can be seen in the use of the terminology of spatial justice in the later writings of Edward Soja (2001; 2010; 2014). Indeed, his long-term project to 'reassert the spatiality of social life' through the development of a 'postmodern critical human geography' can be seen, in one sense, as an attempt to escape the narrowness of the orthodox Marxist orientation that is often associated with much of Harvey's work (Soja 1985; 1989). Despite this melding of eclectic influences, Soja does not arrive at an understanding of the relationships between space and justice that moves very far beyond Harvey's position. It is certainly true that Soja's 'search' for spatial justice is genuine, in the sense that he is clearly searching for a language or a conceptual frame through which he can ground a radical politics of difference. But in the end he is primarily offering up a rhetorical gesture more than a substantive formulation of spatial justice.

A more deliberate attempt to conceptualise the relationship between justice and spatiality can be seen in the early work of Mustafa Dikeç, formerly one of Soja's graduate students (Dikeç 2001; 2009). Dikeç recognises that a meaningful account of the notion of spatial justice inevitably requires an alternative to both the abstraction and aspatial assumptions of Rawls's liberal theory of justice and the 'inchoate' pluralism of Young's politics of difference (Dikeç 2001, 1787–1788). The approach he takes to this task is to understand spatial justice as a 'critique of systemic exclusion, domination, and oppression' which can be articulated through the two classic assertions of contemporary urban politics – Henri Lefebvre's concepts of 'right to the city' and the 'right to difference' (Dikeç 2001, 1790–1791). In bringing together these two rights with what Dikeç refers to as the 'spatial dialectics of injustice', he interrogates the theoretical and political bases of spatial justice much more thoroughly than the treatments by Harvey and Soja (Dikeç

6 Assembling spaces of justice

2001, 1794). This provides an important acknowledgement of the relevance of Lefebvre's work to our understanding of spatial justice, but by deferring to Balibar's concept of *égaliberté* as a means of grounding spatial justice in a 'spatially informed emancipatory politics', Dikeç appears to shift his analysis back to a focus on the 'suppression of discrimination and repression', rather than a theorisation of the spatial character of this form of justice (Dikeç 2001, 1799–800).[6]

What is common to each of these approaches from within the disciplines of geography, planning and urban studies is their curious hesitation in exploring what an explicitly *spatial* justice might mean. This conceptual lacuna has been the catalyst for the questioning of the complacency of these accounts of spatial justice and the theoretical inadequacies of their shared conceptual paradigm within recent critical legal scholarship. Attuned to the potentially 'disturbing' implications that flow from law's spatial turn, Andreas Philippopoulos-Mihalopoulos has recently posed a radical challenge to this existing scholarship on spatial justice by insisting that 'there can be no justice which is not spatial' (Philippopoulos-Mihalopoulos 2015, 25, 181; 2010; 2011). Spatial justice must therefore be conceptualised in a way that moves beyond treating space as an 'adjectival context, a background against which considerations of the surrounding space are thrown into relief' (Philippopoulos-Mihalopoulos 2015, 182).

For Philippopoulos-Mihalopoulos, addressing the limitations of the distributive paradigm and pluralist attempts to achieve social unity requires a recognition that law's spatial turn is premised on a space which is 'non-Euclidean, non-measurable, non-directional, non-unitary, non-linear and non-metaphorical' (Philippopoulos-Mihalopoulos 2015, 16). Drawing on the post-human influences of scholarship exploring new materialisms and object-oriented ontologies, he argues that spatial justice can best be understood as

> the conflict between bodies that are moved by a desire to occupy the same space at the same time. This is neither merely distributive justice, nor regional democracy, but an embodied desire that presents itself ontologically.
>
> (Philippopoulos-Mihalopoulos 2015, 3)

Rather than proposing a blueprint or definitive solution to such a conflict, spatial justice is premised here on the withdrawal of a body from the political, legal and normative obligations that are imposed on it through its enclosure within an 'engineered atmosphere' (Philippopoulos-Mihalopoulos 2015; 2016; 2010).

---

6 This piece is Dikeç's most detailed engagement with spatial justice, and while he has considered the topic in more recent writings, the focus of his work has now shifted somewhat to the political and aesthetic dimensions of spatial forms and distributions, which draws on the work of Arendt, Nancy and Rancière (Dikeç 2005; 2015).

From law's spatial turn to spaces of justice

During the last two decades, there have been numerous edited collections and special issues of journals which have been devoted to juridical aspects of specific spatial phenomena such as the city (Philippopoulos-Mihalopoulos 2007) or borders (*Stanford Law Review* 1996), and several books have showcased the cross-disciplinary influences between legal scholars and geographers (Blomley et al. 2001; Holder and Harrison 2003; Braverman et al. 2014b). While there has been an increasing interest in the exploration of other disciplinary contexts, there has been less interest in taking the theoretical implications of the complex spatiality of law and justice seriously.[7] Furthermore, while there has been a steady growth of scholarship which has attempted to invoke the concept of 'spatial justice', there has been a perplexing avoidance of serious consideration of legal questions or juridical institutions (Soja 2010; *City* 2010; *City* 2011). This collection takes its place within this conceptual region as both an inquiry into the meaning of spatial justice, and an exploration of the spaces through which justice might flow. Through inhabiting this intellectual field, the book contributes to the unfolding and expanding of the disciplinary parameters of law's 'spatial turn' and the ongoing destabilisation of the boundaries between law and the broader humanities (Braverman et al. 2014b; Bartel et al. 2013).[8]

The title of this collection, *Spaces of Justice*, indicates something more than just a conjugation of themes and parameters for the relationships between space and justice. In their exploration of the contours of spatial justice, the contributions to this collection can be understood as gesturing away from some of the more familiar concerns associated with law's 'spatial turn' and instead moving towards something particular to what we have called 'spaces of justice'. The term *spaces* here is not the plural of space or the spatial, but rather of '*a space*'. This distinction potentially opens up some important perspectives on the forms which the interdisciplinary interrogation of space and justice has taken. For instance, to the extent that *space* itself is able to constitute a kind of abstract transcendental field that subtends all kinds of planes of political, social, legal and cultural activity, our specific disciplinary engagements with the relation it has to justice can tend to remain beholden, to some degree, to certain universalising trajectories. To address 'spaces of justice' on the other hand offers a more circumspect avenue of inquiry. It opens up the possibility for a space of encounter. It takes us to scenes, settings, locations, situations, dwellings, squares, offices, roads, passages, paths and itineraries that

---

7 The most significant of exceptions to this generalisation include Manderson 2005; FitzGerald and Philippopoulos-Mihalopoulos 2008; Delaney 2010; Philippopoulos-Mihalopoulos 2015.
8 Irus Braverman and her colleagues chart the progression of legal geography through three modes of scholarly endeavour. The first of these is disciplinary work within law or geography that uses a method of 'import and export'. The second mode involves an interdisciplinary combination of the two disciplines in the development of a common project, and the third involves a move beyond the idea of legal geography to 'transdisciplinary or perhaps even postdisciplinary' investigations (Braverman et al. 2014a).

8 Assembling spaces of justice

– being merely *spaces* and not more than that – are able to sit adequately, patiently enough with the limits that justice inherently comes up against in *space* and, at the same time, to attend to the instantiations and localisations that give it a tangible reality. To address these 'spaces of justice' in this way is to acknowledge that justice cannot necessarily be given a pure determination in space *as such*, in a single space, and yet neither is it without 'a space': justice can do no more than oscillate when it is positioned between a single *topos* and an abstract *utopia*.

In his introduction to the 'Legal Spaces' special issue of *Law, Text, Culture*, Desmond Manderson (2005) links the study of 'legal spaces' to a legal pluralism concerned not just with what law means, but with 'where' it means; not just with the order and meaning that law imposes onto space, but with the materiality of how space also shapes and transforms law and its normative effects and presuppositions. He neatly explains the kind of interdisciplinary stakes involved in a project that attempts to take 'law spatially and space legally' (2005, 1). A work on 'spaces of justice' also necessarily has to navigate the answers to this kind of interdisciplinary problem. However, there is also a potential risk encoded in this formulation, which is not readily acknowledged, where the stakes may indeed be raised *too* high. There would be a great deal required on behalf of the scholar to respond to the call to take 'justice spatially and space justly', for example if these concepts were to remain strung together by the narrow philosophical co-ordinates that are usually reserved for them. Caught by the immensity of such a task, the urge for interdisciplinarity may end up causing us to ignore the encounter that particular disciplines have with their 'spaces', whether that be in a political, ethical, technical, aesthetic or any other sense.

Law for example, as one discipline concerned with the problem of justice, never pretends to tackle something as metaphysically universalising as space in itself. It is content, in the most part, to admit whatever evidence of it is necessary to register and determine disputes confined to the circumstance of particular parties and also to further localise such disputes, preventing them from expanding beyond the contrived, invented space to which they have been artificially restricted. Far from just constituting one particular disciplinary lens onto something that can remain for lawyers, philosophers, surveyors, geographers and architects, one and the same space – a space that each discipline in its turn comes to reach toward like some transparent yet contested plane of shared material or social reality – the encounter that a discipline has with justice, it seems, is unravelled only within spaces that remain incommensurable to one another.

The chapters by Illan Wall and Olivia Barr in this book both speak of the spaces of crowds that have a relation to justice irrespective of any 'cause'. The spatio-temporal contours of a crowd are not purely the experience that a crowd makes of the space it occupies, let alone of space in general. It is the invention of 'a space' corresponding to the crowd. In this way, even if justice is not necessarily in any single cause that a crowd might find itself agitating for with a common purpose, one can still find traces of it when it seems the crowd appears without purpose, yet as a singular alternative to the possibility of living without a space.

Conversely, Edward Mussawir argues that within the juridical and jurisprudential concept of a cause or proceedings, where justice is formally understood, there is a space of its own that is distinct from the commonplace and the coordinates of philosophical inquiry.

The shift from the 'spatial' in the abstract to the singularity of 'spaces' is equally apparent in the other chapters of this book, whether in the spaces that are materialised by La Pietra's devices, invented for reappropriating the streets of Milan in Alexandra Brown's contribution, Zanny Begg's exposition of role of public art in the cultural politics of western Sydney, or in the footsteps of the coroner in the process of constructing a lawful place for the dead in colonial Melbourne in Marc Trabsky's piece. Chris Butler highlights the importance of acknowledging the character of the 'space' through which justice can be inhabited, by charting the influence of Leibniz's rejection of Newtonian 'absolute space' on Lefebvre's articulation of a politics of inhabitance, and in Andreas Philippopoulos-Mihalopoulos's chapter, where the language of 'spatial justice' insists most strongly on a single 'continuum' enclosed within its 'atmosphere', there is also an acknowledgement that there may be a 'space of spatial justice' itself – 'a space of a humble, everyday, quiet justice'.

From this perspective, it is the individuality of the *spaces* that each author in this book has engaged with and the individuality of their encounters with such spaces, more than the universalisability of any theory, that orients the contributions in this book to the question of justice. This study tries not to lose sight of the notion that space is not a given but rather *produced* and *invented*. As such, the justice that is addressed in this book is one that tends to emerge through an attention to the difference in various disciplinary, practical, political and aesthetic engagements and operations of space. In this way, even within the most simple, singular encounter that one has with 'a space', one may be, in Nietzsche's words, 'a hundred steps closer to justice', than in the attempt somehow to verify, survey and apportion space in an attempt to appeal towards what he calls some 'nuance of scientific fairness' (Nietzsche 1998, II, 11). The contributors to this book have embraced the need to take the materiality, unpredictability and manifold possibilities of space seriously, and have also sought to elicit various disciplinary encounters with space to distinctly problematise the question of justice.

Peripheries/passages/appropriations

Spaces of Justice is organised around three broad orientations: Peripheries, Passages and Appropriations. In Part I of the book, contributors consider the limits and edges of spatial form and the possibility of an outside – beyond the ubiquity of violence, truth beyond the limits of space as truth – both in fiction and jurisprudence and the role of public forms of artistic practice in intervening and challenging the impact of dual processes of urban sprawl and gentrification in the development of metropolitan space. The term 'peripheries' acknowledges the fact that spaces of justice are necessarily subtended by limits: limits of truth, experience, presence and absence, the seen and unseen, the limits of violence and the body, as well as the limits imposed by class, capital and culture, especially in the question of access to space. When it comes to spaces of justice, one can say that the 'periphery' always takes precedence over the 'centre'. It is not these limits and peripheries that necessarily enclose space and give the subject a relative centrality and relative marginality in space. Rather it is only by tracing the limits, the edges, the peripheries and the folds in the shape and deployment of space that it becomes possible to understand space not as a transcendental plane in which one is placed, but as a form of exteriority that is inseparable from the cases, tactics, manoeuvres and struggles intimate to the problem of justice. To focus on the 'peripheries' is thus to acknowledge that the constitution of space is itself a tracing of the limits of justice.

Andreas Philippopoulos-Mihalopoulos opens the book with his latest contribution to his comprehensive project of re-theorising spatial justice with a piece titled 'Spatial justice in a world of violence'. Through a close reading of the photographic series *Fortunes of War, Life Day* by artist Eric Lesdema, Philippopoulos-Mihalopoulos is interested in how these images reveal peripheral spaces at the edge of violence which impose an ethic of spatial responsibility on the viewer in the act of turning away and looking elsewhere. While no acts of explicit violence are shown in the images, we are left with no doubt that violence is ubiquitous along the spatio-temporal continuum. This continuum of violence between bodies raises questions of complicity and responsibility. Do we submit to a state of affairs in which space is saturated with the everyday and immobilised violence of the 'engineered atmosphere' – or is it also possible for bodies to withdraw from the atmosphere, through ruptures and folds within the continuum? Such a notion raises the ethical possibility of the 'emergence of spatial justice'.

In the next chapter, 'Justice "From room to room": toward a concept of procedural space in Kafka's *The Trial* and the Fictional work of western jurisprudence', **Edward Mussawir** moves from the aesthetic and ontological register of law and justice to the fictional and procedural. Mussawir puts forward a hypothesis on the relation between space and justice by suggesting the possibility of isolating a peculiar procedural shape that space takes on in the fictional work of Western jurisprudence. Challenging the notion that jurisprudential craft and legal science (to the extent that they attempt to speak in the name of justice) straightforwardly entrench a central, dominant, commonplace or ideological conception of space, Mussawir looks instead to the peripheries of juridical thought, where fiction operates to imperiously displace the plane of 'truth' that any commonplace conception depends upon. In particular, Mussawir places an analysis of the fictional topography in Franz Kafka's *The Trial* alongside consideration of the place of fiction in Roman law. The effect is to show that, far from constituting a merely figurative play of language, the procedural fictional space that these works describe is in fact the product of a more radical and pragmatic manoeuvre. Mussawir thus suggests that we are able to get closer to the constitutive connection between space and justice by isolating these juridical and procedural registers in which space is distorted by fiction.

Zanny Begg concludes this section of the book by tracing the spatial intersections between art, processes of gentrification and struggles for justice on the urban peripheries. In 'Artists and gentrification: is that warehouse conversion my fault?' Begg is particularly interested in how forms of public art contribute to the cultural and political relationships between the city centre and the Western suburbs of Sydney. Questioning the ambitious rhetoric of the proponents of tactical urbanism and the uncritical boosterism associated with Richard Florida's concept of the 'creative class', Begg details the ways in which artists are caught up within the mirrored socio-spatial processes of gentrification and ex-urban sprawl, which push the poor and precarious to the outer suburbs, where services are inadequately resourced. Begg draws on writers from the Italian *operaismo* tradition of autonomist-Marxism, such Antonio Negri, Michael Hardt and Maurizio Lazzarato, in order to understand how the immateriality of creative work creates both new social and spatial relationships alongside emergent 'fields of exploitation'. This highlights the ambivalent role that 'art in the public interest' plays in the politics of urban space. While public art is necessarily constrained by broader economic, social and cultural processes and can be used by the state as a temporary and low-cost form of urban infrastructure, the production and consumption of these works can simultaneously be used to document and confront such processes in everyday struggles that emerge from specific localities. Any investigation of the relationship between art and spatial justice requires an awareness of the difficulties faced by artists in ensuring that their participation and creative works are not incorporated into an institutionalised and commodified urban agenda.

Part II of the book, 'Passages', shifts our concerns from justice considered as a space of withdrawal, displacement and distortion, to justice as a space of *navigation*. Here, it should be noted, the idea of passage is not necessarily aimed at emphasising any redemptive nature of justice, nor clearly does it have a straightforward relation to justice seen as *aporia*. Passages don't just join two spaces together – the before and after of injustice, the fractured and the restored community, the inside and outside of the Good or the moment of the undecidable and the moment of decision. They don't offer the means primarily of getting from one place to another. By virtue simply of the movement that it makes possible, a passage is itself a space of justice. The chapters that form this part of the book are thus concerned first of all with movement, with space as a sign of movement and with justice as something travelled, as something reached essentially by moving and especially by foot. In this sense, part of what is at stake is to turn the so-called *aporias* of justice toward the passages, the roads and the itineraries along which the experience of justice traces the simple and complex movements of bodies.

To explore this frame for the relation between space and justice, the authors in this section give special attention to the space of the dead. It is not so much a reference to the metaphor of passage that traditionally attends the idea of the dead in their transition to 'other' worlds. Rather, justice as movement becomes clearer in relation to the dead when the body is the subject not just of subjective duties, rights, passions and so forth – the whole realm of justice traditionally attached to

12   Assembling spaces of justice

the 'responsible agent' – but of ceremonies that answer only to the question of why, how and where such a body moves.

In **Olivia Barr**'s 'Mourning place', which opens this part, the problem of justice posed following the event of the rape and murder of Gillian (Jill) Meagher in 2012 is drawn away from an analysis of the criminal justice processes that narrowly stage the form of state response to crime, and instead toward the community practices that, as a massive public response, converged upon a particular stretch of road: Sydney Road, Brunswick. Barr analyses first the important way in which pieces of visual evidence of the crime were mediated, projected and thus imagined by the public. She then shows how the peculiar paralysis of justice that affects the visual field in this evidence – the powerlessness of the viewer before a meaning that refuses itself especially in the CCTV footage of Meagher and her killer Bayley outside a bridal shop moments before the murder – becomes transferred onto the one thing that the image does happen to reproduce relatively objectively for the viewer – the everyday movement of Sydney Road in the background. It is the road that then forms the setting for a massive unofficial peace march that took place in response to the murder and which Barr analyses as a work of public ceremonial law and public mourning.

Barr sees this mourning through a number of lenses: it is neither solely mourning for the loss of an individual (Jill Meagher), nor simply mourning for the loss of place (Sydney Road). For Barr, it is the walkers that create a 'mourning place', a mourning and a place that does not allow loss to be unlocalised. It is thus the *place* that mourns alongside the walker. In the way that the peace march took shape, the act of walking was not to make a statement (political or otherwise), nor necessarily to make an appeal to justice. According to Barr it constituted the space of justice itself – an authentic movement that only the road could properly materialise and ground for an act of mourning situated beyond the blinkered and freeze-framed perspective that criminal justice makes of an event. In this way, even before justice speaks to the foundations of political community and so on, it traces itself on the ground and is felt by the contact between feet and earth.

In the following chapter, 'Walking with the dead: coronial law and spatial justice in the necropolis', **Marc Trabsky** takes up related themes of place-making, justice and the dead in an historical study of the coroner in the colonial period of the same city: Melbourne, Australia. For Trabsky, in contrast to Barr, the question of justice can indeed be situated within the parameters of jurisdiction, the affairs of public administration and the ordinary fulfilling of public office. However, far from presenting a purely procedural rationalisation of the juridical, public and civic duties of the nineteenth-century coroner in his administration of justice, Trabsky depicts this office in all the material pungency and intimacy of its everyday relations and surroundings. He sees justice in the colonial period in question as fundamentally bound up with an experience of the place of the living and the dead and with the question of securing continuity between the present and past. To understand the potentiality of inhabiting and colonising land, was to understand not just the necessary preparations, the orderly, rationalised designs made for the co-existence of the living, but more fundamentally to understand the preparations made for the dead. Trabsky sees the office of coroner as revealing in this sense – an official whose task it was to carry the dead through the city streets and set up makeshift inquests into the deaths of persons whose bodies, in that era, followed a trajectory dictated by the swiftness of their decomposition. The dead and the administration of coronial functions were both accommodated, Trabsky shows, in the everyday haunts of the living such as pubs, taverns and brothels. The paths followed, the maps, the itineraries and tracks between these sites constituted both the space of the coroner's office and an unparalleled jurisdiction over colonial lands. Trabsky reads the activity of the coroner, in attending to and walking with the dead, as an activity of spatial justice, the historical importance of which should not be neglected.

The concluding section of the book, Part III, is concerned with the relationships between 'appropriations' of space and spatial justice. The concept of appropriation has of course historically played a central role in Marxist accounts of the interaction between humanity and nature. A classic example appears in Bertell Ollman's book *Alienation*, where he defines appropriation as building 'by incorporating' (Ollman 1976, 91). On one interpretation, this may suggest a unidirectional transference of value to humans through their objectification of the non-human world. But as Henri Lefebvre insists, it is important to distinguish between the appropriation of space as a process of aesthetic experience and creative transformation, and the 'domination' of space as an instrumental deployment of technological functionalism to impose a 'rectilinear' order on space (Lefebvre 1991, 165). In contrasting ways, the chapters in this section trace the spatial intersections between aesthetics, politics, embodiment and affect which arise from the inhabitance of space, the mapping of urban experience and the occupation practices of the political crowd. Through their distinctive arguments about how specific forms of appropriation can open up opportunities to challenge entrenched relations of power, each of these contributions raise crucial questions about the very possibility of spatial justice.

Chris Butler opens this section with his chapter 'Space, politics, justice', in which he explores the characteristics of the space that can ground the concept of spatial justice. Beginning with one of the most influential works in contemporary critical geography, Butler traces the theoretical influences that inform Henri Lefebvre's *The Production of Space*. In this work, Lefebvre embraces a number of aspects of Leibniz's relational theory of space, and Butler discusses how this approach leads Lefebvre to argue for the centrality of bodily inhabitance in conceptualising spatial relations. Lefebvre's idea of inhabitance is concerned with both aesthetic and creative experience and an orientation towards the appropriation of space as a form of political practice. Such a 'politics of inhabitance' can be understood as linking Lefebvre's relational account of space to a second aspect of his work which also owes a debt to the philosophy of Leibniz. This is Lefebvre's theory of 'moments' – understood as fleeting eruptions from within the spatio-temporal relations of everyday life, which breach the 'artificial divide between

14 Assembling spaces of justice

the possible and the impossible'. Butler argues that Lefebvre's brief sketch of the 'moment of justice' can be deepened by reading it in light of Walter Benjamin's 'weak messianism', which presents justice as simultaneously dwelling within the human world, while remaining beyond our capacities to quantify and capture. It is in this sense that spatial justice can be understood as exceeding the limitations of the paradigm of distributive justice and emerges as a ruptural moment, which opens up the question of the possibility of the impossible.

In 'Immersing, comprehending and reappropriating', **Alexandra Brown** introduces us to the installation and film works of Milanese architect, artist and designer Ugo La Pietra. Throughout the 1960s and 1970s, La Pietra utilised a range of experimental and non-traditional architectural practices to explore the potential of individual experiences and agency within the city. While often situated in relation to the Italian *architettura radicale* movement, Brown argues that La Pietra's work needs to be seen as distinct from some of the more prominent contributors to this movement, such as Archizoom and Superstudio. This is particularly so in both his experimental installations and in short films such as *La riappropriazione della città*, where La Pietra was interested in the ways in which architectural design and material practices of reappropriation could be harnessed to enhance the individual's experience of the city. While there are some similarities between La Pietra's rejection of formal urban planning processes and realised built forms and the Situationist practice of *dérive* (or the unplanned drift through the city), Brown identifies how La Pietra's work is distinguished by its lack of explicit interest in 'structural change'. Through its immersion in the practices of the everyday, his interest in mapping as a form of architecture can be understood as an attempt to comprehend the experience and agency of the individual amidst the totalising systems that attempt to govern the so-called 'public space' of the city. Here Brown draws a spatial analogy with the Derridean exposition of the irreconcilable relation between the generality of law and the singularity of justice.

The final chapter in the collection is **Illan rua Wall**'s 'This agitated veil', in which he explores the sublime and radical potential of the crowd as an improper occupation of space. Embracing Walter Benjamin's characterisation of the crowd as the 'agitated veil' which mediated Baudelaire's experience and vision of Paris, Wall begins by identifying the way in which the crowd of the post-Fordist city attains a naturalism and even invisibility, when set against the solidity of the urban built environment (Benjamin 2003, 323). This can be contrasted with the widely expressed unease with the idea of the political crowd, which is often associated with uncontrollable fluidity, irrationality and violence. In tracing the history of crowd theory since the late 1800s, Wall explains the limitations of both the thesis of 'deindividuation' (as proposed by Tarde and Le Bon) and theories which emphasise the crowd as a process of identity formation. Drawing on the work of Canetti and Brennan, Wall conceptualises the crowd as a 'genus of modes of action' which generates a 'sticky' atmosphere and binds its participants together. While it is obvious that, in the abstract, the crowd provides no guarantee of any fundamental political orientation, the ways in which political crowds challenge 'proper' modes of occupation allow us to potentially glimpse a 'momentary flash of justice in the present'. Through their spatial, temporal and affective 'depropriation' of the city, occupation crowds are but one mode of marking spatial injustice, rupturing established orders and initiating the task of assembling spaces of justice.

References

Bartel, R., Graham, N., Jackson, S., Prior, J., Robinson, D., Sherval, M. and Williams, S. 2013. Legal geography: An Australian perspective. *Geographical Research* 51(4): 339–353.

Benjamin, W. 2003. On some motifs in Baudelaire. In *Selected Writings Vol. 4: 1938–1940*, eds Eiland, H. and Jennings, M., 313–355. Belknap Press.

Blomley, N., Delaney, D. and Ford, R. T., eds. 2001. *The Legal Geographies Reader: Law, Power, and Space*. Blackwell.

Braverman, I., Blomley, N., Delaney, D. and Kedar, A. 2014a. Expanding the spaces of law. In *The Expanding Spaces of Law: A Timely Legal Geography*, eds Braverman, I. Blomley, N., Delaney, D. and Kedar, A., 1–29. Stanford University Press.

Braverman, I. Blomley, N., Delaney, D. and Kedar, A., eds. 2014b. *The Expanding Spaces of Law: A Timely Legal Geography*. Stanford University Press.

Buchanan, A. 1982. *Marx and Justice: The Radical Critique of Liberalism*. Methuen.

City. 2010. 'Seeking Spatial Justice': Responses to and comments from Edward Soja. *City* 14(6): 497–635.

City. 2011. 'Seeking Spatial Justice': Part Two. *City* 15(1): 63–102.

Delaney, D. 2010. *The Spatial, the Legal and the Pragmatics of World-Making: Nomospheric Investigations*. Routledge.

Dikeç, M. 2001. Justice and the spatial imagination. *Environment and Planning A* 33(10): 1785–1805.

Dikeç, M. 2005. Space, politics, and the political. *Environment and Planning D: Society and Space* 23: 171–188.

Dikeç, M. 2009. Space, politics and (in)justice. *Justice Spatiale/Spatial Justice*, 1, available at: www.jssj.org

Dikeç, M. 2015. *Space, Politics and Aesthetics*, Edinburgh University Press.

Douzinas, C. and Warrington, R. 1986. Domination, exploitation, and suffering: Marxism and the opening of closed systems. *Law and Social Inquiry* 11(4): 801–828.

Evans, R. 1992. Early racial conflict on Stradbroke Island. In *Whose Island? The Past and Future of North Stradbroke*, ed. Ganter, R., 23–25. Queensland Studies Centre, Griffith University.

Evans, R. 2008. On the utmost verge: Race and ethnic relations at Moreton Bay, 1799–1842. *Queensland Review* 15(1): 1–31.

Fainstein, S. 2010. *The Just City*. Cornell University Press.

FitzGerald, S. and Philippopoulos-Mihalopoulos, A., eds. 2008. Invisible laws, visible cities (Special Issue). *Griffith Law Review* 17(2): 435–576.

Geras, N. 1985. The controversy about Marx and justice. *New Left Review* 150: 47–85.

Harvey, D. 1969. *Explanation in Geography*. Edward Arnold.

Harvey, D. 1973. *Social Justice and the City*. Johns Hopkins University Press.

Harvey, D. 1982. *The Limits to Capital*. Verso.

Harvey, D. 1992. Social justice, postmodernism and the city. *International Journal of Urban and Regional Research* 6: 588–601.

16 Assembling spaces of justice

Harvey, D. 1996. *Justice, Nature and the Geography of Difference*. Blackwell.

Holder, J. and Harrison, C., eds. 2003. *Law and Geography: Current Legal Issues Vol. 5*. Oxford University Press.

Hunt, A. 1985. The future of rights and justice. *Contemporary Crises* 9(4): 309–326.

Lefebvre, H. 1991. *The Production of Space*. Blackwell.

Lukes, S. 1985. *Marxism and Morality*. Oxford University Press.

Manderson, D., ed. 2005. Legal spaces (Special Issue). *Law Text Culture* 9: 1–244.

Marcuse, P. 2009. Spatial justice: Derivative but causal of social injustice. *Spatial Justice* 1 (September). Available at: www.jssj.org

Marcuse, P. Connolly, J., Novy, J., Olivo, I., Potter, C. and Steil, J., eds. 2009. *Searching for the Just City: Debates in Urban Theory and Practice*. Routledge.

Mendieta, E. 2011. The spatial metaphorics of justice: On Edward W. Soja. *City* 15(1): 81–84.

Merrifield, A. and Swyngedouw, E., eds. 1999. *The Urbanization of Injustice*. New York University Press.

Nietzsche, F. 1998. *On the Genealogy of Morality*. Clark, M. and Swensen, A. J. trans. Hackett.

Ollman, B. 1976. *Alienation: Marx's Conception of Man in Capitalist Society*. Cambridge University Press.

Peacock, E. 2001. *History, Life and Times of Robert Anderson: Gheebelum, Ngugi, Mulgumpin*. Uniikup Productions.

Philippopoulos-Mihalopoulos, A., ed. 2007. *Law and the City*. Routledge-Cavendish.

Philippopoulos-Mihalopoulos, A. 2010. Spatial justice: Law and the geography of withdrawal. *International Journal of Law in Context* 6(3): 201–216.

Philippopoulos-Mihalopoulos, A. 2011. Law's spatial turn: Geography, justice and a certain fear of space. *Law, Culture and the Humanities* 7(2): 187–202.

Philippopoulos-Mihalopoulos, A. 2015. *Spatial Justice: Body, Lawscape, Atmosphere*. Routledge.

Philippopoulos-Mihalopoulos, A. 2016. Withdrawing from atmosphere: An ontology of air partitioning and affective engineering. *Environment and Planning D: Society and Space*. 34(1): 150–167

Pirie, G. 1983. On spatial justice. *Environment and Planning A* 15: 465–73.

Plato. 1987. *The Republic*. Lee, D. trans. Penguin.

Rawls, J. 1999. *A Theory of Justice*. Belknap Press.

Smith, D. 1994. *Geography and Social Justice*. Blackwell.

Soja, E. 1985. The spatiality of social life: Towards a transformative retheorisation. In *Social Relations and Spatial Structures*, eds Gregory, D. and Urry, J., 90–127. Macmillan.

Soja, E. 1989. *Postmodern Geographies: The Reassertion of Space in Critical Social Theory*. Verso.

Soja, E. 2001. *Postmetropolis*. Blackwell.

Soja, E. 2010. *Seeking Spatial Justice*. University of Minnesota Press.

Soja, E. 2014. *My Los Angeles: From Urban Restructuring to Regional Urbanization*. University of California Press.

Stanford Law Review. 1996. Symposium: Surveying Law and Borders. *Stanford Law Review* 48(5): 1037–1430.

Wolff, R. P. 1977. *Understanding Rawls: A Reconstruction and Critique of* A Theory of Justice. Princeton University Press.

Young, I. M. 1990. *Justice and the Politics of Difference*. Princeton University Press.

Cases

Delaney on behalf of the Quandamooka People v State of Queensland [2011] FCA 741.

Legislation

North Stradbroke Island Protection and Sustainability Act 2011.

Part I

Peripheries

Chapter 1

Spatial justice in a world of violence

Andreas Philippopoulos-Mihalopoulos[1]

We are all complicit

Figure 1.1 Eric Lesdema, Untitled, c-type from the series *Life Day – Fortunes of War*

1 The author would like to express his gratitude to Eric Lesdema for his generous permission to use his work for this text, as well as the editors of this volume for their patience.

22   Peripheries

Where is the conflict? This is the question Eric Lesdema asks with his photographic series *Life Day – Fortunes of War*.[2] The question is asked obliquely yet relentlessly, haunting the bodies, and the spaces between those bodies. Every single image booms with the question, planting in the viewer the compulsive urge to find the conflict, folded somewhere between the material of the image and the bodies represented in it. We are all captured in this search, in our turn performing what we unconsciously do anyway: we populate space with conflict and its violence, and we position ourselves in relation to it, whether this might be in the deep end or at a distance, taking sides or blocking the conflict from our view. These images render one complicit with the conflict they capture. They set up their temporal and spatial parameters in such a way that they annul any easy hope of escaping violence. They render conflict the main ontological condition of our time, and us complicit with its emergence. This is the reason for which Lesdema's work has stirred so much interest in terms of thinking, observation and analysis.[3]

Here, I would like to take advantage of my experience of working with Lesdema and employ his *Life Day – Fortunes of War* series, not as illustrative tools but as main focal points, around which to construct and present my arguments concerning issues of spatiotemporal continuum, complicity and responsibility, engineered atmospherics and spatial justice. I would like to focus specifically on the spatiality of the series, and especially the way it captures the distribution of bodies in space. Spatiality is of course important in photography in general,[4] but here, at least in my reading, it emerges as the main protagonist claiming the first locus of violence. It would seem that space itself distributes the bodies (human and non-human, material and immaterial) in such a way that they turn against each other, or inhabit spaces of earlier or future violence, haunting them in advance of the advent of violence. Space is saturated with a casual, quotidian, and for this reason deeply entrenched and invisibilised violence. This, aided by some of the other characteristics of the photographs I will be expanding on below, generates an atmosphere so close and all-comprising, that even the illusion of escape is ingested. This is not to say, however, that Lesdema's spaces are without hope. It is just that whatever hope there is, it does not come from the usual avenues. This is the discussion I reserve for the final section, where spatial justice emerges.

---

2 The series was first presented in 1993 and since then, it has been shown across the world. It has been awarded the UN Nikon International Photography Grand Prix in 1997.

3 A volume on this particular work with various contributions, including from myself, is forthcoming from Intellect Books, 2017. See also Hall and Sealy (2001) and www.practicevonstroheim.org for Lesdema's work.

4 See for example the editorial 'On Spatiality' and whole issue 5(1), 2012, of *Photographies*.

Looking away

Figure 1.2 Eric Lesdema, Untitled, c-type from the series *Life Day – Fortunes of War*

Despite the title of the series, there is nothing gory, battlefield-like or even palpably aggressive in these photographs. There is, however, a feeling that somewhere next to what we are looking at, something is happening. Perhaps the main feature of the series is that the camera is looking away from any explicit moment of violence. But looking away is usually associated with indifference or fear, and often displacement of responsibility. It can be a way of putting some distance between the beholder and the thing that is proving too difficult to behold. It is often an attempt at interrupting the continuity between what we see and what we feel, inserting a chunk of denial often garnished with well-rehearsed arguments. Looking away is politically suspicious.

Eric Lesdema makes us rethink the act of looking away. He positions it centre-stage in what is otherwise the steep political and ethical curve of his work. The

24 Peripheries

gesture remains that of turning one's vision away from the spectacle. But here it results in a lateral looking that plunges the viewer in a *continuum* between herself and whatever is-not-to-be-seen. Nothing is left out of this continuum. Above all, this is a continuum brimming with responsibility. Looking away in this case is neither indifferent nor complicit; rather it is a way of confirming the need for ethical positions with regards both to what we see and, significantly, to what we do not.

The whole series is without doubt about conflict, depicting the atrocities of violence (in every conceivable form, such as military, capitalist, consumerist, gendered, racialised, and so on) in a deeply affective way. The photographs, however, are characterised by two traits that eschew the relatively narrow confines of the above category (see Fassl 2014). First, as already mentioned, they never focus on the conflict itself. Second, they feel quick, fuzzy, snappy, unstudied, so much so that they presage the era of the quick, contingent spatiality of iphoneography (this is a 1993 series). These two characteristics construct a new and very difficult language of violence which, additionally, is intensely spatialised in a way unlike the traditional spatiality of war or conflict photography. The photographs tell us this: that violence is *everywhere*, and that even a cursory, haphazard, indeed *peripheral* look reveals this. Lesdema unveils the violence of space at its most ironic: space, he tells us, is inherently violent but its violence is often dissimulated behind sunny posters, colourful packaging, representations rather than substances. Yet, there is something inalienable in our connection to space: we are all bodies vying for the same space, excluding other bodies along the way. We generate space, we are space, and we are constantly on the move, generating more space, but also more conflict with other bodies. The movement captured in the frames is always one of displacement. The camera moves along: it captures the movement of the bodies but also points away from that violence of displacement, towards the new spaces of violence that emerge with every such move.

The photographs stop and look at those peripheral spaces, and challenge us in doing the same. But we are not used to this. We never stop at these peripheries.[5] We are attracted to the centrality of violence because only in this way can we bracket it and isolate it. Centring in on the violence is our way to treat it as an exception, specific instance, specific geography, at a safe distance from us. We are, however, not allowed to do this here. The Elsewhere is central in the series, while the centre remains decidedly off-focus. Not unlike the Renaissance painting thematic technique of mixing the sublime with the quotidian, where the main story of a crucifixion, a biblical murder or a mythological rape would play second fiddle to the labours of a farmer clearing his stable, Lesdema's imagery veils the sublime spectacle of violence behind the quotidian detail of the seemingly insignificant. But, just like a Renaissance painting, *Life Day – Fortunes of War* opens up the possibility of a ubiquity that transcends habitual spatial boundaries. It shows how all bodies, human and non-human, animate and inanimate, are saturated

---

5 Kafka famously said 'We photograph things in order to drive them out of our minds' (cited in Barthes 2000, 53).

in and complicit with violence – the violence of Renaissance crucifixion becomes that of war permeating all movement and rest, all actuality and virtuality. The unsuspected labours or pilgrims roaming around are not only connected to the violence of the centre but positively instigating it, making violence possible by being present in its periphery. Nicolette Barsdorff-Liebchen (2017) talks about how the oblique is the deterritorialised elsewhere, while the main event of the territory (the 'Event') remains 'hidden as it is in plain sight'. Deleuzoguattarian deterritorialisation is a way of resisting the aggressive seduction of capitalism by breaking down the spatially and temporally fixed corridors of consumerist obsession, and imagining new lines of flight (Deleuze and Guattari 1988). And while there are lines of flight in Lesdema's work, they are all folded in the quiet persistence of despair that comes with the ubiquity of violence.

For Jan Baetens (2017) the pictures 'are not violent because of what they show, but because of what they tell or, more exactly, because of the way they tell us what we should think of what they show'. Indeed, their message is delivered with the lateral force of the affect. They often make little sense, they are decontextualised, they feel incomplete, lying unobserved next to the vanishing point of the larger but never-to-be-seen picture, on the margins of towns, cities, villages, in back streets, in community halls, in temporary fairs, as Jane Tormey (2017) writes. Yet, they hit the viewer from within, with the uncontrollable force of an affective deluge, where emotions, symbols and senses comingle to engineer an atmosphere of intense discomfort, yet seduction (Philippopoulos-Mihalopoulos 2015). This is the glasshouse of global consumerism. As Gerald Moore (2017) puts it, 'this collection is remarkable in its capture of the persistence of advertisements, their lingering trace amidst apocalypse disturbing and reassuring in equal measure'.

How to choose where to *point* when deterritorialising? The main event, the Grand Reterritorialiser, is convenient in its centrality, soft in its seduction, steadfast in its persuasion. The main event is always obvious. But where is the Elsewhere? Everything that surrounds the main event is potentially elsewhere. All bodies lead to violence. Which one to choose and point at? This is perhaps one of the strongest qualities of the images, as I have already intimated: they appear accidental and of a temporality that merely floats above the event rather than contributing to it. They often include in the frame the movement that the photographer performed in his turning away from the main event. The images pulsate with a movement *away-from* rather than *towards*. This has a terrifying outcome: wherever you point, accidentally, in panic or aversion to the main event of war, everything is saturated with violence. Obliqueness means: the Elsewhere is already here.

Oblique is to space, what anterior is to time. And time is not left out of complicity either. Lesdema has written extensively about his methodology, which he calls the *Ant-Optic* (Lesdema 2015). *Ant-Optic* anticipates the future of conflict by rooting it into the banal everyday, itself always in the forgettable past or the unobservable present. *Ant-Optic* is anterior to the conflict. It is also oblique to it. It looks to the future askance, leaving it outside the frame. The images wallow in distraction, obsession, lethargy – all conditions of forgetting that the future is already here.

Anteriority is always obliqueness: there is no other way of looking at the future and not being subsumed to it. For this very reason of anteriority, the future is captured. These photographic images *anticipate*. We do not know what, but it feels inescapable. We do not know when, but it has already begun – or rather, it has always been here. Our complicity with the conflict ensures it. We anticipate future sadness, solitary death, ecological disaster, resource depletion; we anticipate violence, war, conflict; we have always been complicit with the waves of refugees, the unequal power distribution, the unjust emplacement of human and non-human bodies. Future itself is made complicit to the conflict.

There are various modes of future-capturing for photography. One of the most irreverent ones is to challenge the traditional belief, as Jan Baetens (2017) puts it, that photographs are traces of what has already been. Here instead we have the traces of what is to come, a future anterior that never exhausts itself in production but hovers, perennially peripheral, above the present. These traces open up fractally to capture the multiplicity of the future, leaving no space devoid of conflict. The anticipatory gaze unearths the archaeology of the causes of violence in their minuscule details, such as consumerist desire, faint traces of nationalism, landscapes marred by militarised semi-presences, insignia of categorisations and exclusions; its post-facto gaze looks at the ruins of plastic enclosures, melancholy disorder and fake sunbeams that replace the real thing, like some Benjaminian angel of history turning back upon himself. We have the before and the after but never the thing itself. Jane Tormey (2017) compares Walter Benjamin's *Arcades Project* with *Life Day – Fortunes of War*, re-semiologising the photographic production process. Quoting from Benjamin, Tormey (2017) writes: 'in an assemblage of small constituent parts, each "individual moment" has the potential to gather "temporal momentum" in its confrontation with other concepts. In the course of that process a conception of history is *constructed* – it isn't fixed or conclusive'. Each piece of matter opens fractally, a fan-like gaping awning, funnelling a history yet to happen, reinstating a history that has never stopped happening. The temporal momentum is paralysing in its banality, irresistible in its familiarity, and atrocious in its relentlessly repeated resolution.

The continuum

The immediate effect of this saturation is an all-consuming spatiotemporality: not only normal everyday spaces (in their full banality) are now seen in a light that allows the violence to bubble up; not only are new spaces generated that go beyond the frame of the photograph, anticipating the violence; but, most significantly, these spaces are all joined up: the most compelling space created by the act of looking away is indeed the continuum. This continuum extends between the viewer and the thing not-viewed, the seen and the unseen, as well as the original and the end viewer. Imagine a flat space where violence is both folded in and spread out, clamping up in densities that hide or opening up in piazzas that reveal the mechanics of violence. Imagine trying to look away from the moment of

Figure 1.3 Eric Lesdema, Untitled, c-type from the series *Life Day – Fortunes of War*

violence, and discovering that there is nowhere to look which would not be replete with the visceral coagulations of this violence.

On the continuum, the eye travels fast and far, unable to arrive at any imaginary outside that would entertain the idea of non-violence. The continuum is the flat ontology of the indistinguishability between the human and the non-human, the animate and the inanimate, the material and the abstract (Bennett 2010): all contained here, whether this is Spinoza's Nature (Spinoza 2000), Deleuze and Guattari's plane of immanence (Deleuze and Guattari 1988), or the flat ontology of new materialism (Bryant 2011). Looking away initiates this continuum and paradoxically, leaves nothing out. Yet, its all-inclusive brutality is countered by its ethical positioning: I want to suggest a continuum built on the urge for seeing and respecting difference; on the necessity to show and view and feel without the risk of being co-opted; and even on a sort of manic courage that is often the result of a revolutionary force.

This is why this continuum is not some cosy flatness of togetherness or of democratic processes and other antidotes. The continuum established here is of a brutal hyperconnectivity, full of ruptures, of high velocity and also high inequality. The stronger, more powerful bodies pull this continuum down, a body weight crunching the plane, making it fold and unfold in undulating configurations determined by the bodies themselves. We are in the presence of corporations, the 1 per cent, the holders of legitimated violence such as the state, the police, the army, the jovial nationalism, the suburban whiteness: all strong bodies that push the one end of the continuum down in an infernal seesaw that makes the lighter bodies the obvious externalities of the move. This might be a flat continuum, but it is also tilted, unequal, biased.

This tilted continuum is also relentless. Not just because it precludes any space of rest, having us sliding constantly on the unequal distribution of power and desire; but also, and perhaps more cruelly, because it plays with our illusions. Where is the violence in a supermarket shelf, an amusement parlour, or innocuous military paraphernalia? There is no violence here, just some innocent horseplay and perhaps some sort of desire to do this, buy that, try the other. The illusion comes crashing down, however, as soon as one sees that one does not see: outside the frame but seeping in through every pore of the animate and inanimate bodies captured by the lens, violence is raging, conflict is the order of the day, ruptures (of any illusion one might have had) indelibly cracking the surface. The wonder of the continuum is that what-is-not-to-be-seen is part of the affective constitution of what is seen. The illusion is the possibility of looking away and avoiding what-is-not-to-be-seen. The end of the illusion is the realisation that, wherever one turns, there is a continuum of violence; and that we, the viewers, the readers, the frames, the bodies in the frame, the bodies outside the frame, the objects and surfaces passing through the frame, are all complicit with the emergence of violence. There is no outside to the continuum.

Atmospheric capturing

There is a sense of plastic in the air, a taste of metal on the tongue, the smell of something burnt a bit further down, a harsh and slimy tactility on the surfaces. The series *Life Day – Fortunes of War* is permeated by a specific atmosphere. By 'atmosphere' here I do not only mean the usual vernacular understanding of the term. That too, since atmosphere has to do with a phenomenological apperception of surrounding conditions – what Gernot Böhme calls 'the common reality of the perceiver and the perceived' (1995, 34, author's translation). We are used to thinking of atmospheres as architectural or design constructions, often in confined interiors, that communicate specific affects, whether pleasing or displeasing. Or we think of atmosphere in its grand geological emanation as the protective mantle around the earth. Lesdema's series, however, questions these understandings and offers in their stead an engineered, air-conditioned atmosphere that claims an ontological status.

Spatial justice in a world of violence 29

Figure 1.4 Eric Lesdema, Untitled, c-type from the series *Life Day – Fortunes of War*

The atmosphere captured by the photographer and in which I am interested here is one of affective circulation between bodies, human and non-human. But not the free-flowing openness of affect. Rather, the atmosphere I would like to focus on is the engineered one. On a first level, the photographer is not a passive receiver of this atmosphere. Rather, he *engineers* the atmosphere through the photographs in order to create a bubble of violent continuum, in which even moments of seeming harmless carelessness and everyday happiness are conditioned by the atmospheric affects. Everything in the engineered atmosphere of Lesdema is tainted by an excess of violence.

This atmosphere defies traditional phenomenological approaches because it renders the viewer obsolete. No longer at a distance, or even immersed in it, the viewer *is* it. The ontological atmosphere bubbles up on the continuum between seer and seen, as well as seen and not-to-be-seen. A veritable offspring of the indistinguishability between the various bodies, an atmosphere goes on regardless of who casts their eyes on it. It defies phenomenology because it *is* fully present,

30 Peripheries

regardless of how it is perceived. Its presence unfolds in the haphazard, casual, unobservable, irrelevant, seemingly trivial nature of the photographs: the captured event would be meaningless even if you were there to watch it. It only works because it is placed *within* an atmospherics of pure ontology, in its turn affected by the fractal shards of ontological continuum.

The photographs serve a function of capturing affective circulation, in the sense of trying to freeze it as an epistemological snapshot. Yet here we are characterised by the sheer impossibility of even moderate affective containment. Affects always exceed the bodies of their emergence (Deleuze and Guattari 1988), filling up those interspheral spaces where nothing remains, except for affective radiation emanating from the floating bodies. An ontological atmosphere is the excess of affect that keeps bodies together, through and against each other. Atmosphere slides amongst the various bodies that circulate in it and freezes them like a sticky, gooey substance – the affective excess at work. There is no atmosphere without bodies, and there are no bodies deprived of affects.

Still, excess does not have to be fiery or indeed excessive in its expression. There are no explosions in these photographs. The crowds are subdued. The laughs are soft. The shops are quiet. If the main event is bombastic in its destruction, here we are in a space of minor politics of dissidence – a politics of quiet persistence and muffled despair. This is not the politics of revolutionary bravado and fanfare but of *stasis*, revolt and pause at the same time, small waves coming from the margins, glimmers of hope that might flow into each other and cause a bigger wave. Even so, the images never show the horizon as the better world elsewhere. Any hope is contained within: 'there is another world, but it is in this one' (attributed to Paul Eluard; see Philippopoulos-Mihalopoulos 2013). Reality does not change, but the frame does. Several frames are characterised by an artifice, luminous and moribund like the sun, packaged brightly, painted badly, pasted unconvincingly. It is not the sun. It is a representation. But it is the only gift that the photographer can offer. Let us sing with Zarathustra, then: 'There is no outside! But we forget this . . . How lovely it is that we forget!' (Nietzsche 2005, 175).

The series is a manifesto against another quiet force: that of capitalism, with its slowly percolating effect of mutilated desire. With this we reach the deeper level of engineered atmosphere, which the photographer can only fleetingly capture with the photographs and the way in which, in his turn, he engineers their atmosphere. One of the most prominent tools of capitalist atmospheric engineering is advertising. Just as various branded products are placed 'accidentally' in films and television, capturing the viewer in their peripheral radiance, in the same way advertising becomes here the stronghold of the location of violence. Perversely, advertising makes us feel comfortable. In a confusing world, where ungraspable narratives are replete with discomfort, a can of Coke operates like the cubists' inclusion of a naturalistic nail in an otherwise cubist painting: something to hook on. Its effect is so absolute as it is quietly subdermal. Gerald Moore (2017) writes on this: 'when we are programmed to fall in love on Impulse and collapse in ecstasy before a vision of Diet Coke, is it surprising that the demands made on desire – and our failure to meet them – leave us cognitively off kilter, affectively overwhelmed?'

Other spaces bloom, inhabited by other bodies, all seemingly innocent, quotidian skins that wear their racism lightly, their anti-foreigner stance humorously, their pro-intervention ideas liberally. None of them is apparently connected to the violent event, yet they are all steeped in the folds of the atmosphere, contributing to its targeted engineering, serving the conative perpetuation of the atmosphere. There are countless bodies here, both human and non-human, trapped in their own desire (for more atmosphere) and illusionary satisfaction (by the atmospheric offerings). Not easily dismissible as frivolous or inanely enslaved to desires, these bodies are real humans exhibiting their vulnerability and real objects donning their fragility, looking to sate their desire to carry on existing in misjudged ways: in supermarkets, in narcosexual stupor, in isolating collectivities – and always in quiet despair.

Once again, there is a looking-away at work. The atmosphere circles the event of violence, both temporally and spatially, without ever touching upon it. Temporally, as I have shown above, it anticipates the advent and at the same time mourns the aftermath of violence, while eschewing the actual event. Spatially, the violent event is brought to the fore by the continuum. This is significant for the following reason: in the core of the atmosphere there is a withdrawal. Violence has withdrawn, sucked in by its own gravitational pull, yet juddering the whole continuum up like a cosmic dervish skirt fissured around a whirling body of ecstatic implosion. Violence is connected, web-like, radiating an excess of affect on all the bodies that populate the continuum, while itself progressively withdrawing. In the core of the ontological atmosphere of violence, there is a withdrawal that informs everything around it.[6]

The feat of the series *Life Day – Fortunes of War* is that it manages to focus on this very movement of withdrawal, spatially and temporally mapping the departing scent of violence without ever focusing on it. Rather, it traces violence as it appears in the bodies of its withdrawal, namely the bodies that are left behind or hanging around at the scene of the future crime in anticipation. It is rare to find such a consistent depiction of withdrawal in its full ontology of a violence that never goes away, however much it withdraws. Withdrawal is not disappearance, but all-emanating, all-thematising ontological presence. The melancholy of this mapping is evident: the continuum is soaked in a violence that can never be dealt with directly because it is always already elsewhere.

We are complicit with this atmosphere, not because we look at its depiction through the photographs, but because the photographs ontologically include us in the atmosphere, before we even get the opportunity for phenomenological immersion. We are already in there, one of these bodies that walk or stand or play or lie down, interacting with the objects seemingly randomly spread around.

6 On withdrawal, see Philippopoulos-Mihalopoulos (2016).

32 Peripheries

We identify with them, egging them to carry on what they are doing, hoping that something will be revealed. This is perhaps our greatest complicity: that we try to give meaning to the meaninglessness of violence. But isn't this to be expected? We are enveloped in a vast glasshouse of excess, atmospherically conditioned to live side by side with violence and not even bat an eyelid. Lesdema's atmospherics are irresistible because they do not allow for a space of resistance. They take away from us the past and the future, the away and the elsewhere, and return it to us bathed in casual violence, with ourselves in its centre.

Spatial justice: closed for judging

Figure 1.5 Eric Lesdema, Untitled, c-type from the series *Life Day – Fortunes of War*

The continuum of violence is inescapable. Apart from the complicity with anonymous material (Negarestani 2008), so guilt-ridden and so absolute as to become the unobserved day in the life of anyone; apart from the inescapability of violence and conflict, mushrooming everywhere like damp covering every surface of every body that has been captured in the picture; apart even from the inescapability of atmospherics, so refreshingly asphyxiating, so castrating yet so desirable: apart from all these, there is the grand inescapability of the world as captured by Lesdema – a world with no other world, no better world outside, no easy illusion, not even a promise of change. Space contorts bodies in forced but compulsive postures, late mannerists of late capitalism, interacting without connecting with other bodies and objects, devoid of community. Likewise, bodies force space in niches of violence, making it co-extensive with their struggle to maintain the atmosphere of compulsion. The bodies draw violence from the space around them: the space is not only a receptacle for but also a storage of violence. Piled up, folded in, spread through, violence has a deleterious effect on space, and the space of the bodies that move in it. Violence is inscribed on bodies and spaces like dams on the skin of the earth. The history of violence is spatial, marked on the anthropocenic layers of our behaviour, anticipating our actions and demise.

The atmosphere is engineered to feel that everything that exists or could exist is contained irredeemably in here, inescapably violent, relentlessly continuous. The whole continuum is enclosed within this atmosphere. Yet, there might be a way of counteracting, resisting, going against, breaking the atmosphere and withdrawing from it. The way out comes from within: every continuum is ruptured. Since the continuum has no outside ('there is no edge! We can't jump out of the universe' (Morton 2013, 17)), ruptures are ontologically included in the continuum in the form of folds (that is, connections), invisibilisations, withdrawals, atmospheric enclosures that rupture the continuum. Ruptures contribute to the continuity of the continuum by allowing it to gain momentum and carry on spreading spatially and temporally. Their necessity is as overwhelming as their constitutive presence: the continuum is too much. No outside means a vast inside that cannot be understood, handled, manipulated. This inside is untenable for humans and non-humans alike. The continuum must be ruptured in order to become liveable, bearable. And so we do: we split it into rooms, property, territories, packs, relations, time. We split it into human and non-human, races and genders, spaces of withdrawal and those of visibilisation. These are Spinozan fictions, extensions of imagination that are necessary for understanding (Spinoza 2009). We dissimulate the continuum. Moira Gatens and Genevieve Lloyd (1999, 34) refer to it as 'the capacity to feign'. So we construct material and immaterial boundaries that separate bodies from each other, we elevate skin into a severing screen, we exclude future generations from our present actions, we put distance between us and the effects of intrahuman, planetary, affective violence, we cover it up with our hind legs, hastily, patchily, unconvincingly. This is often adequate. We take recourse to what Teresa Brennan (2004) calls the foundational fantasy of the difference between the self and the environment, or what Timothy Morton (2013) calls the rift between ontology and epistemology. In this way we carry on with the world, 'forever taking leave' (Rilke 1995, 381). This means only one thing: that there is no difference between illusion and necessity. All ruptures are necessary, all ruptures are illusionary. Neither inherently good, nor bad, ruptures

34 Peripheries

are necessary illusions. We need to pause and rest. It is too fast and fiery out there, in the thick traffic of the continuum. Ruptures are boundaries, borders, property walls, locks and fences. But they are also blankets, gatherings, privacy, oblivion, imagination.

Lesdema's continuum, so brimful with violence, is in its turn ruptured by an endless series of further enclosures, all fractally reproducing the inescapability of the larger atmosphere. In the photograph introducing this section, the camera points to a white barrier stick. The stick is reminiscent of a solitary cemetery cross because of the sign that has been stuck across it. The sign reads 'Closed for Judging'. We are left outside looking in, separated by the prohibitive sign and barrier. On the other side, a handful of people are stooping over some ballot papers or such, we assume. We are on the other side of judging and its atmospherics of enclosure and control. Withdrawing from the atmosphere is a movement that allows a momentary rupture: during the length of a retained, withdrawn breath, the importance of air becomes asphyxiating. While it is difficult to withdraw from earth's atmosphere,[7] it is only marginally less difficult to withdraw from an engineered atmosphere. We are all part of its emergence. We perpetuate it with our positioning, political choices, legal embodiments, body functions. Bodies *desire* atmosphere. Withdrawing from an atmosphere is a withdrawal from the desire of the body itself. Removing the body from the atmosphere is not enough. Atmospheres are preconscious, affective events that cannot be fought headlong because there is nowhere from where to fight them. 'We are always inside an object' (Morton 2013, 17). One needs to remove one's body from the body of its desire. A political withdrawal is always self-withdrawal from the regimes of violent judging.

In this space where we stand, we are still neither outside, nor self-withdrawn. But at least we have withdrawn from that space of judgment where violence takes place in the form of binaries, exclusions, rejections, theological extractions and demonic excursions. Deleuze (1997) talks about the difference between judgment on the one hand, theologically formed, raining upon bodies with the weight of eternal debt for existence; and a justice negotiated between the bodies themselves, without recourse to higher levels, but rather steeped in the continuum. Deleuze writes: 'there exists a justice that is opposed to all judgment, according to which bodies are marked by each other, and the debt is inscribed directly on the body following the finite blocks that circulate in a territory' (Deleuze 1997, 127–128). We are still complicit with it (there is no space free from violence, and the violence of judgment more specifically) but we are at least hiding behind the impossibility of reaching across by claiming the force of the movement of withdrawal: how to move beyond death, marked by the solitary white cross 'closed for judging'? We are fortunate to be allowed to linger here. In this brief, almost benevolent rupture, Lesdema has placed himself (and us with him, sharing his gaze) at a

---

7 Although see Negarestani (2008) on how we are moving underneath the surface of the earth in a cthuloid movement of the war against the sun; and Colebrook (2014) on the death of the posthuman as the ultimate withdrawal from the atmosphere.

distance from the atmospherics of violence. He has managed to capture this distance, however short-lived, minor or desperate. This is the space of spatial justice. *Spatial justice emerges from a movement of withdrawal from the atmosphere.* We are moving towards a new space, on the other side of judging: no longer a space of theologically conditioned atmosphere that comes imposed from above in divine awe and magnificence, backs turned to us and intent on regulating the infinite process of judging; but a space of a humble, everyday, quiet justice that circulates amongst bodies unobservable. We allow ourselves to claim the movement of withdrawal and indeed of looking-away as our just emplacement.

References

Baetens, J. 2017. Right on target. In *Fortunes of War, Life Day: A Reading in Retrospection.* Intellect (forthcoming).

Barsdorff-Liebchen, N. 2017. *Fortunes of War, Life Day: A Reading, in Retrospection.* Intellect (forthcoming).

Barthes, R. 2000. *Camera Lucida.* Howard, R. trans. Vintage.

Bennett, J. 2010. *Vibrant Matter: A Political Ecology of Things.* Duke University Press.

Böhme, G. 1995. *Atmosphäre.* Suhrkamp.

Brennan, T. 2004. *The Transmission of Affect.* Cornell University Press.

Bryant, L. 2011. *The Democracy of Objects.* Open Humanities Press.

Colebrook, C. 2014. *Death of the Post Human: Essays on Extinction, Vol. 1.* Open Humanities Press.

Deleuze, G. 1997. *Essays Critical and Clinical.* Smith, D. and Greco, M. trans. Verso.

Deleuze, G. and Guattari, F. 1988. *A Thousand Plateaus: Capitalism and Schizophrenia.* Massumi, B. trans. Athlone Press.

Fassl, J. 2014. 'We photograph things to drive them out of our minds': war, vision, and the decoding of memory in the photography of Iraq veteran Russell Chapman. *Intervalla: Platform for Intellectual Exchange* 2: 127–140.

Gatens, M. and Lloyd, G. 1999. *Collective Imaginings: Spinoza, Past and Present.* Routledge.

Hall, S. and Sealy, M., eds. 2001. *Different.* Phaidon.

Lesdema, E. 2015. Drowning the moon. www.formatfestival.com/artists/eric-lesdema-0. Accessed 7 July 2016.

Moore, G. 2017. . . . *pro foro mori.* In *Fortunes of War, Life Day: A Reading in Retrospection.* Intellect (forthcoming).

Morton, T. 2013. *Hyperobjects: Philosophy and Ecology after the End of the World.* University of Minnesota Press.

Negarestani, R. 2008. *Cyclonopedia: Complicity with Anonymous Materials.* Re-press.

Nietzsche, F. 2005. *Thus Spoke Zarathustra.* Parkes, G. trans. Oxford University Press.

Philippopoulos-Mihalopoulos, A. 2013. The world without outside. *Angelaki: Journal of the Theoretical Humanities* 18(4): 165–177.

Philippopoulos-Mihalopoulos, A. 2015. *Spatial Justice: Body, Lawscape, Atmosphere.* Routledge.

Philippopoulos-Mihalopoulos, A. 2016. Withdrawing from atmosphere: An ontology of air partitioning and affective engineering. *Environment and Planning D: Society and Space* 34(1): 150–167.

Rilke, R. M. 1995. The Eighth Elegy: dedicated to Rudolf Kassner. Mitchell, S. trans.

In *Ahead of All Parting: the Selected Poetry and Prose of Rainer Maria Rilke*, ed. Mitchell, S., 376–381. The Modern Library.

Spinoza, B. 2000. *Ethics*. Parkinson, G. H. R. trans. Oxford University Press.

Spinoza, B. 2009. *Treatise on the Emendation of the Intellect (On the Improvement of the Understanding)*. Elwes, R. H. M. trans. Dodo Press.

Tormey, J. 2017. Life Day: A visual historiography. In *Fortunes of War, Life Day: A Reading in Retrospection*. Intellect (forthcoming).

Chapter 2

Justice 'from room to room'
Toward a concept of procedural space in Kafka's *The Trial* and the fictional work of Western jurisprudence

Edward Mussawir[1]

Justice, space and the vocation of jurisprudence

The opening paragraph of Justinian's *Digest* records a fragment – taken from the first book of Ulpian's *Institutiones* – on the relation between law (*ius*) and justice (*iustitia*). 'For he who intends to devote himself to law (*ius*)', the fragment from Ulpian states, 'first it is necessary to know from where the very name of law [*ius*] derives. It is called such from justice [*iustitia*]. For . . . the law is the art of goodness and fairness' (Ulpian, *Digest* 1, 1, 1). To derive the concept of law from that of justice today is nothing controversial. Modern legal thought easily presupposes that justice is meant to take us to the philosophical root of that which law explores and demands only in an outer, incomplete or derivative shape. And many contemporary theorists of law have no trouble acknowledging, whether or not directly in Derrida's footsteps, the possibility and even imperative in critiquing and deconstructing the law as such, alongside the radical impossibility of doing the same to 'justice'. Yet Aldo Schiavone (2012), in his close reading of this fragment, allows a different story to be told when he observes that of course the opposite of the statement was true in the historical and etymological sense: that '*iustitia* derived from *ius*, and not the other way around', and that Ulpian, the great classical Roman jurist, could not have been unaware of this (Schiavone 2012, 419).

The meaning of this textual reversal will offer for Schiavone an important clue about the relation of the philosophies of justice to the distinct practical art of jurisprudence. The Roman jurists did not just start off with the same problem that the Greek philosophers had set themselves, for instance, in being able to know, or to be able to frame a proper philosophical receptacle for a thought that has never

---

1 I'm indebted to all the help and good humour of those who listened to and commented upon an earlier version of this paper at the Spaces of Justice symposium in December 2013: Marc Trabsky, Olivia Barr, Andreas Philippopoulos-Mihalopoulos, Anne Bottomley, Lee Stickells, Amelia Thorpe, Zanny Begg, Illan rua Wall and Chris Butler. Part of the research for this paper was conducted as part of a Griffith University New Researcher Grant in 2013. I'm thankful for the support that the university provided for that project. I'm also especially grateful to the help of Marta Madero, Paolo Napoli and to the research support of Lucy Barker for their help in discovering some of the texts of Yan Thomas. Any errors in the interpretation and translation of those texts are my own.

38 Peripheries

stopped asking the question 'what is. . . ?': 'what is justice. . . ?', 'what is truth. . . ?' and so on. Jurisprudence was content to stay within the practical, procedural and ritual dimensions of *ius* (of right) that made the problem of justice revolve around the necessity for a response to other kinds of questions: 'when?', 'where?', 'in what measure?' etc. What Schiavone shows is that this obvious inversion of the truth in Ulpian's fragment had a rhetorical aspect. It 'was used to emphasize a word – *iustitia* – which, as we know, was a rarity in the language and conceptual baggage of the jurists ...' (Schiavone 2012, 419). In this context, far from being simply a piece of dogmatic flourish, the fragment allows one to recognise something of the clarity with which the jurist no doubt perceived the true nature and importance of his craft. Schiavone concludes, about the riddle enclosed in this fragment, that it shows Ulpian, speaking earnestly to those ancient students who were entering the vocational domain of law, defending – even at the height of their renown – the true philosophical life of the jurists: those scholars of law who he thought held a real and practical knowledge of justice in its ritual and procedural dimensions as against those who, calling themselves philosophers, tended to transcendentalise it through introspection and asceticism.

The ancient fragment in other words involves an idiomatic reversal that the contemporary reader easily misses. Ulpian was not relegating *ius* in relation to *iustitia*, a concept from which it was supposed to be derived. On the contrary, he was affirming with this neat inversion, that the art of jurisprudence and the vocation of the jurists who were the custodians, the 'priests', of the very old tradition of *ius* was a real philosophy of justice. As such, those who intended to devote themselves to this tradition, he intimates, should see it as more than entering a profession but as living a kind of life alongside the problem of justice, in the same way that one speaks of living the 'philosophical life'.

I begin with this brief note or story to introduce and frame a study that intends to take the question of 'spaces of justice' through what one can call a distinctly *jurisprudential* register. An approach to such a topic already requires some delimitation of terrain and in particular an acknowledgement of some of the incommensurable contexts and limits through which something, including something as abstract and as immediate as space, might come under the sign and the language of justice. Even in a text like Ulpian's: without a way of acknowledging the distinctly philosophical and jurisprudential conceptions of justice that circulate there and which do not necessarily share intersecting co-ordinates, we are left with what could become effectively a blank page for all kinds of commonplace conceptions to be projected. The relation that justice has to space is surveyed by law and jurisprudence in a way that is not at all the same as that which is posed in philosophical reflection and speculation. And in this way, contrary to the assumption that any study of 'spaces of justice' should go beyond mere jurisdictional limits, that it should tackle increasingly universal problems, insistent spatial injustices to which the law on its own finds no easy or adequate answers, there may be much to be gained by modestly inquiring into a type of space that has a relation to justice only through a distinct jurisdiction: a mode in which that space is spoken in and as law.

Procedural space in Kafka's *The Trial*   39

My aim in this chapter is in this sense to consider and describe a particular type of space in relation to justice: a space of justice that is ordered and shaped in jurisprudence. Jurisprudence is a discipline which turns the problem of justice toward the realm of law, and to the pragmatism, artifice, technology and fiction inherent in the juridical art. It draws this question, that is, away from the theologies, metaphysics, rhetoric and philosophies that transcendentalise the question of 'what is justice?' and threaten to make of it a mode of pure meditation or an experience of impossibility. If it is possible to describe on the other hand a space that is unravelled not necessarily within universalisable and fixed philosophical co-ordinates (such as that of the relation between subject and object), as we shall see, but according to the peculiar procedural contours of jurisprudence – the topology of a 'proceedings' or the shape of space as it is qualified procedurally – then this potentially allows one to observe an important dimension to the concept of justice. Others have shown why it is important not to confuse the territorial aspect of jurisdiction with a pre-given space or spatial arrangement as such (see especially Dorsett and McVeigh, 2012). One assumes that if law acts, it does so either upon a space that has its own nature determined *outside* law, or else as merely one of a number of social institutions that construct space according to a dominant ideology. But the tendency to see a 'spatial' or 'territorial' bias in the concept of jurisdiction has its correlate in a corresponding difficulty in paying attention to the specificity of the shape which legal science and legal fiction in particular give to a space of justice.

To undertake this exposition, I want to focus on two works of fiction. The first is that of Franz Kafka's unfinished novel *The Trial*, a work of literary fiction that reveals one of the most striking descriptions of the procedural space of modern law. The second is the work of legal fiction in Roman law and Western jurisprudence which, likewise unfinished, draws us to the various receptions, continuities and mis-receptions of law and procedure. Assistance for interpreting these works is found in that of the French jurist and historian of Roman law Yan Thomas, who offers a contemporary renewal of understanding fiction as well as juridical procedural space from the point of view of the Western jurisprudential tradition.

The Trial: some fictional topographies

Let's begin with the first work of fiction. Franz Kafka's unfinished novel *The Trial (Der Prozeß)*, as is well known, relates a story of a bank clerk named Josef K. who is interrupted one morning in his bedroom by officers who place him under arrest for something that he is never informed of (Kafka, 1994).[2] From the very beginning, *The Trial* presents K.'s exploration – if not with an attempt to clear his name of this unknown accusation, then at least to access the law in which this accusation is registered – of the strange space of the proceedings. It is a space

---

2 The novel was first published in German as *Der Prozeß* in 1925. The secondary literature on the novel in English alone is prolific and too voluminous to list here.

40 Peripheries

of unexpected contours where it seems that K., left to his own devices, finds that everyone and everything is concerned with his 'trial'[3] and at the same time seemingly unconcerned with bringing it to any resolution. The space of the court is completely contiguous with or indistinguishable from the domestic settings of the people. Apartment rooms, dwellings, ordinary work spaces serve as makeshift courtrooms, interrogation rooms, torture chambers. The most diverse characters reveal themselves to belong to juridical offices, some of which seem to withhold advice on the law where one surely expected it, others which eagerly offer advice where one least expected it. Everything is at once mundane and deeply enigmatic. There is strictly no space that remains outside of that of the legal proceedings: a proceedings that enlarges to be virtually co-extensive with ordinary life and, in its ubiquitousness, is devoid of any content and appears to never get beyond its odd preliminary stages.

I want to focus on the construction of space in this text, first because the kind of space that the novel describes is imbued with some remarkable fictional distortions and exaggerations, and second because these distortions, deeply characteristic of the fictional world of *The Trial*, are – I want to suggest – far from peripheral to the sober procedural world of jurisprudence and the problem of what I will call *procedural space*. There are at least four distinct elements to the peculiar spatial construction in the novel.

1. Door and passageway / topology of the contiguous and faraway

The first aspect is the creation in *The Trial* of a topology of what Deleuze and Guattari have called the 'contiguous' and the 'faraway' (Deleuze and Guattari 1986). The contiguous is not opposed to what is faraway. Two faraway places are shown through some back door to in fact be directly in contact and adjacent to one another like the law courts which K. finds can be accessed through the back of the painter Titorelli's apartment just as they are in nearly every attic. There are thus fictional discontinuities in space in *The Trial* that are shown up by doors, acting like portholes or wormholes, that bridge long distances and which the characters forever either guard or wait for some permission to enter (like a recursion of the parable 'Before the Law' which appears in the novel itself in the chapter titled 'In the Cathedral').

Deleuze and Guattari (1986) in fact notice two types of space in Kafka's work which are particularly exemplified in *The Trial*: the astronomical space of the tower with its orbiting fragments of wall corresponding to the spatial relation of distant–close, and on the other hand an underground space of endless corridors and secret passages which corresponds to the relation faraway–contiguous. This

---

3 The translation of the German title of the novel *Der Prozeß* as *The Trial* in English is not without a certain bias. The German word connotes not just the idea of a trial in the specifically legal sense, but also of legal procedure, proceedings, lawsuit, etc. The English word 'trial' has additional connotations of test or examination.

isn't, as they say, only a 'mental' representation (Deleuze and Guattari 1986, 73). These relations don't just appear as occasional or confused observations made by the main characters; they constitute a concrete diagram of space itself in the novel. A door does not just connect two spaces that one might easily and continuously move between: it introduces a split into space, annulling any continuity itself and in effect holding a particular character before its threshold. At his initial arrest, K. – already within his own home – encounters the space like the segmented space of offices protected by unknown passwords. 'Perhaps if he were to open the door into the next room or even the door into the hall, these two [warders] would not dare get in his way . . . But perhaps they might get hold of him all the same' (Kafka 1994, 6). Passageways on the other hand run like tunnels without end or beginning. They nullify more than they traverse very great distances. They spin and throw one out in unknown directions. And offices themselves, as Deleuze and Guattari (1986) note: 'become contiguous, even though they are quite separated from each other; they also lose their exact boundaries to the benefit of moving frontiers that shift and come together with them in a continuous segmentation' (Deleuze and Guattari 1986, 78).

2. Room to room / ad hoc scenography

A second related element of space in *The Trial* is that which one could call an ad hoc or provisional scenography. From room to room, space in *The Trial* is composed for a distinctly theatrical purpose: designed only for the type of performance that the space will stage. This is so not just from the point of view of the author and his purposes: to support the effects of a dramatic construction that he deems necessary. The 'setting the scene' is directed less by an attempt to lay the story of justice out in a spatial setting than it is through the point of view of the navigation of juridical space that the characters find themselves in. A room, for instance, constitutes a particular space for the conduct of the proceedings only provisionally. Where one expects to find the institutional space of the law to be stable and enduring, one instead finds that it is purely staged, makeshift, put up only for the particular occasion. The law thus relies on inhabiting a variety of everyday spaces for the purposes of the proceeding. K., for example, is initially arrested in his bedroom and in Frau Grubach's living room where the warders await him. K.'s neighbouring lodger Fräulein Bürstner's room is used for the initial investigating commission. The assembly hall for his first hearing is stumbled upon in a room adjoining that of the domestic space of a washerwoman. Furthermore, when K. returns to this space later he finds the court to be not in session and the washroom restored to a fully furnished living room. The law court offices are found in the attic of a block of flats, its entrance announced only by a small card at the stairs written in childish and scribbled writing. An office at K.'s work is found being used as a flogging room where his two initial warders are being punished. The examining magistrate whose portrait K. observes at the advocate's house is said by Leni the nurse not to be sitting in a judge's chair as expected but in a 'kitchen chair with an old horse-blanket thrown over it' (Kafka 1994, 85). All these spaces are seemingly set up, staged and occupied only for the momentary, ad hoc performance for which they are intended.

3. Cramped and open / postural architecture

The Trial also introduces a particular distortion to architectural space: a kind of reversal between the normal relation between posture on the one hand and walls, doors, ceilings and stairs on the other. It's as if it is no longer the architectural space that inherently determines the postures and bearings of the characters, like the mere building-images, the mere settings in which one experiences the shape of a fictional account indifferent to the precise technical spatial dimensions in which it occurs. The architecture of *The Trial* is deformable, distorted, unreal. In the most part it is decidedly incommodious to its inhabitants and designed less for the characters simply to live and play out the vagaries of their fictional destinies, than for a grotesque form of literary torture to be inflicted on them. A building is designed like a projection of certain mannerisms of those that occupy it. K., in this sense, barely enters any room connected with the proceedings without encountering a radical shift of dimension: the closed, cramped stuffiness of an attic, the wide specularity of a theatre or a church, like the one whose size seemed to K. to 'border on the very limits of what was humanly endurable' (Kafka 1994, 163): relations of space which Deleuze and Guattari (1986) link to the motifs in all of Kafka's work of the head bent in front of a painted image on the one hand and on the other the head straightened by a line of music. In *The Trial*, characters are constantly bending down, to whisper, to console, to peer in and out, to bear some kind of weight. Even when the men in the gallery of the examination hall must bend their necks below the awkwardly low ceiling, one senses that it is not the design of the hall itself that is fictionally out of place here, but rather that these members of the crowd, themselves creatures strangely in the habit of stooping, have found for themselves an opportune, fortuitous niche. The cathedral pulpit is said to appear as though a normal man could not stand upright and as though it were 'designed to be a form of torture for preachers' (Kafka 1994, 161). In *The Trial* it is not just architecture which exerts a certain discipline on bodies in space, bending and twisting them to the dictates of a new model of power; rather space retains an element of singularity, completely causally indeterminable in relation to the inherent postures or mannerisms of those who inhabit it. Kafka's characters find out soon that any apparatus in which they are situated was one 'meant only' for them (Kafka 1994, 166).

4. Orientation of detour / diversionary space

The space of *The Trial* is peculiarly fictional in at least one other aspect. The reader notices that to be disoriented in this space is oddly not opposed to finding the right path. In order to find the place to appear for his initial examination, for example, K. is lost. He knocks on various doors at the apartment building at the address using the made-up pretence of asking whether a joiner named Lanz lived there in order to have the opportunity to look into the rooms. When at the end of his tether, he knocks finally on the door of a washerwoman, the washerwoman surprisingly directs him to the actual room for his hearing that he was looking for. K. suspects that she misunderstood him. He says: "'I asked about a joiner, a certain Lanz." "Yes," said the woman, "please go in"' (Kafka 1994, 30). Further on, while in the attic law court offices, the usher asks K. whether he has already lost his bearings. 'Show me the way,' says K., 'I'll make a mistake, there are so many ways here.' 'There is only one way,' the usher replies (Kafka 1994, 52). In a later chapter, intending to meet an Italian business associate at the cathedral on a rainy day, K. happens to discover a small ancillary pulpit only by having been distracted and by trying to rediscover his original seat. It is a pulpit that 'would certainly not have been noticed by K. but for the lighted lamp above it' (Kafka 1994, 161). K. then finds himself summoned individually before the pulpit by a priest, the prison chaplain, who addresses him in person as if, strangely enough, this priest had been expecting him all along.

In a reciprocal way, to approach any direct object within sight, a character sometimes imagines a straight path (the shortest path) to be sufficient, but then seems to become aware at the last moment that it was reached only by having made a kind of unexplainable detour, the object itself bending all the avenues that would seemingly lead to it. When in search of the painter Titorelli's apartment, for instance, K. was 'going to go straight up', but the hunchback girl shows him that 'he must take a side-turning' (Kafka 1994, 111–112). Also, at his initial arrest, when advised that the supervisor was ready to see him, K. attempts to walk directly into the next room but finds himself pushed back by the warders. Once he is properly dressed, he finds that he 'had to walk . . . through the empty room next door into the adjoining room' (Kafka 1994, 7–8).

The world of *The Trial*, its spatial universe, its strange fictional orientations and one could say its peculiar form of non-Euclidean geometry, bears Kafka's signature in no more obvious way than in these examples. In them, one notices a kind of literary stylistics of space that corresponds to Kafka's fiction: a kind of surreal space which it is tempting to imagine as being dreamt up in the mind of the author alone in order to make the parable of an abstract inaccessibility of the law tangible in something more than just parable form. But what I want to suggest is that we are put on the wrong path by imagining that the law's relation to fiction in the novel is solely or primarily one of allegory. Walter Benjamin once observed that most of the interpretations of Kafka, the psychoanalytic and the theological interpretations just as much as the 'natural' and the 'supernatural', missed the point. (Benjamin 1999, 127). But the thing that seems so difficult for interpreters, at least in the field of legal study, to hold onto closely enough in *The Trial* is what is both an operation of fiction *as well as* a work of jurisprudence. And this does not require further contexts, further layers of clever explication, not even some special interdisciplinary flourish that can make the dourest black-letter lawyer appreciate the colourful metaphorical palette that literature necessarily grants to law. The

44 Peripheries

work of fiction would not be simply a neat allegorical decoding of (or disguised commentary on) thoughts borne by the world of legal theory. On the contrary, what one needs is a way of cutting through the contexts, the proliferating judgments, in order to arrive upon a more isolated, delimited, discrete jurisdiction. What makes Kafka's fictional topography in *The Trial* a kind of 'space of justice' is not the metaphor it introduces in order to represent the (in)accessibility of justice or of the law. It is much more the tracing of an increasingly precise, forced, non-figurative manoeuvre. This manoeuvre, even if it annuls metaphor in language, does not annul the work of fiction which justice necessitates in a definite jurisprudential manner: in its procedural space.

Legal fictional space

Why does procedural space not correspond simply to the material structures of the law – the courtroom, the office, the prison, etc. – even when these structures distinctly order, rule, proceduralise bodies according to a form of legal institution? Legal procedure does not operate purely, nor even primarily, as a straightforward code for actions that are undertaken in the *name* of law only and in spaces that are external to the innovation in its form and its thought. The law is usually seen to project its conception of space through pre-existing technologies of representation – the technologies of surveying, cartography, geometry and so forth – in order that it may be technically measured against a standard more or less approximating some measurable 'truth', and as far as possible from those purely subjective or, worse, purely 'fictional' representations which one imagines may make any proceedings descend toward uncertainty. Where there is acknowledgement, on the other hand, of the independence that law takes from material reality, it is more often than not only to emphasise the power of abstraction at its heart: the discursive hold that it makes on the general and the universal. Yet legal fiction describes a manoeuvre that is singular rather than universal and far from a departure from the properly procedural consideration of space. It constitutes a distinctive mode of departure from the realm of 'truth' that is in some ways the reverse of what we otherwise tend to see in the meaning of 'fiction'. Divorced, for instance, as it necessarily is from any material reality, but far from a mere figurative play of meaning, legal fiction comes to describe a precise technical universe all of its own.

In '*Fictio legis*: l'empire de la fiction romaine et ses limites médiévales' [*Fictio legis*: the empire of Roman fiction and its medieval limits], the legal historian Yan Thomas (1995) situates some elements to the study of legal fiction in the work of Western jurisprudence today. Fiction is not, according to Thomas, merely a convenient idiom in which the law expresses its tendency to conservation and internal abstract coherence. Nor is it a simple metaphor or analogy, relatively imperfect, in which legal principle often finds itself commodiously lodged. Rather it involves, according to the way the Romanistic tradition had defined it, a more complete, more definitive and entirely unambiguous reversal of the normal relation to truth and to nature. As the medieval interpreters described it: 'Fiction takes as true that which is certainly contrary to the truth' (Thomas 1995, 17).[4] It has a discrete technical function. It doesn't bathe in the delirium of false appearance. It doesn't simply introduce a displacement between the words and their meaning, which as Thomas says would hardly distinguish it from ordinary language. And it doesn't just manage the relative discrepancy in what is declared and what exists – the doubt or the paucity of evidence for which it would be enough to rely on the form of presumption rather than a resort to fiction *per se* (Thomas 1995, 17). Legal fiction directly negates what is manifestly true.

Thomas prefers to highlight the full extent of this radical reversal and exceptional artificiality to the techniques of right (*ius*) in Roman law. Fiction, in the ancient juridical technique of the Romans, appears to be virtually boundless. It was capable of directly modifying everything from 'being and non-being, quantity, quality, relation, time, place, etc.' (Thomas 1995, 21). Legal fiction even operated over such things as biological givens, going so far as to suppose that someone alive was dead, that a deceased person was still alive, that someone who didn't exist like an unborn child was already born, and so on. It was used, moreover, not simply for making some analogy or equivalence in a typical mode of expression, but rather in order to express the functional distance law took with nature and reality. 'There is no insignificance', Thomas says, 'in a mode which, even for suggesting some analogy, takes the detour of supposing the existence of that which is not' (Thomas 1995, 25). The Romans preferred in this way the fiction of the strict *non-existence* of an impossible or unintelligible clause, rather than the idea of it being simply a nullity. They preferred the fiction, in the law of *postliminium*, that a dead prisoner had not fallen into enemy hands at all – that he had died in Rome – in order to preserve the inheritance, than the more direct expression, for instance, that the law chooses to institute the succession of Romans dead in captivity (as one interpreter renders it) (Thomas 1995, 34).

This distinctly juridical function of *as if*, Thomas suggests, constitutes a remarkable and lasting innovation of Roman jurisprudence; a pragmatic, functional 'denaturing' of the world underlying the very invention of juridical art and juridical technique, that we are able to observe and reconstruct only by taking stock of the long Christian medieval detour of interpretation that this tradition has undergone, and whose traces are still left in contemporary habits of legal thought. The medieval jurists, Thomas reminds us, never stopped trying to rein in the functional limitlessness of Roman fiction: working to bring it within the bounds of a properly Christian sacralised notion of 'nature', 'truth' and 'reality'.[5] Thus, according to

4 The quote is from the medieval jurist Cino da Pistoia, whose formulation Thomas says condenses a good century of doctrine on legal fiction. All quotes from Thomas in the present work are the author's own translation of the original French.

5 The most instructive example that Thomas provides of the work of this medieval re-interpretation of Roman fiction is that of Accursius's gloss on the section of the *Institutes* which denied the right to adopt to those who had undergone voluntary castration as a punishment for rendering themselves feminine. This gloss, Thomas notes, copies the word *castratus* remarkably as *caste natus*, excluding in this way the right to adopt not in relation to those who had undergone voluntary castration (*castratus*)

46 Peripheries

them, fiction could not go unrestrained. It could not go as far as to 'take the place of truth' itself (Thomas 1995, 51, citing Baldus on Digest 17, 2, 3). Fiction was still able to operate in the medieval law, but not to the extent of postulating what was, according to the divine and natural world, impossible. Fiction could feign that a living man for example be taken as having died or a dead man to have died at a particular fictional moment in time, since it was always possible in nature for this man to have died at a moment other than what he had. Yet one could not stretch the law as far as feigning that this dead man had fathered a child, since that fact would not just be untrue but indeed against the very order of nature itself. Thomas explains that it's only because of these very distortions and limitations which the medieval scholastic interpreters introduced to their rendering of the text of legal fiction and which are central to modern thought that, he says 'inversely, the Roman *ius civile* can appear to us in its unmistakable originality' (Thomas 1995, 52).

What Thomas's remarkable analysis of Roman fiction allows us to see, above all, is that what constitutes juridical art at its base – its origin, originality and invention – is the overt and direct discrepancy, the unlimited independence and the exceptional artificiality that it takes with regard not just to the 'facts' as they are but to the entire ontological realm of 'truth' and 'nature'. This is not to suggest, as Thomas comments about the tendency in the thought of someone like Ernst Kantorowicz, the author of *The King's Two Bodies*, that there is anything metaphysical or supernatural in this artifice of legal fiction. It belongs only to the sober world of casuistry and, he says, to the 'cold analysis of juridical technique' (Thomas 1995, 36).[6] It's an analysis and a perspective, however, that for our purposes helps to isolate part of the distinctly juridical and procedural shape given to something which we are so accustomed to conceive within a metaphysical or subjective-intuitive universalism as space itself. Space is not immune from the fictive operations of legal procedure and jurisprudence. Thomas gives the example, for instance, that the legitimacy of the formulary process, limited to the border

---

but to individuals who were impotent from birth (*caste natus*): the opposite in effect of the original meaning. Whereas the Roman jurists perceived no limits of nature to the fictive functionality of the right to adopt, the medieval reception implicitly reins it within the confines of a form of natural possibility, a nature ordained and ensured by God. Fiction can thus, for the medieval interpreters, easily feign that a castrated man may adopt since he otherwise would have naturally had that capacity, but it cannot feign it for a man impotent from birth, since the latter was excluded by nature itself and the truth of such nature or fact cannot be circumvented by a mere fiction of the law (Thomas 1995, 50; 2005, 125–126).

6 It is interesting also to compare Giambattista Vico, who attributed the legal fiction of the Romans more to a form of poetics. '[A]ncient jurisprudence was thoroughly poetic. It imagined the real as unreal, the unreal as real, the living as dead, and (in case of pending legacies) the dead as still alive. It introduced many empty masks without subjects, *iura imaginaria*, rights invented by the imagination. Its entire reputation depended on the invention of myths which could preserve the dignity of the laws and administer justice to the facts. Thus all the fictions of ancient jurisprudence were masked truths. And since their strict measures used exactly so many words, the formulas in which the laws spoke were called songs, *carmina*, which is Livy's term for the formula condemning Horatius to death' (Vico, 1999, 454–455).

marked by the one-mile radius around the city, was extended in effect in Cisalpine Gaul by way of the fiction that it had 'taken place at Rome'. 'The fiction of locality', Thomas adds about this relation, 'maintained the city as a unique space of legal procedure, despite the municipalisation of Italy: the passage of the city to the territorial State was both enabled and abolished by the fictitious attachment to the city' (Thomas 1995, 28).

Just as law was able to postulate, in order solely to think and construct a right, a fictional temporality divorced from any subjective experience (such as in supposing that an unborn child of a deceased had already been born at the time of death), it was similarly capable of describing a spatiality that, like in Kafka's *The Trial*, constituted a definite distortion to the plane in which the subject normally finds themselves situated. This distortion, this detour through unreality, again, is no whimsy or accident of the imagination either in Kafka's case or in Roman jurisprudence. The conception of space that the novel presents, just as much as that presented in jurisprudence, is not just any fictional figuration or arrangement. It is fictional in that it draws us into a world that is not our own. But its fiction operates more immediately on a pragmatic, technical plane: constituting a sober 'way out' more than a free play of signification; a conscious suspension of the normal relation to truth in order to hold to the matter of right. Legal fictional space, if we can read it in this way, is not just a result of an excursion that the imagination has taken with reality; it is also a result of a certain prudence taken with law – the tracing of a juridical space of procedure that can be, and sometimes can *only* be technically described in fiction.

Res and the procedural qualification of space

The space of procedure is not the space in which the procedure occurs. The universe of *The Trial*, for instance, gives us no definite juridical setting, no locus for any 'trial' as such. If one gets the semblance of there being a courtroom, it is soon displaced, hidden, collapsing under its warped dimensions and annexed to some temporary washroom. If there is any actual trial or proceedings in the novel it is one that unfolds *as* and not *in* space. Like the space of legal fiction, procedure tends to bend space to the shape of what it demands in a form independent from the co-ordinates of a physical external world we find in experience. Not, that is, by being completely abstracted from this experience, but on the contrary by pragmatically isolating what in it can still be salvaged for the composition of a right.

Thus, it's not necessarily by doing a kind of empirical analytical work that one is able to arrive at a more precise picture of this type of space. Within critical legal studies, Piyel Haldar (1994), for example, has been able to give architecture a more central place in the possible analytics of legal procedure in affirming that 'forms of architectonic construction – walls, windows, doors, gates, steps, pathways' provide the material basis for separating the inside and outside of procedure, making an unordered exterior come within the bounds of law, representation and justice (Haldar 1994, 186–187). 'The axioms of the built environment', he says, 'the height, length and width of a court room, mark both the accommodation of a trial as well as the coordination and management of its procedure' (Haldar 1994, 186). Yet, while such an analysis of courtroom space can show an otherwise hidden facet underlying juridical procedure (the fact that it is always performed and constructed in a spatial environment operating with an aesthetic, ideological and material force), at the same time, space considered from its strictly procedural dimension, as the analysis of legal fiction has shown, takes on attributes that seem to have no equivalent in experience. It is not a view of the dependency of the trial or legal judgment or legal reason upon the structures of the material world that is decisive here, but rather the strange *independence* that jurisprudence acquires from it, the detour, in other words, that it takes through a world that it makes all its own.

One concept through which one might try to trace with more precision something of this peculiar fictional independence that characterises procedural space – an independence from the truth and from the common intuition of space – is that of the juridical concept of *res* ('thing'). It is necessary to return here to certain works of Yan Thomas (1980; 2002a) for an analysis of the properly procedural function and meaning of *res* in jurisprudence, and again more specifically in Roman jurisprudence. Thomas shows the precise way in which the philosophies and ontologies of the 'thing', tied as they tend to be to a 'presupposed' subject, to the exteriority of the subject–object relation and the transcendentality of the 'thing-in-itself', send us on the wrong track with respect to the things of (Roman) law (Thomas 2002a, 1449). Roman law divided things (*res*), Thomas tells us, according precisely to the procedural element that defined their inauguration and consecration in the juridical world: not, that is, according to some absolute ontological criteria, but by criteria marked by the lawful processes of having a relation with the thing – a legal contestation, a contested 'matter'. The various procedural orders of things (*res*) for Thomas thus correspond with institutions that do not have any kind of natural basis. The law classifying things as *res sacrae* (sacred things), *res sanctae* (sanctified things such as walls and gates), *res publicae* (public things) and *res religiosae* (tombs), did not express social prohibitions or mystical taboos over dealing with such religious or sacred or public things in Roman society. It made the technical space of their legal inaccessibility – their mode of being outside commerce – a tool for grounding the ordinary world of legal exchange. Thomas (2004) shows, more specifically, how the status of *res* in the Roman category of *res religiosae*, applying to tombs and removing them from the world of ownership, concerned the precise mode of definition in which these spaces were prescribed as extending no further than the structure which housed the actual body of the dead. The presence of the body in this way was strictly insisted upon in law not as a concern for the inviolability of a body, but as a concern for imparting the relative certainty of the limits of a body to the potentially unstable juridical category of tomb within legal proceedings.

In two notable articles (Thomas 1980; 2002a), the legal historian shows that *res* ('things') in Roman law were far from having the ontological meaning ascribed to any things/objects of the external world, but were rather a distinct mode of qualification and evaluation, inscribing them in the world strictly and solely according to the regime of their valuation in legal proceedings. *Res* meant, according to Thomas, at its origin in Roman jurisprudence, 'the idea of litigation, the litigious circumstance and the object providing the occasion for dispute' (Thomas 1980, 416). What's important, for our purposes, is that this jurisprudence did not necessarily think 'things' in the pre-given space of an 'external' world, namely in their relation to a (particular or universal) subject, but in their *relation of integration to the law*: through the lens that qualified them uniquely for juridical treatment (Thomas 1980, 418). Never situated in a pure exteriority, Thomas thus tells us, these things 'entirely escape . . . the Cartesian category of extension or the Kantian and Hegelian notion of "*Sache*"' (Thomas 1980, 425). The purely procedural meaning of *res* is held onto with a remarkable tenacity.

To take one example, the Roman jurists, holding to this concept of *res* as both the thing and the proceedings (the thing as and for the proceedings), were capable of thinking it through certain apparently fictional manoeuvres of presence and absence. Once again, while tending to distort the presuppositions of ordinary experience of things in space, these fictions nevertheless held a practical rather than a mystical or metaphysical significance. Thomas points for instance to the following passage from the *Digest* where the jurist Paulus says:

> Labeo and Sabinus think that if clothing is returned torn, or any article is returned spoiled, as, for instance, a cup with the edge crushed, or a tablet with a painting erased, it is said to be an absent thing (*rem abesse*) . . . Likewise, if an owner ignorantly purchases something which has been stolen from him, it is very properly said to be absent, even if he should afterwards ascertain the fact; because where the value of anything is absent, the thing itself is considered to be absent.
>
> (Paulus, *Digest* 50, 16, 14, cited in Thomas 2002a, 1453)

The 'thing' (*res*) here, as Thomas shows, is not a thing like any other object of the external world, but the thing strictly as it is for the proceedings. Only from this perspective does the jurist's particular formulation become clear: the absence is not of the ordinary object (the cup) in itself or in one's experience of it, but of the value that it must necessarily hold in the proceedings, the identity of which must continue unchanged throughout this proceedings so long as it relates to what the parties plead and so that, in effect, the judge is able strictly to evaluate this 'thing in question' and nothing else. In this way, the thing which had been stolen and then unknowingly rebought by the one who had lost it, although it changes nothing in the object itself considered ontologically, nonetheless at the moment it is returned it is said paradoxically to become 'absent', as the jurist emphasises, from the point of view of the proceedings. It's not that the thing itself is missing in the ordinary sense; it's that the circumstance means that it is necessary for a new proceedings, or a proceedings for a new 'thing' *per se*, which here is not equivalent to its mere exchange value, to be instituted. The fact that the Romans preferred

50 Peripheries

to express the idea through the fiction of an *absence* here, rather than through a more direct route, shows the extent to which their procedural conception of things was able to give itself a distinctly spatial formulation. It's preferable, in other words, to think of the necessity for a thing to be fictionally considered absent in space than for the simple need for pleadings to be altered. This procedural Roman *res*, Thomas reminds us, finds itself denatured when, through the Kantian and Hegelian philosophy, it is grafted to a transcendental spatial field where for instance *res* becomes opposed to *persona* like an object is opposed to a subject of right. In Roman law, he explains, 'one can no longer think in terms of the antithesis of the subject–object relation' (Thomas 1980, 425).

In *The Trial* one can also witness a space that has its co-ordinates and dimensions established not by the content of a law, transcendent or otherwise, but by the avenues of a purely procedural logic. In the chapter titled 'Advocate – Manufacturer – Painter', the painter Titorelli gives K. a kind of blueprint for navigating this procedural space. He explains the existence of three dimensions. First, that of a kind of *utopia*: the unheard-of space of what he calls 'actual acquittal' where 'not only the charge but also the proceedings and even the acquittal' disappear from the record and where one may rely for obtaining an acquittal upon nothing other than one's own 'innocence' (Kafka 1994, 124). Second, the space of 'apparent acquittal', where more practically, with great efforts of influence, and with certain formal certifications vouching for one's innocence within prescribed forms, one may convince the judge to make a favourable decision. The procedural difference here, as the painter notes, being 'expressed in regulations issued to the court offices', is that with apparent acquittal the 'certification of innocence, the acquittal and the reasons for acquittal' are added to the record of the charge; however, the matter stays within the court and oscillates between the higher and lower levels with the possibility of starting up again at any moment with a new arrest (Kafka 1994, 124). Finally, the space of 'prolongation' which, as Titorelli explains, means that 'the proceedings are kept permanently in their first stages'. It involves the constant protraction of the minor proceedings to keep them from ever reaching a conclusion. Thus, although the defendant is not free, he can avoid a conviction without too much concerted effort just by keeping the case 'constantly moving in the small area to which it has been artificially restricted' (Kafka 1994, 126).

The fictional distortions of space in the novel are easier to navigate when they are linked to the technical procedural apparatus that is staging it, not as some transcendent, inaccessible 'beyond' to the law itself, but as the purely immanent 'procedural space' where one is left only to make certain forced, sober, pragmatic manoeuvres. The choice of a procedural avenue to take may turn out to be decisive. But even more immediately, the procedural space which K. tends to approach is experienced only in the guise of some *res*, neither subject nor object, a being qualified purely juridically. This procedural thing is merely received when it comes and relinquished when it goes. Giorgio Agamben (2008), writing on Kafka's novels, seems to support this account when he indicates that what K.

stands for in *The Trial* is not a subject, but a false accusation (*kalumnia*), the accusation being

> the juridical 'category' par excellence . . . the implication of being in the law . . . And the being – implicated, accused in the law – . . . becomes a *cosa*, that is, a cause, an object of dispute (for the Romans, *causa*, *res* and *lis* were, in this sense synonyms).
>
> (Agamben 2008, 15; see also Trüstedt 2015)

What's missing from the space of the novel is a certain image of judgment – the element that would otherwise co-ordinate and orient all the various procedures toward a plane on which they would find some coherence and some conclusion. But the *res* – the thing in contestation – remains. The novel in this way reverses the ordinary relation that the procedures of law would have to a truth, a reality and a justice within the situations portrayed. Accusation, arrest, interrogation, examination, court hearing, advocacy, all of those practices which for the protagonist K. and the reader would normally operate within the precise machinery of legal judgment or at least in its shadow, in *The Trial* strangely operate just as precisely to remove it, avoid it, to break it down, to hold it at bay. And this seems to be the result of an act of fiction that is concerned to situate itself entirely from within the space of procedure.

Frames of analysis for procedural space

I would like to conclude this brief exploratory study with some methodological reflections. These relate to some habits within contemporary scholarship in the humanities and social sciences (of which legal scholarship is part) that it seems to me to foreclose some useful avenues for investigating the relation between space and justice. The contemporary sociological study of space tends to bypass some important dimensions when it leaves law as just one amongst a number of sociological operations and institutions constituting an essentially ideological superstructure of the modern world. There is no doubt an important epistemological problem at the heart of these studies – namely of how to produce a knowledge of space without replicating the political ideologies that continue to separate us from it practically, materially, etc. But the approaches to this problem often leave open the distinct form that this problem takes on in jurisprudence, that is not so much of knowledge and truth, the passage in general from a mental to a social space, but something more circumspect and enduring: the peculiar procedural meaning that space acquires within the formal domain of law. The work of jurisprudence here – the science of law – is left relatively untouched by that of sociology, even history, physics, geometry, etc. Jurisprudence need not pretend to offer an account of space from the point of view of its natural or objective reality, let alone its physical, metaphysical, ideological or religious dimensions; it can afford to trace only the necessary, technical (and sometimes strange) shape and meaning that it takes within the confines of the procedural categories and qualifications that law establishes.

To address a spatial conception of justice as founded on jurisprudence is in some ways, then, to return the question of justice to its legal relations, to dwell within law and to hold to the element that gives any social relation of space its 'lawfulness'. Jurisprudence is capable of approaching space in quite a unique way which is very rarely addressed directly and which will give its own set of reference points through which to speak of 'justice'. This is not to suggest that this kind of analysis can afford to remain on a strictly doctrinal level, as though we would only be able to appreciate the distinctly lawful relation of space by being insulated from other disciplinary engagements that might otherwise only confuse the picture. This would be to somehow substitute the object for the tools of the analysis. At the same time, however, there is merit in acknowledging the limits to a form of interdisciplinarity that leaves the surface of law merely glossed by other forms of knowledge such as geography, architecture, sociology and political science. One of course needs a multitude of disciplinary tools in order to be able to cast into relief the relation of space – if one can put it in these terms – particular to law. But what's at stake is not the capacity of these tools to reach somehow behind the normative assumptions of one discipline or another, caught within their disciplinary limits, in order to make transparent a reality supposedly obscured by the opaque surface of law. On the contrary, to the extent that these disciplinary tools are capable of putting themselves in the service of a jurisprudence, a science that holds itself up to one particular form of relation – that of law and lawfulness – one is able to move beyond the comfortable borders between which each discipline makes a merely casual excursion into foreign terrain.

Against this backdrop, this study has tried to follow a course that is all the closer to the surface of a juridical mode of thought and – in doing so – has attempted to keep at arm's length a commonplace conception of space that does not just find itself immediately confirmed in our subjective 'good sense' or 'common sense' but which also tends to be taken as a single transcendental plane intersecting whatever disciplinary frame we want and thus allowing a thinker to easily annul the gap that separates reality from the fictions through which juridical procedure acts upon the world. Instead, the aim here has been to try and hold to the order of space implied by this legal procedural form itself, with all the distortions that this textual condition may demand. Only in this way can one assess a 'space of justice', not by relying on some transcendent perspective, but from within the 'formal mediations' themselves, as Thomas puts it, by which law is 'interposed between the subjects and themselves, between society and itself' (Thomas 2002b, 1425).

References

Agamben, G. 2008. 'K.' Heron, N. trans. In *The Work of Giorgio Agamben: Law, Literature, Life*, eds Clemens, J., Heron, N. and Murray, A., 13–27. Edinburgh University Press.
Benjamin, W. 1999. *Illuminations*. Zorn, H. trans. Pimlico.

Deleuze, G. and Guattari, F. 1986. *Kafka: Toward a Minor Literature*. Polan, D. trans. University of Minnesota Press.

Dorsett, S. and McVeigh, S. 2012. *Jurisdiction*. Routledge.

Haldar, P. 1994. In and out of court: On topographies of law and the architecture of court buildings. *International Journal for the Semiotics of Law* 7: 185–200.

Kafka, F. 1994. *The Trial*. Parry, I. trans. Penguin.

Schiavone, A. 2012. *The Invention of Law in the West*. Carden, J. and Schugaar, A. trans. Harvard University Press.

Thomas, Y. 1980. Res, chose et patrimoine (Note sure le rapport sujet–objet en droit romain). *Archives de Philosophie du Droit* 25: 413–426.

Thomas, Y. 1995. *Fictio legis*: l'empire de la fiction romaine et ses limites médiévales. *Droits* 21: 17–63.

Thomas, Y. 2002a. La valeur des choses: Le droit romain hors la religion. *Annales. Histoire, Sciences Sociales* 6: 1431–1462.

Thomas, Y. 2002b. Présentation. *Annales. Histoire, Sciences Sociales* 6: 1425–1428.

Thomas, Y. 2004. *Res Religiosae*: On the categories of religion and commerce in Roman law. Pottage, A. trans. In *Law, Anthropology and the Constitution of the Social: Making Persons and Things*, eds Pottage, A. and Mundy, M., 40–72. Cambridge University Press.

Thomas, Y. 2005. Les artifices de la vérité en droit commun médiéval. *L'Homme* 175–176: 113–130.

Trüstedt, K. 2015. Execution without verdict: Kafka's (non)-person. *Law and Critique* 26: 135–164.

Vico, Giambattista. 1999. *New Science*. Marsh, D. trans. Penguin.

Watson, A., ed. 1985. *The Digest of Justinian, Volumes 1–4*. Watson, A. trans. University of Pennsylvania Press.

Chapter 3

Artists and gentrification
Is that warehouse conversion my fault?

Zanny Begg

> No amount of 'new urbanism' understood as urban design, can promote a
> greater sense of civic responsibility and participation if the intensity of private
> property arrangements and the organisation of commodity as spectacle . . .
> remains untouched.
>
> (Harvey n.d.)

In a cultural context shaped by growing tensions over art's impact on urban
development – between the enthusiasm of the place-makers on the one hand,
and the protests of anti-gentrification activists on the other – David Harvey sets
a sobering limit. The progressive character of these urban interventions must be
tested against their ability to challenge the spatial dysfunction that often forms the
motivation for their creation. In his dry way Harvey cuts to the heart of the problem for the burgeoning industry of place-making, community gardens and public
art: where these urban manifestations leave the intensity of commodity, spectacle
and private property untouched, they may ultimately fail to foster the greater civic
responsibility or participation on which their very existence is premised.

In this chapter I will explore the tensions generated by the intersections between
art, gentrification and spatial justice, by looking at some specific examples from
Sydney. Through this process I hope to question the causality or blame for gentrification that has been historically attributed to artists (most notably by Rosalyn
Deutsche), looking instead at the broader dynamics shaping the urban landscape.
In addressing this question, I will explore the conundrum that both gentrification
(neighbourhoods becoming exclusive) and its opposite (neighbourhoods staying
very poor) are equally real and unjust. The challenge for artists is to find ways
to engage in public art projects that enlarge the spaces of justice rather those of
injustice.

Miwon Kwon has developed three paradigms to schematically distinguish different forms of public art: (1) *art in public places*: a modernist object placed outdoors
to 'decorate' or 'enrich' urban spaces; (2) *art as public spaces*: less object-oriented art
that sought greater integration between art, architecture, and the landscape, and
(3) *art in the public interest*: often temporary programmes focusing on social issues
rather than the built environment that involve collaborations with marginalised

social groups (Kwon 2002). It is this last form of public art – often called New Genre Public Art – that will be the focus of this contribution as it purports to heal the urban social fabric and thus by its nature invites an evaluation against the criteria outlined above.

Art in the public interest

The importance of public art to urban planning was highlighted in Sydney by several recent announcements. I was a guest speaker at the City of Sydney's launch of its public art policy in 2011, and in mid-2014, Lord Mayor Clover Moore announced the first of a series of public art commissions for the city's million-dollar city plan (Gorman 2014a). In 2014 Kaldor Public Art Projects launched their 45th Anniversary Project, for the first time, selecting an Australian artist, Jonathan Jones, to create a site-specific work especially for Sydney. In late 2013 Jamie Packer announced he would contribute $60 million to cultural projects in Sydney as part of a deal negotiated with the state government for Crown Resorts to operate a VIP-only casino at Barangaroo, half of which would be spent on Western Sydney. In 2006 the Museum of Contemporary Art began a long-term programme, C3West, focused on community engagement in Greater Sydney. These are just a few of the projects that have sought to connect art, urban planning and community engagement within the city of Sydney.

The emergence of 'art in the public interest' (as defined by Kwon) is often traced to the influential early 1990s exhibition, *Culture in Action: A Public Art Program of Sculpture Chicago*, which helped transform expectations of the genre from the creation of objects in space into a series of community engagements and experiences. This important exhibition, curated by Mary Jane Jacobs, drew together the lineages of minimalism, conceptualism and performance art into a new way of commissioning and engaging with making art in public. No description of these forms of practice would be complete, however, without also noting the significance of new forms of architecture and urban planning (called 'new urbanism' by David Harvey), which have fused with these forms of contemporary art to create a globally recognisable type of public art.

'New urbanism', or what is increasingly referred to as 'tactical urbanism', has powerful roots in North America. The vibrancy of these roots was documented in the American Pavilion at the 2012 Venice Biennale of Architecture with hundreds of case studies on urban activism on display. The visual tropes of these forms should now be well recognised: recycled urban detritus such as packing crates, jars and tyres; ecological reclamation projects such as urban farms and gardens; and relational encounters such as walks, talks, classes and meals. According to Mike Lydon, editor of the *Tactical Urbanism Manuals*,

> Tactical Urbanism incorporates a deliberate, phased approach to instigating change; local solutions for local planning challenges; short-term commitment and realistic expectations; low-risks, with a possibly a high reward; and the

56 Peripheries

development of social capital between citizens and the building of organizational capacity between public-private institutions, non-profits, and their constituents.

(Malhotra 2012)

For those familiar with the debates over gentrification, proponents of these forms of urbanism use some worrying language. Lydon enthusiastically explains 'North American cities are seeing influxes of educated young adults who want to re-make neighbourhoods to their liking' (Malhotra 2012). This cheerful embrace of the incursion of middle-class educated 'creatives' into poor and underdeveloped neighbourhoods may raise a red flag for those who have followed the history of the literature in this field, particularly Ruth Glass's 1964 work on gentrification. Ruth Glass, Director of Social Research at University College London, coined the term gentrification to describe the displacement of working-class communities by middle-class households. In the late 1980s Rosalyn Deutsche singled out artists as the 'shock troops' of this trend in her stinging critique of the gentrification of the Lower East Side of New York. Deutsche railed against small-scale entrepreneurs (artists) and elite businesses (galleries and dealers) who were making incursions into working-class neighbourhoods, taking advantage of cheap real estate, to create and distribute culture (Deutsche and Ryan 1987).

The debates over the connection between art and gentrification are often heated. To see the passion this discussion provokes, you only need to look through the comments section for some recent articles: Matt Bolton, 'Is Art to Blame for Gentrification?' (Bolton 2013); Marcus Westbury, 'Artists Kick-start Gentrification' (Westbury 2010), or Joe Kennedy, 'On Gentrification and the Avant Garde' (Kennedy 2013). The debate predictably breaks down into a clash between those who argue that 'creatives' are white, middle-class and fetishise the allure of working-class or migrant areas (whilst simultaneously destroying them), versus those who argue that mourning the development of former industrial areas is nostalgic and out of touch with the working class's own aspirations for culture and change.

It is my contention that the heat in these debates has served to obscure dramatic shifts in the patterns of urban life that artists have, in fact, proved relatively marginal to. In his influential book *The Social Production of Urban Space*, Mark Gottdiener argues that the power of the 'central city is on the wane' subsumed by more messy forms of urban sprawl that have created a spatial landscape of suburban centres, shopping malls and regional hubs criss-crossed by the long commute. According to Gottdiener, if the phenomenal form of industrial capitalism was the city, and its productive form the factory, today the dominant phenomenal form is 'the poly-nucleation of deconcentrated space', and its productive form is the multinational corporation (Gottdiener 1994, 267). In Sydney the flashpoints of the gentrification debate have focused on a variety of areas, from Redfern to Chippendale, that were built for an inner city working class whose jobs, and places of residence, have long since been dispersed into the far-flung regions of suburbia. This point is demonstrated by a recent article in the *Sydney Morning Herald* that documents how workers in essential services now regularly commute over an hour from the city hinterland to work (Gair and Saulwick 2015).

There goes the neighbourhood

The inner city suburb of Redfern is an interesting example of how these issues can intersect, and for me they do so both theoretically and personally. Deutsche's critique was an inspiration for me when I engaged in my own reckoning with gentrification in a project titled *There Goes the Neighbourhood* that I co-curated with Keg de Souza in 2009. The exhibition angrily challenged the displacement of the area's Indigenous, migrant and working-class communities (de Souza and Begg 2009). Seven years later, it is hard to find traces of these communities. The median price to buy a house in Redfern has jumped from $547,000 (Redwatch 2010) in 2005 to $1,178,000 in 2015, clearly out of range for all but the wealthiest (Domain House Price Guide 2015). The median rent was $839 a week in 2014–2015, up 9 per cent from the preceding year. Today the once semi-derelict apartments at the top of Eveleigh Street have been internally renovated and are being rented at $1,000–$1,200 a week (Gorman 2014b). I have found myself caught up in these changes and have moved out of the area for cheaper housing in Fairfield, Western Sydney.

Redfern was not only a working-class area, but also one of significance to the Indigenous community. In a catalogue essay for *There Goes the Neighbourhood* Gary Foley explained the militant Aboriginal history of Redfern in the 1960s and 1970s, including the emergence of the Black Power Movement and the Aboriginal Tent Embassy (Foley 2009). Redfern was the centre of an urban Land Rights claim, with whole streets purchased for the Aboriginal Housing Company in the 1970s. In the 1990s, as land prices began to rise, the AHC began demolishing these houses and shifting tenants to properties they owned in outer suburbs like Mount Druitt. The development company Deicorp caused a furore in late 2015 when its advertising campaign for a new apartment block boasted, 'The Aboriginals have already moved out, now Redfern is the last virgin suburb close to the city, it will have great potential for capital growth in the near future' (Karvelas and Rushton 2015).

The AHC is poised to build a $70 million new complex, incidentally *with* Deicorp, which includes housing for students at nearby Sydney University. The commitment to house Aboriginal people was to be deferred until the availability of 'further funding' (Living Black 2014). The Redfern Aboriginal Tent Embassy was established on Sorry Day 2014 on the vacant land at the centre of The Block, demanding that the area stays in Aboriginal hands. The protesters were concerned that the AHC lacked a transparent commitment to house Aboriginal people and that their removal was tantamount to 'social cleansing' (Feneley 2015). The lengthy and public campaign eventually extracted a commitment to specifically include sixty-two homes for Indigenous families as part of the new development (McNally 2015).

The specific connection Aboriginal people have to The Block is a reminder of the importance of the politics of place and the brutal and often racist aspects of the gentrification process. Poor, migrant and Indigenous communities are being 'cleansed' from the city centre and displaced into less conspicuous, isolated suburban areas in Western Sydney or the city hinterland. Gottdiener argues that such forms of spatial segregation place poverty out of sight of the new inner city elites, thus liberating them from 'responsibility for the less advantaged' (Gottdiener 1994, 272). As Friedrich Engels pointed out as early as 1872, the bourgeoisie has only one way of solving the housing problem – that is to recreate it somewhere else, further out of sight (Engels 1872).

Yet to say that artists were the 'shock troops' of this process is over-stating the case. Deutsche railed against a wave of neo-expressionist artists and galleries that crowded into the Lower East Side with little engagement with its particularities. In Sydney, artists followed similar patterns of location in the former slums and industrial heartlands, opening galleries, bars and cafes across the inner city that no doubt added to their urban chic. Yet while artists contributed to the 'ambience' of a neighbourhood, their arrival and/or departure appears to reflect far broader shifts in the production and reorganisation of urban space than they can be rightly credited or blamed for. The lag between the factories closing and the million dollar warehouse conversions was significant and in some areas, like Chippendale, it allowed three generations of artists to reimagine the city from the same dusty space – from Jellyheads in the 1980s to Serial Space in the 2000s. As the area started to gentrify in the mid-2000s artists might have felt pangs of guilt at the expensive cafes that were mushrooming around them. But when the brewery closed in 2006, taking with it the smell of malted barley and 300 jobs, and an entire block emerged, rebranded as Central Park with 255,000 m^2 of commercial and residential space, more powerful dynamics revealed themselves.

The website for Central Park proudly proclaims its working-class heritage with photos of the brewery workers and a short essay about bar brawls and urban slums. The website also identifies with the urban chic of artists by offering a 'home with personality'. Yet the reality of the commercial spaces inside Central Park is more Superdry than Jellyheads. Suburbs like Chippendale, Redfern and Surry Hills were all beacons for artistic communities that have aggressively gentrified, yet areas such as Green Square or Alexandria, which were less known for their artistic communities, have been subsumed by the same dynamic as part of a general recolonisation of the inner city as a place for elite consumerism rather than working-class production. The flip side of this is that inner city living is no longer the idiosyncratic aspiration of artists, but has become a mainstream dream for upper middle-class families who want easy access to parks, culture, shopping and infrastructure without the drag of the long commute. The urban chic that artists created has been just one of a range of other factors that made these areas attractive, and in places where this chic might be lacking, it can be easily inserted through new public art commissions and the promotion of small-scale retail opportunities.

Artists are attracted to poor neighbourhoods because they have insecure incomes, and they are often displaced alongside other poor residents as rents and prices rise. Rather than shock troops of gentrification, they appear more like canaries in the mine, sniffing out cheap land and then suffocating in the foul air of real estate speculation as inner city land values rise. This is not to let artists 'off the hook' for how they engage with the process of gentrification, nor to gloss over the impact public art can have on the identity of urban areas, but to reassess art's causal role within broader changes of industrialisation and land use. Artists form an eye-catching fringe to the powerful forces of real estate speculation and property development that have aggressively shifted inner city neighbourhoods from sites of industrial production to enclaves of post-Fordist consumption.

The uncomfortable conundrum for scholarly work on gentrification has always been that any effort to improve a neighbourhood could lead to an improvement in the value of land and the changing of the composition of that community (i.e. gentrification). Yet it would be impossible to sustain an argument that working-class communities, with or without artists, should not act to improve their local environments, especially when many are saddled with high crime rates, capital abandonment and severe environmental issues. To return to the case of Redfern, while we mourn the unsustainable rise in house prices and the displacement of sections of the Aboriginal community, who could say it wasn't a good thing that cases of armed robbery fell 48.8 per cent between 2007 and 2009? Or to use a different example: Potts Point today is one of Sydney's most expensive suburbs, yet much of its architecture was saved by militant environmental and working-class struggle through the Green Bans in the 1970s. Challenging the direct causality between creative attempts to improve or protect neighbourhoods and their gentrification might focus attention on more worthy culprits and invite artists to think a little more carefully and specifically about in whose interests they work.

Speculative speculation

Mark Gottdiener makes a strong case against using organic terms like 'ecology' or 'landscape' to describe the urban predicament we find ourselves in, as these terms falsely lend it a sense of Darwinian natural evolution. He argues there is nothing evolutionary about how our cities function, and while they may not be precisely planned, the framework for certain types of land use are firmly established, protected and rewarded. According to Gottdiener, real estate capital, developers, government and business have formed a 'pro-growth' front, which is driving patterns of land use and exclusion, creating violent divisions between enclaves for the wealthy, and sprawl and ghettos for the majority.

In Sydney it is now commonplace for articles in mainstream newspapers to decry the unaffordability of the city, with Clover Moore recently telling a summit on housing that 84 per cent of lower-income households in Sydney are experiencing 'housing stress', with more than 30 per cent of their gross income spent on housing: 'We will not be sustainable unless people in our essential, low-paid service industries can afford to live here, rather than being condemned to lengthy congested commutes from far-flung cheaper housing on Sydney's fringes' (Duke 2015). The first step to challenging the vested interests of investors, developers and real estate agents is to recognise that their dominance is a political choice, which springs from myriad laws relating to taxation and land use, and is not a natural part of the growth of cities, nor the fault of artists for falling in love with the generous ceiling heights of abandoned industrial architecture.

Since the publication of Deutsche and Ryan's 'The Fine Art of Gentrification', the categories 'artists' and 'middle class' have become interchangeable in many of the debates over gentrification. In more recent years this has been challenged by a number of studies on the income of artists, which have revealed that most artists sit in the lowest income strata. For example, an Australian survey by David Throsby and Anita Zednik found that the median income earned by visual artists in the 2007/2008 financial year was $25,800 (Throsby and Zednik 2010) – $10,000 below the poverty line (Melbourne Institute 2007). Similar studies in the USA found that the median income for artists in 2011 was under US$28,000 (Nicodemus 2013). Both of these studies revealed that artists come from culturally and educationally diverse backgrounds that do not neatly match the white, middle-class tag.

While I hope to have demonstrated why it is incorrect to blame artists for the process of gentrification, this does not absolve them from making choices over how they engage with this process, particularly in a context where they are being increasingly called on to help improve the fabric of the urban environment through new forms of public art. Central to the discourse surrounding the 'regeneration' of global cities emerging from a period of industrial decline has been the much-feted 'creative class' who, it is argued, will fill inner city areas with flexible offices, cafes, art galleries, pop-up shops and spontaneous/temporary creativity. Richard Florida is the ideological father of this 'class', arguing that it is no longer industrial production, but 'creativity' which is the source of 'new technologies, new industries, new wealth and all other good economic things' (Bolton 2013).

In various forms Florida's argument has entered the mainstream of government planning. A 2013 NSW Government report, *A Platform for Growth NSW Creative Industries* (New South Wales Department of Industry 2013a), revealed that employment growth in the NSW creative industries nearly doubled that of the rest of the state's workforce (2.6 per cent versus 1.4 per cent per annum from 2006 to 2011) and that more people work in creative jobs than in all of mining and agriculture put together. 'Creativity' is now a core concern of government and business. The conservative state government in NSW has launched a Creative Industries Action Plan (IAP) that is one of six IAPs commissioned by the NSW Government to 'help rebuild the NSW economy' (NSW Department of Industry 2013b).

The preamble to the plan argues for 'recognition of the importance of the creative industries to Australia's future social and economic prosperity', urging a 'strong focus on education and investing in developing creative careers; and the importance of maximising the use of high-speed broadband . . . to improve market access and connect with new national and international audiences'. The recognition of creativity comes hand in glove with new urban planning models. The City of Sydney announced it would spend $1.2 billion over the next decade on creating a more convivial inner city ambiance befitting a 'creative city'. This included $400 million to revitalise Green Square, $220 million to transform George Street into a pedestrian spine with integrated art commissions, $37 million to integrate the Barangaroo development with Millers Point and, as mentioned earlier, $7 million on public art (Government News 2013).

Farewell to the urban working class?

What does the Floridian explosion of 'creativity' and 'creative industries' mean for the poor? In the mid-1970s, Antonio Negri argued that capital's attempt to control working-class struggles, by socialising the wage and restructuring giant plants like Fiat, had backfired and that although the working class had been devastated it had also entailed a greater socialisation of capital with a related 'further massification of abstract labour, and therefore' the generation 'of socially diffused labour predisposed to struggle'. While the category of the working class had 'gone into crisis', Negri explained, 'it continues to produce its own effects on the entire social terrain as proletariat' (Negri n.d.).

Negri thus shifted his analysis of class away from the site of production towards the 'social factory' where layers of unemployed, house workers, students, artists' communities and the poor fell under the category of core sectors of the working class. He emphasised that the growth in job mobility, part-time and casual work, the diffusion of production into the informal economy, and the growth in intellectual labour did not mean the end of the working class. As he explains, 'the only possible answer to this, from the working-class viewpoint, was to insist on and fight for the broadest definition of class unity, to modify and to extend the concept of working class productive labour' (Negri 1982). Negri extended this definition to cover a 'wide range of behaviours in social struggles, above all in the mass movements of women and youth, affirming all these activities collectively as labour' (Negri 1982).

Echoing Gottdiener's arguments on the spatial transformation of cities from the centralised factory to the 'polynucleation of deconcentrated space', Negri and his collaborator Michael Hardt argued that there has been a transformation in the basis of capitalist production from the early industrial capitalism of Marx's time through to the current global order of 'Empire'. While Marx saw industrial labour as hegemonic in the times that he wrote *Capital*, today this role has been replaced by immaterial labour. As they explain, 'in the final decades of the twentieth century industrial labour lost its hegemony and in its stead emerged "immaterial labour", that is labour which creates immaterial products such as knowledge, information, communication, a relationship, or an emotional response' (Hardt and Negri 2004, 108).

Hardt and Negri go on to explain that while industrial labour imposed its own imprint on society – the discipline of the factory, the regimentation of school, the structure of the military – immaterial labour also imposes its own values of communication, networks and affect. Immaterial labour 'transforms the linear relationships of the assembly line into distributed networks' of collaboration (Hardt and Negri 2004, 111). According to Negri, 'if we pose the multitude as a class concept, the notion of exploitation will be defined as exploitation of cooperation' (Negri n.d.). Hardt and Negri are at pains to point out that by the *qualitative* dominance of immaterial labour they do not necessarily mean a corresponding *quantitative* one: 'when we say immaterial labour is tending towards the hegemonic position we are not saying that most of the workers in the world today are primarily producing immaterial goods. On the contrary, agricultural labour remains, as it has for centuries, dominant in quantitive terms, and industrial labour has not declined in terms of numbers globally' (Hardt and Negri 2004, 109).

Central to the development of Hardt and Negri's argument has been the work of another theorist from within the *operaismo* tradition, Maurizio Lazzarato. Lazzarato used the term 'mass intellectuality' to describe the dual impact of the demands of capitalists for the inclusion of subjectivity within the process of production itself and the contrapuntal effects of workers' struggle for 'self-valorisation' and against work. According to Lazzarato, post-Fordism is premised on the 'defeat' of the Fordist worker but also the 'paradoxical' strength of intellectualised living labour within production itself (Lazzarato n.d.). Lazzarato argues that immaterial labour can be defined as labour that produces the 'informational and cultural content of the commodity' (Lazzarato n.d.). This form of labour has broken down old divisions between manual and intellectual, material and immaterial labour by transforming the split between conception, execution, labour and creativity. What is specific about immaterial labour, according to Lazzarato, is that it produces a 'social relationship'. Rather than material products which can be consumed and destroyed by the individual consumer, immaterial labour enlarges, transforms and 'creates' the ideological environment of consumption.

The spatial consequences of this are marked. In the past, working-class neighbourhoods such as Redfern or Chippendale were spatially grouped around sites of production – the railways or the brewery. Today, working-class communities have become more geographically dispersed and fragmented. As Mark Gottdiener explains, we are witnessing the decline of the city neighbourhood, which is being replaced by 'personalised networks of people who commute across regional space in order to experience social communion' (Gottdiener 1994, 264). Concurrent with this physical dispersion is the dispersal of the field of exploitation mentioned above as a new generation of workers find themselves working in creative, caring and service industries where they are being exploited not only for their labour power but their ability to collaborate, care, communicate and initiate.

These two factors have had two inter-related effects. On the one hand the rise of new forms of public art (gardens, meeting centres and community initiatives) can be viewed as springing from a longing to connect a sense of community to

Artists and gentrification 63

a geographic place – a connection that is no longer provided by the large-scale factories and the working-class neighbourhoods of the past. On the other hand, it can be seen as the natural evolution of the expanding field of exploitation with the provision of temporary, low cost urban infrastructure necessary to sustain the productive cycles of the 'precariate'. This tension underlies a sense of ambivalence that can sit at the heart of many contemporary public art projects.

Creative consumers

Crucial to an understanding of these forms of creativity, premised as they are on art's abilities to heal rifts in the social fabric, is the approach they demonstrate to what Chris Butler calls the 'complexity and ambiguity' of everyday life (Butler 2012, 109). There are two opposing ideas that dominate approaches to art and everyday life that frame this discussion: Henri Lefebvre's notion that everyday life presents opportunities for revolutionary praxis, and de Certeau's focus on everyday life as the site for the productive or creative consumer. These two approaches have roughly shaped the scope of the debates over art and everyday life historically, and a wide variety of differing views can be loosely grouped around these two poles of the discussion.

According to John Roberts, author of *Philosophizing the Everyday*, there have been three timelines through which art and everyday life have been theorised. The first is the Russian Revolution, which under the auspices of 'modernism shattered the class-exclusions and genteel aestheticisms of the old bourgeois culture and academy across Europe and North America'. The second is the end of World War II, which 'unleashed popular and intellectual dissent from the old pre-war bourgeois ruling parties and culture'. The third was the counter-culture ascendency of the 1960s, which continued a critique of 'high culture and political economy' (Roberts 2006, 6–7). After 1975, Roberts argues, the discourse on art and everyday life was hegemonised through de Certeau's idea of the productive consumer, which has led to a dehistoricisation of the category of the everyday and a philosophical foreshortening of its potential (Roberts 2006, 122–123). *Philosophizing the Everyday* is a sustained attempt to re-foreground the earlier debates on art and everyday life and to rearticulate the Lefebvrean notion of the everyday as a basis for a '*critique of culture*' (Roberts 2006, 3).

The instrumentalising of a de Certeauian approach to everyday life has allowed a proliferation of art practices that sit alongside, or even directly facilitate, experiences of consumption. The danger of this is that the creative consumer operates in what Lefebvre might call a 'privileged space', one where consumption offers choices for adaptive reuse, reimagining and play. For these practices to retain their criticality they need to be extended beyond 'privileged space' into areas where 'the exigencies of daily living affect everyday experiences but remain beyond the control of local residents' (Lefebvre 2009, 193).

Breaking with this logic requires the reversal of the polarities of choice assumed within the logic of consumption. To conclude this chapter I want to look at a few

64 Peripheries

examples of cultural projects that provide glimpses of how this might be possible. *Fun Park*, curated by Karen Therese, initiated a long-term engagement with one of Sydney's most disadvantaged neighbourhoods, Bidwill in Western Sydney. The project was included within the 2014 Sydney Festival, an expensive inner city middle-class arts festival, yet demanded that, in order to participate, audiences had to make the long and inconvenient trip to Bidwill – a suburb poorly serviced by public transport. The project avoided obvious dangers of voyeurism by opening up a genuinely collaborative space between locals and outsiders, under the artistic control of local residents. *Cup of Tea with Therese*, for example, invited audiences into Therese's house for a tea and a chat. Therese is a long-term public housing resident who is devastatingly articulate about the experience of poverty in Sydney's fringe suburbs.

Fun Park took over a year to create, and the relationships it forged between artists and locals ran deep. The project aimed to occupy the local shopping centre, which was built in the 1990s but never opened, leaving local residents dependent on the local bottle shop, or fish and chip shop, to buy food. When this proved impossible the event took place in the car park and surrounding area. Demonstrating the positive capacity for art-related activities to improve the economics of an area, a FoodWorks supermarket opened in the shopping centre after the event and artists involved have been urging supporters to 'shop at Bidwill' as a form of consumer solidarity aimed at keeping services in the area and the business open.

In May 2015, SBS Television aired an inflammatory documentary about residents of Bidwill and Mount Druitt called *Struggle Street*. The documentary caused a huge controversy when released, with residents complaining they had been duped into participating and then portrayed in the worst possible light as drug-crazed, itinerant, desperate and criminal. In response, *Fun Park* reconvened for a special one-day event that allowed a more nuanced view of life in Bidwill to emerge. When discussing the TV show, Therese explained that 'it was poverty porn, they just wanted to show how bad we are and nothing about how we help each other to survive' (Fun Park 2015). Similarly during the event, a video screening of *Social Revolutionaries Press Conference* was held which provided a space for young people from the area to talk back to the media and explain in their own way the issues for their neighbourhood. Projects such as *Fun Park* were able to challenge what Bek Conroy described, in an essay for the project, as the 'postcode violence' of the distribution of culture and agency in Sydney (Conroy n.d.).

Responding to the slightly different debates between Marx and the utopian socialists, Mark Gottdiener offers some insights into the potential for a détente between the de Certeauian notion of the creative consumer and the Lefebvrean idea of the everyday as a site for revolutionary praxis. He argues that neither can work alone and that radical consumerism and political struggle need to be linked as forms of resistance to urban injustice. As he explains, we need to 'tie together class struggle with ideas aimed at radically transforming personal relations and community space' (Gottdiener 1994, 271). It is within this détente, where consumerism becomes a radical tool that benefits buyers and sellers alike, that possibilities open up between public art, social struggles and everyday life. Through this process it might be possible to create small 'tears' in the fabric of the everyday that might sublate what Butler describes as 'everydayness as a set of social practices mediating individual participation within the world of consumption' and its existence 'as an object of commodification in itself' (Butler 2012, 109).

Another example of a project which provides some glimpses of how art can help improve the 'urban fabric' without necessarily feeding cycles of consumerism and real estate speculation, was *Little Baghdad*, also curated by Karen Therese, this time through her directorship at Powerhouse Youth Theatre, Fairfield. Fairfield is 40 minutes by train from the city centre and is a largely ungentrified neighbourhood with a majority migrant population, including a large community of Iraqi refugees. After leaving Redfern I moved to Fairfield and was an artist involved in *Little Baghdad*. The project had many aspects, but the one I want to focus on here was a series of three dinners called *The Long Table* that brought together the Iraqi population and the broader Sydney cultural milieu. The dinners were catered for by the Parent Café, a community garden and catering company located in a local school. The Parent Café was established by Haitham Jaju, an Iraqi refugee, to ease the alienation and isolation for refugee families through building a sense of community around education and food. The dinners were served in full Iraqi attire, and contributions to the night were made by Iraqi and non-Iraqi artists and activists in both English and Arabic, sometimes without translation. The purpose of the night was cross-cultural dialogue, and non-Iraqi participants like myself were ushered into a space where passionate discussions were held on difficult questions such as ISIS, feminism, religion, refugees and imperialism. The Long

Figure 3.1 Still from *1001 Nights in Fairfield*, single channel video by Zanny Begg, 2015, commissioned by Powerhouse Youth Theatre, Fairfield and STARTTS (Service for the Treatment and Rehabilitation of Torture and Trauma Survivors)

66 Peripheries

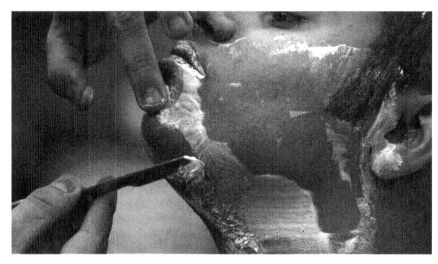

Figure 3.2 Still from *1001 Nights in Fairfield*, single channel video by Zanny Begg, 2015, commissioned by Powerhouse Youth Theatre, Fairfield and STARTTS (Service for the Treatment and Rehabilitation of Torture and Trauma Survivors)

Figure 3.3 Still from *1001 Nights in Fairfield*, single channel video by Zanny Begg, 2015, commissioned by Powerhouse Youth Theatre, Fairfield and STARTTS (Service for the Treatment and Rehabilitation of Torture and Trauma Survivors)

Table did not try to gloss over these issues, nor did it try and make palatable 'Iraqi culture' for an art audience: the event was a 'Welcome to Fairfield' in all its difference and un-homogenised urban culture.

Of course, Fairfield is not immune from the pressures of real estate speculation. Over the last year land prices have risen sharply, making it harder for low-income residents to call it their home. Interestingly this rise has not been accompanied by many of the trappings of gentrification – the one artisanal coffee shop has closed, there are no goget car hubs, bookshops, water-fountains in the parks or organic food outlets. In Fairfield it is possible to observe how the early dynamics of rising land prices, gentrification and cultural projects have played out to their own particular rhythms.

To conclude I want to return to David Harvey's warning on the limitations of 'new urbanism' that I began this contribution with. Artists and 'creatives' have become a key plank in the replanning of public space within the city. Yet as Jill Grant warns, this reorganisation 'calls for democratic and participatory communities and an egalitarian social vision' whilst often 'producing developments for elite consumers' (Grant 2006, 161). Artists face difficult choices about how they participate and contribute their 'creativity' to this urban agenda. When millions of dollars in public money are being handed out for large scale and ambitious projects, the pressure to participate is intense, especially for a social group that is precarious, often unwaged and cash-poor. Yet the desire to resist wholesale incorporation into this agenda will sustain what Matt Bolton calls the 'antagonistic grit' that makes art more than just culturally sophisticated commercialisation of our cities. The luxury warehouse conversion might not be our fault, but our consciences will hardly be clear if we only end up decorating its foyer.

References

Bolton, M. 2013. Is art to blame for gentrification? *Guardian*, 30 August 2013. www.theguardian.com/commentisfree/2013/aug/30/art-blame-gentrification-peckham. Accessed 28 April 2016.

Butler, C. 2012. *Henri Lefebvre: Spatial Politics, Everyday Life and the Right to the City.* Routledge.

Conroy, B. n.d. In the car park of my dreams, https://getfunparked.wordpress.com/in-the-car-park-of-my-dreams-rebecca-conroy/. Accessed 28 April 2016.

de Souza K. and Begg, Z. 2009. *There Goes the Neighbourhood.* Performance Space.

Deutsche, R. and Ryan C. G. 1987. The fine art of gentrification. *The Portable Lower East Side* 4(1). www.abcnorio.org/about/history/fine_art.html. Accessed 28 April 2016.

Domain Home Price Guide, https://www.homepriceguide.com.au/Research/? Location Type=Suburb&State=NSW&SuburbID=36922. Accessed 28 April 2016.

Duke, J. 2015. Affordable housing at crisis point: Clover Moore. *Domain.* 13 March 2015. http://news.domain.com.au/domain/real-estate-news/affordable-housing-at-crisis-point-clover-moore-20150313-143hsw.html. Accessed 28 April 2016.

Engels, F. 1872. The housing question. *Marxists Internet Archive.* https://www.marxists.org/archive/marx/works/1872/housing-question/ch02.htm. Accessed 31 March 31 2016.

Feneley, R. 2015. Aboriginal Tent Embassy in Redfern: We'll evict them from the block, says Aboriginal housing boss Mick Mundine. *Sydney Morning Herald*, 23 February. www.smh.com.au/nsw/aboriginal-tent-embassy-in-redfern-well-evict-them-from-the-block-says-aboriginal-housing-boss-mick-mundine-20150223-13m6md.html. Accessed 6 August 2015.

Foley, G. 2009. Black power in Redfern: 1968–1972. In *There Goes the Neighbourhood*, eds Begg, Z. and de Souza, K., 12–21. Break Out Press.

Fun Park. 2015. https://getfunparked.wordpress.com/in-the-car-park-of-my-dreams-rebecca-conroy/

Gair, K. and Saulwick, J. 2015. Housing affordability crisis has essential workers fleeing Sydney. *Sydney Morning Herald*, 14 July 2015. www.smh.com.au/nsw/housing-affordability-crisis-has-essential-workers-fleeing-sydney-20150707-gi70bl.html. Accessed 28 April 2016.

Gorman, J. 2014a. Clover Moore unveils ambitious $9m public art plan for CBD including a 50m high 'cloud' and a giant milk crate. *Daily Telegraph*, 29 July 2014. www.dailytelegraph.com.au/newslocal/city-east/clover-moore-unveils-ambitious-9m-public-art-plan-for-cbd-including-a-50m-high-cloud-and-a-giant-milk-crate/story-fngr8h22-1227005448024. Accessed 28 April 2016.

Gorman, J. 2014b. Redfern's gentrification continues as families and young couples flock to the inner city suburb. *The Australian*, 20 January 2014. www.theaustralian.com.au/news/redferns-gentrification-continues-as-families-and-young-couples-flock-to-the-inner-city-suburb/story-e6frg6n6-1226806547038. Accessed 28 April 2016.

Gottdiener, M. 1994. *The Social Production of Urban Space*, 2nd edn. University of Texas Press.

Government News. 2013. www.governmentnews.com.au/2013/05/14/article/Clover-to-spend-1-9-billion-on-City-of-Sydneys-infrastructure/GBSDQWBZKH.htm. Accessed 6 August 2015.

Grant, J. 2006. The ironies of new urbanism. *Canadian Journal of Urban Research* 15(2): 158–174.

Hardt, M. and Negri, A. 2004. *Multitude: War and Democracy in the Age of Empire*. Penguin.

Harvey, D. n.d. The political economy of public space. http://davidharvey.org/media/public.pdf. Accessed 28 April 2016.

Karvelas, P. and Rushton, G. 2015. Redfern apartment marketer spruiks 'Aboriginal Exit'. *The Australian*, 8 March 2015. www.theaustralian.com.au/business/property/redfern-apartment-marketer-spruiks-aboriginal-exit/story-fn9656lz-1127150438149. Accessed 6 August 2015.

Kennedy, J. 2013. Strategies against estate agents? On gentrification and the avant garde. *The Quietus*, 22 August 2013. http://thequietus.com/articles/13174-gentrification-art-london-contemporary-music-festival. Accessed 28 April 2016.

Kwon, M. 2002. Public art and urban identities. *European Institute for Progressive Cultural Policies*. http://eipcp.net/transversal/0102/kwon/en, Accessed 28 April 2016.

Lazzarato, M. n.d. General intellect: Towards an inquiry into immaterial labour. Emery, E. trans. www.geocities.ws/immateriallabour/lazzarato-immaterial-labour.html. Accessed 28 April 2016.

Lefebvre, H. 2009. Space: Social product and use value. In *State, Space, World: Selected Essays*, eds Brenner, N. and Elden, S., 185–195. University of Minnesota Press.

Living Black, SBS on Demand, 20 June 2014.

Malhotra, S. 2012. Mike Lydon: Tactical urbanism for urban replanning. Interview. *Partizaning*, 29 May 2012, http://eng.partizaning.org/?p=1441. Accessed 28 April 2016.

McNally, L. 2015. Redfern tent embassy claims victory with Aboriginal housing deal. *ABC News*, 27 August 2015. www.abc.net.au/news/2015-08-27/redfern-tent-embassy-claim-victory-after-aboriginal-housing-deal/6728342. Accessed 31 March 2016.

Melbourne Institute. 2007. Poverty lines. http://melbourneinstitute.com/downloads/publications/Poverty%20Lines/poverty-lines-australia-dec-2007.pdf. Accessed 28 April 2016.

Negri, A. 1982. Archaeology and project: the mass worker and the social worker. www.elkilombo.org/archaeology-and-project-the-mass-worker-and-the-social-worker/. Accessed 30 May 2016.

Negri, A. n.d. Towards an ontological definition of multitude. Bove, A. trans. www.generation-online.org/t/approximations.htm. Accessed 6 August 2015.

New South Wales Department of Industry. 2013a. www.business.nsw.gov.au/_data/assets/pdf_file/0014/30173/Summary-Brochure-of-the-Government-Response.pdf. Accessed 6 August 2015.

New South Wales Department of Industry. 2013b. www.business.nsw.gov.au/_data/assets/pdf_file/0013/30172/iap_nsw_creative_industries.pdf. Accessed August 6, 2015.

Nicodemus, A. 2013. Artists and gentrification: Sticky myths, slippery realities. http://createquity.com/2013/04/artists-and-gentrification-sticky-myths-slippery-realities/. Accessed 28 April 2016.

Redwatch. 2010. The changing face of Redfern and Waterloo: Crime down, housing prices up, jobs and opportunity for the community. www.redwatch.org.au/RWA/statements/2010/100215nswg. Accessed 28 April 2016.

Roberts, J. 2006. *Philosophizing the Everyday*. Pluto Press.

Throsby, D. and Zednik, A. 2010. *Do You Really Expect to Get Paid? An Economic Study of Professional Artists in Australia*. Australia Council for the Arts. Available at http://australiacouncil.gov.au/workspace/uploads/files/research/do_you_really_expect_to_get_pa-54325a3748d81.pdf. Accessed 23 August 2016.

Westbury, M. 2010. Artists kick-start gentrification. *The Age*, 7 June 2010. www.theage.com.au/entertainment/art-and-design/artists-kickstart-gentrification-20100607-xnrm.html. Accessed 28 April 2016.

Part II

Passages

Chapter 4

Mourning place

Olivia Barr[*]

In late 2012, in an inner city suburb of Melbourne, Australia, called Brunswick, or more affectionately, 'the Republic of Brunswick', a woman walked home along the main street of Sydney Road. She did not make it home safely; she did not make it home. One week later, two days after her body was found in a roadside grave in the far north of Melbourne where suburbs end and small towns scatter, more than 30,000 people walked down that same road – Sydney Road, Brunswick – in a peace march in what was, in effect, a ceremonial act of public mourning. While there are infinite reasons as to why so many walked, some knowable, most unknowable, this chapter attends to a slightly different question. That is, rather than contemplating the reasons why each individual walked, or attempting to think collectively as to why so many might have walked, this chapter is concerned with thinking more carefully about *how* those that walked, walked, and how through the practice of a certain form of walking, those that walked, walked lawfully, together. In doing so, this chapter pays attention to a distinctive form of lawful walking conducted in a public ceremony of mourning, and asks how this walking relates to the place of law.

To be clear, this is neither a chapter about the violent death of Gillian ('Jill') Meagher, nor one about Adrian Bayley, who was sentenced to life imprisonment in 2013 after pleading guilty to her rape and murder.[1] Instead, this chapter concerns

---

[*] Thank you to Edward Mussawir, Chris Butler and Griffith Law School for the invitation to participate in the delightfully creative *Spaces of Justice* workshop at Minjerribah in December 2013. I owe much to those island conversations, and to many other conversations with friends and colleagues since this time, but especially to those who call Sydney Road home. All websites are current as of 8 February 2016.

[1] Bayley's sentence was upheld on appeal: *Bayley v R* (2013) 43 VR 335, which was an appeal from *R v Bayley* [2013] VSC 313. In May 2015, in separate proceedings, Bayley was convicted in the County Court of Victoria by Justice Pullen for three further offences involving the rape of three women between October 2000 and July 2012. Sentenced to 18 years' imprisonment to be served concurrently with the life sentence for the murder of Jill Meagher, Pullen also imposed a new non-parole period of 43 years, which extended the previous non-parole period of 35 years. Justice Pullen recognised that this extension of non-parole, having regard to his age (Bayley was 44 at the time), 'most likely extinguished any hope of him being released from prison on parole' (cited in *Bayley v Nixon* [2015] VSC 744, para 1). Bayley applied for, but was refused, legal aid to appeal the decision extending his non-parole period. The Supreme Court of Victoria quashed Legal Aid's decision to refuse aid (Bayley v Nixon [2015] VSC 744). Despite remitting the decision, Bayley was

74 Passages

the public response to her death, and focuses on those that walked in memory of Jill Meagher in a peace march, and how that walking constituted a public ceremony of mourning, and also a public ceremony of law.[2] Operating as a lodestar, the philosophical work of Gillian Rose in *Mourning Becomes the Law* (1996) quietly guides this chapter before emerging more overtly towards the end. By way of context, this chapter is a first step in a broader jurisprudential investigation into the question: *how* does mourning become the law. While I do not offer a complete answer here, part of the response, it seems to me, must relate to questions of place. This is because, quite simply, mourning always happens somewhere, especially public mourning. The place of mourning is therefore both a question of where and how.

On this occasion, when 30,000 people walked down Sydney Road in a public ceremony of mourning, it seems to me that a momentary space of justice formed. By engaging with this moment, this chapter enriches understandings of how spaces of justice form, and it does so in the language of lawful place. 'Lawful place' is a phrase I use to describe a place that belongs, or belongs again, to law.[3] As a concept, it offers a way of capturing the critical potential of paying attention to the place of law, and the law of place, as well as attending to the ways in which we live with law in place. Of course, in locations such as Australia, when the law we live with is colonial, and the land on which we live is not only unceded Aboriginal land, but also itself Aboriginal law, then the question of lawful place – of how we live with law in place, and how we might live this life well – is crucial, and demands proper and ongoing attention. Lawful place, therefore, is a concept I am developing as a way of capturing the critical potential of paying attention to the place of law, and the law of place, as well as attending to the ways in which we live with law in place. In this chapter, the question of lawful place relates to Sydney Road, Brunswick, when, one Sunday, a vast tide of people walked this road. Whether the character of the walk is understood as solidarity, reactions to injustice, calls for justice, a peace

ultimately represented by pro bono counsel, not Legal Aid when, on 13 July 2016, the Victorian Court of Appeal quashed one of Bayley's three subsequent convictions, which required Warren CJ, Weinberg and Priest JJA to re-sentence, fixing 'a new non-parole period on all sentences of 40 years' imprisonment' (Adrian Ernest Bayley v R [2016] VCSA 160, para 12) as prior sentences 'were, if anything, moderate', his 'offending was utterly abhorrent . . . [but] not, however, atypical so far as he was concerned' and his 'appalling history leaves little or no room for optimism . . . for rehabilitation' (ibid, para 189–191).

2 This march was recorded widely. For a selection of newspaper articles commenting on the march, see, for example, 'Thousands March to Honour Jill Meagher' 2012; Thousands March in Honour of Meagher' 2012; 'Thousands Take to the Streets of Melbourne for Peace March Following the Death of Irish Journalist Jill Meagher' 2012; 'Jill Meagher Peace March a Victory for Kindness' 2012.

3 The phrase 'lawful place' is indebted to the work of Shaunnagh Dorsett and Shaun McVeigh, especially their work on 'lawful relations' that runs most clearly through their jurisprudential work on jurisdiction (2012). Dorsett and McVeigh's understanding of 'lawful' as denoting a connection to law, and *with* law, is an important influence in my jurisprudential thinking on place, especially as illustrated in a companion article (Barr 2015, 200–201). Also taking as its example Sydney Road, the road in question in the companion article is an earlier Sydney Road (1838 mostly), as well as a much longer 874km road that, both then and now, connects Australia's major cities – Melbourne and Sydney (Barr 2015).

march, a protest against ongoing violence against women or a public remaking of the ripped fabric of a community as a place to live safely, contemplating this walk as the making of a lawful place means decoupling the question of justice from the institutions, systems and official responses that seek to encompass it.

Lawful place is also material. Like Philippopoulos-Mihalopoulos's (2015) emphasis on the materiality of spatial justice exuding well beyond the reach of legal institutional forms into the atmosphere, lawful place also exudes beyond formal institutions into the materiality of the everyday, albeit much less atmospheric and somewhat more mundane. For me, tracing the sites, signs and traces of common law's material practices, and thinking about how we live with law in place, it is not the institution that matters so much as the walker, and the road. Walking with law, and walking in mourning, it is the lawful walker with their feet on the ground that creates spaces of justice through the repetition of footsteps, such imperceptible minor movements, that in turn constitute Sydney Road anew as a lawful place.

Focusing on a road, this chapter builds through the materiality of walls, ground and place. After introducing the events surrounding Jill Meagher's death, the first part focuses on walls through the representation, projection and dislocation of images captured in the iconic CCTV footage so crucial to the public imagining of this event. The second part turns to the ground by listening to the rhythms of footsteps on 2.4km of bitumen tar and cracked concrete as 30,000 people walk in response. Mourning on the ground, and in place, the chapter concludes by framing this public ceremony of mourning as both a place to mourn, and a mourning of place: a mourning place.

Walls: representation, projection, dislocation

In the very early hours of Saturday 22 September 2012, a 29-year-old ABC journalist from Ireland, Jill Meagher, was walking home along Sydney Road after a Friday night out with work colleagues at two local bars, the Brunswick Green and Bar Etiquette.[4] A busy high street; a short walk home; the offer of a lift home with friends refused. Having half-arranged to meet her at the bar, but fallen asleep, Jill Meagher's husband, Tom, was at home in their Brunswick flat, several hundred metres away, literally just around the corner.

Captured in silent CCTV footage is her last image; an image significant to the public response that followed (3AW Radio 2012). In an impossibly long two and half minutes, this closed circuit video shows a number of people walking past a Sydney Road shop front. Moments of stasis are punctuated: by a car, a walker, another car, taxi, tram, taxi, walker, taxi, etc. A man in a blue hoodie crosses the screen three times, twice by himself, first exiting stage left, retracing his steps, exiting stage right, entering again, travelling in his original direction: no longer unaccompanied. This last image of Jill Meagher takes place outside a dress shop called Duchess Boutique on Sydney Road.

---

4 The ABC (Australian Broadcasting Corporation) is Australia's public broadcaster.

Earlier, and only half a block down the hill on Sydney Road, Jill Meagher appears in separate CCTV footage filmed of the footpath outside Crust Pizza (WordswithMeaning! 2013, 10:39).[5] Posted online as an 11-minute collage, this video tracks Meagher through a webbing of CCTV reconstructions from leaving work to the bar to nearly-but-not-quite-home. It also tracks Adrian Bayley. For most of the collage, the cameras are distinct: one shows Meagher, one shows Bayley. Towards the end, however, this changes. The second last CCTV camera is located at Crust Pizza, and displays Jill Meagher walking, talking on the telephone, as she walks first into, then outside, the frame of the image. Having left the frame, the viewer remains, left abandoned to watch the paved footpath as the circulated image cycles, movement paused, the pace of time radically altered as it becomes increasingly unclear whether the camera has frozen or time really has stalled. In this moment of uncertainty, the reconfiguring of time and space is so impossibly tangible it can nearly be tasted. Suddenly, of course, always already suddenly, a man runs into and out of the frame. The same man, the same blue hoodie, running, chasing it seems, running towards, running after, or, at least, running in the same direction.

The frames are interpolated: in the subsequent CCTV footage constituting Jill Meagher's last image outside the Duchess Boutique, some twenty shopfronts and a church up the hill from Crust Pizza, the chaser has already arrived, no longer running, walking alongside. In this final image, at 1:38 a.m. on 22 September 2012, Jill Meagher walks along Sydney Road with a man in a blue hoodie: not with, but with-away, withering-away, pausing, hesitant it seems, unsteadily holding herself with what seems to be both a mix of alcohol and a broader hesitation. Glancing over her shoulder, clasping her phone, the space of her body language distancing, radiating outwards, attempting to expel, as she stands, leans, steps carefully, stands still, in what suggests an unwillingness to walk further alongside this unknown man.

This most affective of moments was a significant contributor to much that followed, including the intensity of the march. Released within days after she was identified as missing, the final CCTV footage of Jill Meagher garnered an intense response which gained rapid momentum across traditional and contemporary social media. The search for the then-missing Jill Meagher was sharp. An independent, professional, young, married, white, well-educated, contemporary, social, inner-city woman, who simply, unapologetically, went for a Friday night after-work drink with friends before walking the short distance home along Sydney Road was, for a host of reasons, instantly identifiable: identified with.

---

5 This is separate CCTV footage to the final CCTV image (ibid.), but unfortunately is no longer available in full. While the specific CCTV collage that serves as the subject of analysis has been removed from YouTube, a substantially similar but incomplete 11-minute CCTV collage is available here: 'New CCTV Footage of Adrian Ernest Bayley and Jill Meagher Timeline (Raw Original Footage Only)' 2013. The specific Crust Pizza footage subject to interpretation can mostly be viewed from 10:39 to 11:19, although unfortunately it does not include the image of Bayley running across the screen, which would occur, presumably, sometime shortly after the end of this shorter, but currently available, CCTV collage.

Whether it was self-identification or identification through a friend, a sister, a mother, a daughter, the underflow seemed to be the repeated heartbeat that we have all walked 'that' road (certainly metaphorically, but for many women in Melbourne also literally) and that we have all walked that road in the same manner: trustingly. As a result, this last silent image of a young woman having just left the intimacy of friends with a besotted husband waiting, this woman with such heartbreaking timing, irrupted, and snowballed through social media forums as police sought to identify those captured in the CCTV footage, especially the man in the blue hoodie; the unknown man walking alongside. Five days after she went missing, less than two days after the CCTV footage was made public, identified and arrested, the man in the blue hoodie led police to her grave. Having pleaded guilty to the rape and murder of Jill Meagher, Adrian Ernest Bayley, then 41, was sentenced to life imprisonment with a non-parole period of 35 years (*R v Bayley* [2013] VSC 313; *Bayley v R* [2013] VSCA 295).[6]

What was it about this final CCTV image that led to such a response? For it really was an unprecedented response. While Melbourne's political identity is often linked to its vibrant social commentary and acts of public protest, whether through peace or protest marches or other forms of public action, as will be explained in more detail in the next part of this chapter, there was something very different about this public walk. Certainly, this CCTV image was central to all that followed, and has, with time, become iconic. Coupled with a repeated image of a smiling Jill Meagher, as well as various after-images of the march of those walking silently, this has become what is remembered. It structures, or at least contributes to the structuring, of collective memories. In what ways, then, might this final CCTV image of Jill Meagher have contributed to the massive, and so very unanticipated, public reaction of so many walking, and walking so silently down Sydney Road together?

Consider an earlier image, similarly iconic. Also a still-frame of moving CCTV footage, this is the image of 2-year-old Jamie Bulger as he places his hand in an older boy's hand, following another boy as he is led through a shopping centre in Bootle, Merseyside on 12 February 1993.[7] Both ten years old at the time, the two older boys were Bulger's soon to be killers, Robert Thompson and Jon Venables, in an event which marked a nation and triggered 'a kind of national collective agony' (Young 1996, 113). As criminologist Alison Young observes (1996, 111–145), the reception of this image and the response it engendered was intimately linked with both the rhetoric and the trauma of the seen and the unseen; the visible and the invisible. Noticing the confusion between semblance

---

6 Bayley's non-parole period was extended to 43 years, but remains subject to a series of appeals and judicial review challenges, see above footnote 1.

7 The still image is taken from a shopping centre CCTV camera in 1993, which was released to the police and is now, arguably, in the public domain. See, for example, Wikipedia, 'James Bulger before being kidnapped by Venables and Thompson (above Bulger)', 12/2/1993, 15:42:32 . For its continued use in media references to this case, see, e.g., McKay (2000). For moving collages of the CCTV footage, see, e.g., jnic0 'James Bulger Killer Jon Venables Back in Prison' 2010, 0:17–0:27; Shanicee151 'James Bulger' 2008, 0:56–1:12.

78   Passages

and substance and the resulting misidentification of appearance and reality that plays out through the witnessing of this image, Young writes in a manner aiming to both hold and speak across these divides to 'exorcize the phantoms and phantasms of the event' (Young 1996, 112). In doing so, Young reveals a number of strands that again appear, albeit somewhat reconfigured, in the final CCTV image of Jill Meagher. Contributing in different ways to the public reception of the image, these strands include the trauma of the unseen, the active distancing of time, issues of identifiability and the consequences of framing.

Consider the first of these strands, the trauma of the unseen. Witnessing or witnessing again this image of Jamie Bulger, there is a trusting intimacy and softness to the way this small child holds the hand of the larger child. Knowing what is to come, what happens outside the frame, the events that follow on the railway line, again out of sight, the witness experiences an interruption of time, and the distinction between materiality, reality and appearance somehow rupture. There is so much that is absent from this image, yet it is this image that came to dominate; this image that haunts. Of course, while obvious, it is important to remember that this image is not located at the site of violence, of the damage that was inflicted, of the torture on the railway tracks: this is the trauma of the unseen. Both spatially and temporally, the innocuous shopping mall is *prior to* the site of violence, and it is this knowledge of what is to come that hermeneutically leaks from this image. This is the second strand which notices how the image actively distances time. Also important to the rupture of this image is the third strand of identifiability in the sense that the childlike childishness of this small child is, as Young observes, as 'an ideal child, or an *idea* of a child' (1996, 115). The attractive ideality of the child emboldens the sense by which the witness witnesses the image as both present and past; experiencing the messiness of time. Here Young (1996, 115) refers to Roland Barthes' *Camera Lucida* (1981), and more specifically, to a passage where Barthes writes about the experience of viewing a photograph of a young man awaiting execution:

> The photograph is handsome, as is the boy: that is the *studium*. But the *punctum* is: *he is going to die*. I read at the same time: *This will be* and *this has been*; I observe with horror an anterior future of which death is the stake . . . I shudder . . . *over a catastrophe which has already occurred.*
>
> (Barthes 1981, 96)[8]

Witnessing the horror of what has been and is yet to come, Young convincingly draws on Barthes' engagement with the photograph of a young man since executed to interpret the CCTV image of Jamie Bulger.

Likewise, the viewer of Jill Meagher's final CCTV footage also experiences what Barthes describes as 'the horror of an anterior future' (1981, 96). She is already dead, the rape and murder completed, her killer now locked up, but in the

---

8 On Barthes' *studium* and *punctum*, see footnote 10 below.

image, they are both present. Represented as human in all their living materiality, there is simultaneously both an action to come and an action that has been. The rapture associated with this young woman seems to emanate from a certain form of ideality, although it is hard to define precisely what is being identified with. Perhaps this attractive ideality relates, somehow, to the idea of an independent, professional, young woman with a contemporary inner-city lifestyle, and one with so much future ahead? Or maybe the relatability stems more directly from the idea of a woman who can – and should be able to do so safely – walk home alone after saying farewell to friends?

Whatever the form might be, there is a relatability in both CCTV stills of Jamie Bulger and Jill Meagher, and as such, there is a tension between the materiality of the image and that which it represents. In the final image of Jill Meagher, there is a woman who is seemingly material in the moment of the image, yet we know is no longer alive. This knowledge we hold coupled with the knowledge of the image itself as an immaterial projection that objectifies and operates as a work of visual memory, projecting and protecting that which is no longer, and masking from our sight that which has not yet been. This tension between materiality and its other also operates as a distancing of time, where the measure of the meter somehow pauses and we are reminded that time has not always been so.[9] From the plough to the grid (Hachamovitch 1991; 2000), through to a dissectible linear coordination of temporality, there is a materiality to time: a bodily experience, a heartbeat, and one that is about to, has already, stopped. This image, this stilled and silent CCTV footage, is active in its rupture of time, revealing the normativity of modernity's temporality and its representation of a projected and lucidly tangible reality. This visual distancing of time as it folds from now to then to not-quite-yet is what haunts the viewer; the witness. This is where the final strand is raised. For an uneasy ethics dwells, and its bodily inhabitance – its residence – is supported, perhaps constituted, by the very distinct framing of this precise and stilled CCTV image.

Instituting the frame of Jill Meagher's final image, the angle of the CCTV camera is directed from the inside of a boutique dress shop, positioned high in one of the shop's interior rooftop corners. From these heady heights, the image appears inside-out, peering down on two rows of dresses lining the shop walls, gazing toward three mannequins garbed in evening gowns in the storefront window, then continuing through the window and glass alcove of the front door entry, peering through to the outside, beyond, onto the footpath and cracked bitumen and tram tracks of Sydney Road. In the image that unfolds, as Jill Meagher pauses, soundlessly communicating with the hooded figure, the disjoint

---

9 Like space, time is a highly contested concept and understood in vastly distinct ways including, for example, Platonic time, Cartesian space-time, and duration in Henri Bergson, *Time and Free Will: An Essay on the Immediate Data of Consciousness* (1910). For an example of the work of time in common law, see Goodrich and Hachamovitch 1991, 167. For an example of the work of non-linear time in Australian Aboriginal law, see Gagudju elder Bill Neidjie, *Story About Feeling* (1989).

of a metallic line forming the top of the shopfront doorframe, coupled with the line of the window sill, actively disrupts the camera's line of sight and there is a visual rupture of the body. In that moment, there is a temporary disembodiment, and what is most noticeable is her legs: *punctum* (Barthes 1981).[10] Knowing what is to come, the image is highly affective, strikingly fragile, vulnerable, evocative, soundlessly intense. Despite the futility, it is hard to smother the desire to call out, swallow the warning, watch the silent footage silently. Jill Meagher walks outside the frame. With the micro-detail of recording technology, police records reveal that one minute later, at 1:39 a.m., her husband sends a text message to see if she is OK. She is not.

The disembodied CCTV image of Jill Meagher where her legs become the focus resonates with a disturbing contemporary discourse which utilises and displays disembodied live female body parts for marketing purposes.[11] It is within this context we must view Jill Meagher's disembodied live body. Slowing down, and looking more closely at the CCTV footage, a house of mirrors moment occurs when she slowly steps one footstep further, and her head instantaneously disappears as the perspective alters (3AW Radio 2012, 1:59). While her legs are what is most noticeable, and remembered and recalled in everyday conversations, for me this is part of the *studium*, while the *punctum* is elsewhere, captured most clearly in the next moment (3AW Radio 2012, 2:00). In this final image, my eye is drawn to the line above her tightly clasped hands, where her head suddenly disappears. It is this line that ruptures and forces the viewer's sight to her legs in the absence of a full body. Perhaps the *punctum* is her wringing hands just below the headless line? Yet, I do not think so. It is not her hands or legs as such, but rather *the line* between her torso and her missing head that jumps out. This is the *punctum*: the line. It is this line

10 In his short but influential book *Camera Lucida: Reflections on Photography* (1981), Roland Barthes searches old photographs for the 'likeness' of his mother as part of the mourning for her recent death. In doing so, Barthes focuses on the experience of viewing a photograph, and famously distinguishes between *studium* and *punctum* (25–28). For Barthes, *studium* is the subject, meaning and context of a photograph, and what creates interest in a photograph as a viewer interprets the intention of the photographer through the activity of viewing. As Barthes writes, '[t]he *studium* is a kind of education (knowledge and civility, "politeness") which allows me to discover the *Operator*' (28). It is often, however, rather forgettable. 'The *studium* is the order of *liking*, not of *loving*' (27). In contrast, *punctum* is that which is memorable and jumps out of a photograph at the viewer, creating a direct relationship: '[a] photograph's *punctum* is that accident which pricks (but also bruises me, is poignant to me)' (27). It is the detail that draws the eye, and holds our gaze, and as a result changes the experience of the photograph, yet, unlike the intentional and planned *studium*, *punctum* is aberrant, and often unnameable.

11 See, for example, Caputi (1987, 158–197). Think, for example, legs on the bonnet of a car; a midriff with washing detergent; bra-wearing breasts unattached to a head or legs; a long ankle in high heels and all manner of other disjointed images so readily recallable. The disembodiment of live women for the market is a normalisation of acceptable forms of gender violence, and its pervasive non-noticeability is worrying. In many respects, what can be seen in contemporary advertising practices is a continuation of Simone de Beauvoir's (1949) infamous statement that 'Woman is made, not born', although in the instance of body parts in advertising, Woman is only 'partially' made.

that pierces as the head floats in absentia, missing, already dissected. In a further macabre twist, while much less noticeable, there is a double layering of dislocated bodies that occurs moments later when, coupled with her headless body, there is a dislocated bodiless Adrian Bayley (3AW Radio 2012, 2:05–2:12). Having stepped outside the image, Bayley has already passed outside of witness, yet ever so briefly his head reappears in the bottom left corner of the screen, a head absent the body, surveilling her headless body.

Walled through windows, representing and projecting, this image is above all an image of dislocation. A dislocated body, dislocated time, dislocated space. With the angle of the camera, the lines run oddly, dissecting what is otherwise an instantly forgettable visual site of a footpath at night, hosting pedestrian passers-by, with cars skimming the road in the background. The weirdly twisted compounding curves of the camera, housed in the top corner of the shop, viewed through the window, offer refracting layers of screens, walls and dreams through which we watch. The image builds on and contributes to a long history of law's relation to violence (Cover 1986), including violence to the female body, the violence of surveillance, and the violent and demanding edge of modernity's ocularcentrism that erases our senses.[12] Yet, it is the materiality – or the disjunct between the image and its material– that harms, tortures, haunts. This woman we cannot save. She has already died. The witness is left without an outcome, helpless in their legal and ethical subjectivity, unable to contribute to, let alone guide, formal legal justice through the navigation of the criminal legal system still to come, which in any event, is never enough. The unease with which the viewer witnesses the disembodiment of Jill Meagher, from full bodied to incomplete, knowing what is to come – just a few minutes after this image and several metres along – calls for and initiates the work of mourning.

The public response, therefore, offers a way of understanding the ceremonial work of both mourning and of law in the aftermath of this event. Driven by the circulation of the image, haunted by what is outside the image, the public response, it seems, is to what is *within* the frame. Unable to see beyond the frame and that which is invisible to the witness, in other words, that which harms, what becomes important is what *is* witnessed, that is, the materiality of Sydney Road. Cars, taxies, trams, pedestrians and above all, a whole lot of very grey cracked concrete. A footpath that leaks into a road, a white line of order, tram tracks, a shop front alcove, glass, metal, a red line in the brown carpet, a painted shop number in bold orange writ-back-to-front '517'. But the gaze of the witness penetrates outside, wanting to see further. The road, the road: Sydney Road. The glass

---

12 For a recent overview of how Australian feminist jurisprudence has raised these and other issues over several decades, see the *Australian Feminist Law Journal* collection 'Occasions and Events' curated by Ann Genovese (2015), which includes interviews and reflections on three key Australian feminist legal texts by Margaret Thornton, *The Liberal Promise: Anti-Discrimination Legislation in Australia* (1990), Reg Graycar and Jenny Morgan, *The Hidden Gender of Law* (1990); and Ngaire Naffine, *Law and the Sexes: Explorations in Feminist Jurisprudence* (1990).

82 Passages

walls of the shop and the walls encasing the camera lens both create an inability for the witness to experience the materiality of the location. Unable to experience the materiality of the woman now gone, of Jill Meagher, unable to protect her as the idea of or ideal woman we all seek to identify with, the projection and subsequent desire for protection is one of locality; a very material, and very particular materiality: the materiality of the ground. And it is this, the ground, which forms the public response. This is a response full of materiality: a public ceremony of law where patterns of movement rest in a material walking of the ground, and a collective mourning of the road.

Ground: movement, materiality, mourning

With the final CCTV image already in circulation to assist the missing person search, the news that Jill Meagher was dead travelled quickly. Having heard the news of her death on the morning of Friday 28 September 2013, less than one week after she went missing, Philip Werner, a Brunswick resident and photographer, decided to organise a peace march for that weekend: Sunday at noon. Instituted without any formal support from the local council, public interest groups or police pre-closing the road, a quickly made flyer posted alongside obsolescent posters on Sydney Road seeking information of the no-longer-missing Jill Meagher, coupled with a largely ignored Facebook post, and several telephone calls to major news outlets, meant that a peace march was, in effect, planned. As the caveat in small type at the bottom of the poster declared:

> In case no-one seems to be in charge, just start marching peacefully down Sydney road at 12:15pm. I'm just a local Brunswick resident who wants to help end violence in general and against women in particular.
>
> (Werner 2012)[13]

In response to the call of an understated poster for a 'peace march', with minimal planning, no formal support, only a few police officers on hand and less than two days' notice, an estimated 30,000 people marched down Sydney Road, Brunswick on Sunday 30 September 2012 (see Figure 4.1).[14] Heading south from Brunswick's

---

13 Philip Werner's poster is available online, see Werner 2012b.
14 For Melbourne, this was not only unusual in its 'unprompted-ness', but also unusual in its size, making it an extremely large march. For instance, to give a sense of the size of the numbers, later Reclaim the Night marches (several marches all several weeks later) were estimated at several thousand (approximately 2,000–3,000), and the 'anniversary' march on 29 September 2013 when people again walked down Sydney Road was estimated as 'thousands' (approximately 5,000) (Lallo 2012; 'Reclaim the Night March for End of Violence Against Women Packs Road in Melbourne' 2012; 'Jill Meagher Remembered as Thousands March Down Sydney Road in Melbourne' 2013; Zielinski 2013). Compare this with another public ceremony of 'national' mourning, the Anzac day dawn service in 2013, when the number of those attending the Melbourne war memorial on St Kilda Road was estimated at 45,000.

Figure 4.1 September 30, 2012. People take part in a peace march down Sydney Road in Brunswick, Melbourne, Victoria in memory of ABC employee Jill Meagher, who was murdered after a night out with colleagues.
Photo by Aaron Francis/Newspix.

northern boundary to one block shy of its southern boundary, 30,000 people walked, slowly, quietly, in contemplation. Bicycles, dogs and prams, muted conversation and the occasional placard; most walked in silence, as people, together. Pausing outside the boutique dress shop, the site of the evocatively silent final CCTV footage where Jill Meagher was last seen, framed inside-out in such poignantly affective images, a street-side memorial of flowers, cards and candles slowly expanded. Yet while this site could have been the end of the march, it was not, and as the march continued down Sydney Road, some came, some went, some slept oblivious. While some still walked with the mass moving south, others – having walked already – weaved back up the road, whether heading home or for a Sunday coffee or somewhere elsewhere, in a rhythm of circulation patterning the road.

The materiality of movement in this public ceremony was performed through the practice of walking. A meditative walk, feet touching the ground, concrete resting under the soles of so many sets of shoes as those who walked, walked. There are, of course, different ways and different modes of walking (Barr 2016). From the dandy to the *flâneur*, the Romantic poet to the walking artist, the armed soldier to the political protester, the practice of walking carries a multitude of political, cultural and aesthetic meanings (Wordsworth 1793; Rousseau 1979; Benjamin 1999; Thoreau 1854; De Certeau 1994; Long 1967; Solnit 2001), as well as juridical meanings (Barr 2016; Barr 2013). Consider the legal subject, and more specifically, consider the legal subject walking. This is most easily understood as portrayed in William Blackstone's aphorism: 'wherever the subject goes, they carry the law with them' (Blackstone 1765, 106).[15] Refraining from the embrace of the metaphor, and taking Blackstone seriously, one way of interpreting, and the way I interpret this is, quite simply, that as the subject walks, the subject carries 'the' law with them, in this case, Anglo-Australian common law: an act of legal movement (Barr, 2016).

Captured within the jurisdictional imagining of the common law subject (Dorsett and McVeigh 2012), therefore, is a mechanism of movement (Barr 2016). As the subject walks, treading lightly or not so lightly depending on their gait, common law moves with the physical movements of the common law subject. As I've argued elsewhere, what this means is that as the subject walks, common law moves through the technology of the jurisdiction of the person, and as a matter of materiality, common law moves through the practice of walking: juridical walking (Barr 2016; Barr 2013). Yet, as with all walking, there is more than one way of juridical walking. Consider the ways in which different persons enter the space of the courtroom: the walk of the judge, the pace of the accused, the hesitant steps of the spectators. Consider too religious forms of walking, whether the walk to confession, a walk in different directions along the marriage aisle or walking before and after sermon. These are all walking practices differently connected to law and indeed, different forms of law. For this public ceremony on Sydney Road, walking in memory of Jill Meagher, in addition to the legal subject walking, carrying and moving common law, there is a further connection between walking and law. This is a connection that moves between people and attaches to the ground: this is the movement of mourning.

On Sydney Road, one Sunday, we can trace the work and practice of mourning through public footsteps. Whether those who walked did so to acknowledge the sadness of the loss of life, to remember, for peace, to protest against violence against women or violence in general, to be together in community or to reclaim and nurture a place that had been so severely scarred, it seems to me that this walk constituted, above all, a place to mourn. Despite a few placards at the beginning of the walk (see Figure 4.1), including signs of a peace march, this was clearly not a political march, not in the same manner as we have come to understand contemporary political marches, and clearly distinct from later Sydney Road marches calling for women to reclaim the night.[16] Despite different political viewpoints,

---

15 'For it is held, that if an uninhabited colony be discovered and planted by English subjects, all the English laws are immediately there in force. For as the law is the birthright of every subject, *so wherever they go they carry their laws with them*' (Blackstone 1765, 106).

16 Examples of these explicitly political 'processions' include a Reclaim the Night march down Sydney Road in October 2012, specifically linked to Jill Meagher's death, see Lallo 2012; 'Reclaim the Night March for End of Violence Against Women Packs Road in Melbourne', *ABC News* (online) 20 October 2012; and the anniversary march one year later, see, e.g., 'Jill Meagher Remembered as Thousands March Down Sydney Road in Melbourne', *ABC News* (online) 30 September 2013; Zielinski 2013.

and different reasons for coming, regardless of whether people knew Jill Meagher or whether they believed in the ideals of a peace march, on this day, walking, people came together. Walking the road in public ceremony, this march was, more than anything, the work of mourning: public mourning.

What is it to mourn, and to mourn publicly? Sigmund Freud's classical distinction between mourning and melancholia, which is set out in his 1917 essay of the same name, provides a helpful entry point into thinking about mourning generally, and public ceremonies of mourning specifically:

> Mourning is regularly the reaction to the loss of a loved person, or to the loss of some abstraction which has taken the place of one, such as one's country, liberty, an ideal, and so on. In some people the same influences produce melancholia instead of mourning and we consequently suspect them of a pathological disposition. . . . [A]lthough mourning involves grave departures from the normal attitude to life, it never occurs to us to regard it as a pathological condition . . . We rely on its being overcome after a certain lapse of time, and we look upon any interference with it as useless or even harmful.
> (Freud 1979, 243–244)

Freud's attention to the work of mourning assists by illustrating how part of the difference between mourning and melancholia is not only a matter of pathology but a matter of finitude, endings, or most simply a matter of time. For Freud (ibid.), in the work of mourning there is an activity of working through the loss of the object, whether literal or symbolic, in a process of relinquishing emotional ties to the lost object that occurs through the labour of memory. The work of mourning is therefore an activity of heightened and hyper-remembering where the lost object is constantly revived in the psyche of the mourner, replacing the actual absence of the object in reality with an imagined presence. It is the slow process of detaching the attachment of this imagined presence that is the 'painful unpleasure' of the work of mourning (Freud 1979, 245). However, it is only where the 'work of mourning is completed [that] the ego becomes free and uninhibited again' (ibid.).

Jurisprudentially, what is particularly interesting is Freud's observation, rephrased by Clewell: that the work of mourning occurs 'whether in response to literal death or symbolic loss' (Clewell 2004, 43). For the march in memory of Jill Meagher, the loss was both: mourning the loss of a person for some, but also a symbolic loss, mourning the loss of an abstraction. Contemplating both forms of loss involves opening up the jurisprudential relation between movement, mourning and place, which in turn leads to a consideration of public ceremonial law and how this might relate to questions of lawful place. My suggestion is that, in and through this march, the abstraction which has been lost has something to do with place, and with the relation between place and law. Further, it is the loss of an abstraction that is particularly important in coming to some understanding of the work of mourning in this time and space, and how the work of mourning

86 Passages

performed through a public ceremony of collective walking might relate to Sydney Road and the institution of lawful place. As Freud observes, the march in memory was a 'grave departure from everyday life' (Freud 1979, 243–244), and it is a grave departure in the sense of walking. Walking, as an everyday practice, is largely forgettable. Yet, on Sydney Road one Sunday, the act of walking in this manner – together, en masse, in silence – was a 'grave departure', transforming an everyday practice of largely forgettable walking along the sides of roads, on footpaths, into a ceremonial form of mourning in the centre of the road.

What, then, was the abstraction which was lost? There are at least two possibilities, both of which locate the abstraction lost in relation to practices of care: caring for the dead, and caring for place. The first abstraction relates to the care of the dead, or more properly, a loss of an ability to care for the dead. What does it mean to care for the dead? In general terms, the care of the dead is a social, political and legal practice performed in many different ways for multiple reasons (Metcalfe and Huntington 1991; Hocart 1970; Hertz 1960; Van Gennep 1960), and is most simply a response to the knowledge that without those that came before, without ancestors, we would not be. This places the dead as inheritance, and as the carriers of tradition. As Giambattista Vico shows, more than biological, genealogical or familial inheritance, it is through the generation and transmission of our human institutions that the dead order the relation between time and space; an institutional inheritance of the ways we order and conduct our lives (Vico 1967; Harrison 2003). To care for the dead, therefore, becomes a fundamental practice of social and legal ordering, and it is ceremonial practices, such as burial, that reveal not only the ways in which we inherit from those that came before, but also the ways in which law comes to be in place (Barr 2016). In the case of this march, this mourning procession, to walk for the dead and to place feet on the material ground is also a mode of care: ceremonial care, and one that occurs in place. While this may relate to the care of a specific dead or to the care of the dead more generally, it is a mode of ceremonial care that also relates to the ideal or the abstraction embedded in the practice of caring for the dead more generally.

This raises the possibility of another abstraction exercised through another mode of care, also exhibited in the mourning work of this public ceremony, namely the practice of caring for place. Displayed through a form of juridical walking, this is movement across material ground where the placing of each foot matters, and it matters as a question of justice and a matter of 'where'. For on this particular day, 30,000 people walked down the road of Sydney Road. Through a silent demand of sheer physical numbers, cars were halted, removed from their usual space, trams paused and the footpath flooded into the bold, open, central lines of the road. Feet reclaimed, the road opens up, and there is a reclamation of space; a reclamation of justice; relocating the dislocation that occurred through the CCTV image in the stark lines of the road with its gauged tram tracks. In response to the final CCTV image of Jill Meagher, and its haunting beyond the edges in the realm of the invisible, this is a material movement in place by 30,000 walkers that is a call for justice; for some form of justice. For this loss was not only a loss of the invisible, but it was also a loss of place: a loss of lawful place; and of living with law in place. Caring through the practice of collective walking, therefore, was a ceremonial gesture for a public mode of care: caring for place.

Therefore, my argument is that this public ceremony of mourning worked in two related ways: both caring for the dead, and caring for place. This provides a partial response to the question I asked earlier about how we might understand the work of mourning in this public ceremony as thousands walked down Sydney Road, and in what ways this work might be connected to law? My suggestion is that the work of mourning addresses the loss of an abstraction relating to place, to being in place, and to being with law in place. Yet this is insufficient; more is needed.

Gillian Rose, in her posthumously published *Mourning Becomes the Law* (1996), offers a way of pushing this line of jurisprudential thinking a little further. In a book which attempts to realign the ruptured relation between metaphysics and ethics as a way of returning philosophy to the city, my interest is the conceptual promise of the title (Rose 1996). Exploring this promise, Rose engages with the work of French baroque painter Nicolas Poussin. In Poussin's 1648 painting, *Landscape with the Gathering of the Ashes of Phocion* ('*Gathering the Ashes*') (Walker Art Gallery, Liverpool, Figure 4.2), Poussin references Plutarch's *Life of Phocion* (1919), and addresses the city of Athens' final judgment of treason against Phocion. Known for his civic virtue, Phocion was a respected Athenian general for much of his life in the fourth century BC, including acting as governor, until he was accused of refusing to attack one of Athens' rivals, Nicanor, and sentenced to

Figure 4.2 Nicolas Poussin, *Landscape with the Gathering of the Ashes of Phocion by His Widow* (1648)

Courtesy National Museums Liverpool, Walker Art Gallery.

88 Passages

death for treason in the same manner as Socrates: by hemlock. As an additional disgrace, as was the case with Polynices in Sophocles' *Antigone* (Sophocles 1947), Phocion's burial within the walls of the city was forbidden. As ordered, the body of Phocion was taken outside the city walls and burnt by a paid alien with his ashes left untended on the pyre. This legal procedure is depicted in Poussin's companion painting, *Landscape with the Funeral of Phocion* (1648, Louvre, Paris), yet it is his *Gathering of the Ashes* that is of most interest to both Rose, myself, and the question of lawful place.

In *Gathering the Ashes* (Figure 4.2), which is best known for its technical landscape that frames the shadowed foreground with such drama, Phocion's wife is depicted with a trusted female companion outside the city walls where the body of Phocion was burnt, gathering the ashes. Focusing on the wife, this painting can be interpreted as portraying the opposition between pure individual love and the unjust city. Consider the gesture of the wife, bending down, scooping up the ashes, as an act of perfect love against the backdrop of the unjust city; as an opposition of the pathos of love to the unjust power in the domination of architectural and political order of the city (Rose 1996, 25).[17] Gillian Rose, however, challenges this interpretation and argues it misses the political work of this painting. Rose suggests we pay attention not just to the bearing of the wife, but to the bearing of her female companion. As Rose explains in these rich quotes, it is not the wife but the servant, looking furtively over her shoulder that reveals political defiance:

> The bearing of the servant displays the political risk; her visible apprehension protects the complete vulnerability of her mourning mistress as she devotes her whole body to retrieving the ashes. This act is not therefore solely one of infinite love: it is a finite act of political injustice.
>
> The magnificent, gleaming, classical buildings, which frame and focus this political act, convey no malignant foreboding, but are perfect displays of the architectural orders: they do not and cannot in themselves stand for the unjust city or for intrinsically unjust law. On the contrary, they present the rational order which throws into relief the specific act of injustice perpetrated by the current representatives of the city – an act which takes place outside the boundary wall of the built city.
>
> The gathering of the ashes is a protest against arbitrary power; it is not a protest against power and law as such. To oppose anarchic individual love or good to civil or public ill is to deny the third which gives meaning to both – this is the other meaning of *the third city* – the just city and just act, the just man and the just woman. In Poussin's painting, this transcendent but mournable justice is configured, its absence given presence, in the architectural perspective that frames and focuses the enacted justice of the two women.
>
> (Rose 1996, 25)

---

17 Rose attributes this interpretation to art historian Sister Wendy Beckett, as explained through her correspondence with Rose (see Rose 1996, 25).

Linking the wife of Phocion to Sophocles' Antigone, and rejecting the contention that these acts are transgressions of the laws of the city, Rose instead posits that in 'these delegitimate acts of tending the dead, these acts of justice, against the current will of the city, women reinvent the political life of community' (Rose 1996, 35). Rose goes on:

> By insisting on the right and rites of mourning, Antigone and the wife of Phocion carry out that intense work of the soul, that gradual rearrangement of its boundaries, which must occur when a loved one is lost – so as to let go, to allow the other fully to depart, and hence fully to be regained beyond sorrow. To acknowledge and to re-experience the justice and the injustice of the partner's life and death is to accept the law, it is not to transgress it – mourning becomes the law. *Mourning draws on transcendent but representable justice, which makes the suffering of immediate experience visible and speakable.* When completed, mourning returns the soul to the city, renewed and reinvigorated for participation, ready to take on the difficulties and injustices of the existing city. The mourner returns to negotiate and challenge the changing inner and outer boundaries of the soul and of the city; she returns to their perennial anxiety.
>
> (Rose 1996, 35–36, emphasis added)

Through her reading of Poussin's art, and Sophocles' *Antigone*, Gillian Rose offers the jurisprudent a glimpse of how mourning becomes the law, in the double sense of becoming, and how we need to think more carefully about the place of mourning both within and without the walls of the city.

While not yet answerable in full, how, then, might Rose's work help us deepen our understanding of this particular public ceremony of mourning as thousands walked down Sydney Road, and its connection to law? While of course the register of mourning differs between the wife of Phocion and 30,000 people that walked a road in Melbourne, in both moments there is a material practice of political defiance that forms part of the work of mourning and how mourning might just somehow and somewhen, yet always temporarily, become the law. In the road and for the road, this act of political defiance is not just an act of love, whether for person or place (for presumably most of those that marched never knew Jill Meagher, and it cannot be assumed that all that walked loved the place of Sydney Road), but an act of justice; a space of justice. In the background rests a criminal legal system that appears structurally incapable of delivering 'justice'; a criminal justice system that is never enough. Whether drawing on 'transcendent but representable justice' or more spatial accounts of justice, by walking the road together in a ceremony of mourning, public suffering is both visible and able to become speakable (Rose 1996, 35). It is this public response to the rape and murder of Jill Meagher that manifests in a public ceremony of law that opens up the possibility of thinking more carefully about the spaces of justice and the grounded place of law, and more specifically, relations between the legal and architectural ordering of the old city and a new ethics of lawful place.

Openings: public ceremonial law, spaces of justice, lawful place

To conclude, I would like to return to the beginning of the walk, one Sunday at noon on the northern boundary of Brunswick, when it was still not yet clear that 30,000 people would walk. In response to an initial request by a police officer for the march to walk down the footpath, before the overwhelming numbers became apparent and the suggestion near-instantaneously redundant, Philip Werner, who instigated the march, commented on the importance of walking down Sydney Road, observing 'the way that marches and festivals can close down, or rather open up, a public road, and give it back to people on foot' (Werner 2012a).

In kind, intrigued by the suggestiveness of Gillian Rose's philosophical work, this chapter has opened up the jurisprudential question of how mourning becomes the law. In September 2012, when 30,000 people walked in a public ceremony of mourning, this was a moment when, somehow, mourning becomes the law. But, as always, the jurisprudential question is one of 'how?' As a public ceremony of mourning, it seems to me this juridical walk was both a place to mourn, and a mourning of place. That is, this march was a *mourning place*, and the work of this public ceremony of mourning was in relation to both the loss of Jill Meagher and a further, abstract loss. This loss was the loss of place; a loss of lawful place; and of living with law in place. In this respect, my argument has been that this public ceremony of mourning has worked in two related ways: both caring for the dead, and caring for place. Through the material practice of care, through the delicate relation between movement and rest in this public ceremony of mourning, there is a connection to law, and a connection, more specifically, to the possibility – or at least the question – of lawful place.

By focusing on an example of a public ceremony of mourning, this chapter has considered ways in which ceremonies of law are integral to the life of law, and to the conduct of life with law. Questions of ceremony and ritual are, of course, intimately connected with the modes, forms and shapes of law. They are also connected with the time, space and place of law. By reconfiguring public ceremonies of mourning as a (somewhat) forgotten aspect of public law, that is, public ceremonial law, the question of how a public ceremony of mourning, such as the march in memory of Jill Meagher, contributed to the institution of the time and space of Sydney Road, Brunswick, has been translated into a question of 'lawful place', that is, how a place belongs (or belongs again) to law. Put boldly, such ceremonies not only inaugurate the time and space of law, but through ceremonial rhythms slowly oscillating between movement and rest, they also contribute to the place of law, and of how we live with law in place. The shared walking of Sydney Road was more than a call for justice awaiting a response, but also a lawful place. This moment of collective walking was a dynamic and legal activity of law moving in place, settling into the material soundtrack of the road, resting in place. In other words, the shared walking of Sydney Road wrote itself into the road to be remembered as a place that could be mourned, and a place to mourn together: a mourning place. Yet the question that still remains, and one that I find myself continually wanting to ask, despite its manifest absurdity is: *how might a road mourn?* Well, figuratively, at least, a road mourns through movement. For it is through material practices of movement, such as walking and public ceremonies of mourning, that mourning becomes the law, and, just perhaps, movement becomes lawful place.

References

Books and journal articles

Barr, O. 2013. Walking with Empire. *Australian Feminist Law Journal* 38: 59–74.

Barr, O. 2015. A jurisprudential tale of a road, an office, and a triangle. *Law and Literature* 27(2): 199–216.

Barr, O. 2016. *A Jurisprudence of Movement: Common Law, Walking, Unsettling Place*. Routledge.

Barthes, R. 1981. *Camera Lucida: Reflections on Photography*. Vintage Books.

Beauvoir, S. de. 1949. *The Second Sex*. Parshley, H. M. trans. Gallimard.

Benjamin, W. 1999. *The Arcades Project*. Belknap Press.

Bergson, H. 1910. *Time and Free Will: An Essay on the Immediate Data of Consciousness*. F. L. Pogson trans. Kessinger.

Blackstone, W. 1765. *Commentaries on the Laws of England*. Clarendon Press.

Caputi, J. 1987. *The Age of Sex Crime*. Women's Press.

Cover, R. 1986. Violence and the word. *Yale Law Review* 95: 1601–1629.

Clewell, T. 2004. Mourning beyond melancholia: Freud's psychoanalysis of loss. *Journal of the American Psychoanalytic Association* 52: 43–67.

De Certeau, M. 1994. *The Practice of Everyday Life*. University of California Press.

Dorsett, S. and McVeigh, S. 2012. *Jurisdiction*. Routledge.

Freud, S. 1979. Mourning and melancholia. In *The Standard Edition of the Complete Psychological Works of Sigmund Freud*, vol. 14, ed. James Strachey. Hogarth Press.

Gennep, A. van. 1960. *The Rites of Passage*. Vicedom, M. and Kimball, S. trans. University of Chicago Press.

Genovese, A., Thornton, M., Naffine, N., Heath, M., Graycar, R., Morgan, J. and Hunter, R. 2015. Occasions and Events. *Australian Feminist Law Journal* 41(1): 1–42.

Goodrich, P. and Hachamovitch, Y. 1991. Time out of mind: An introduction to the semiotics of common law. In *Dangerous Supplements: Resistance and Renewal in Jurisprudence*, ed. Fitzpatrick, P. 159–181. Pluto Press.

Graycar, R. and Morgan, J. 1990. *The Hidden Gender of Law*. Federation Press.

Hachamovitch, Y. 1991. The ideal object of delirium: An essay on the faith which attaches to instruments (*de fide instrumentorum*). *Law and Critique* 2(1): 85–101.

Hachamovitch, Y. 2000. Ploughing the delirium. In *Merleau-Ponty: Difference, Materiality, Painting*, ed. Foti, V. 112–126. Humanity Books.

Harrison, R. P. 2003. *The Dominion of the Dead*. University of Chicago Press.

Hertz, R. 1960. *Death and the Right Hand*. Needham, R. and Needham, C. trans. Cohen & West.

Hocart, A. M. 1970. *Kings and Councillors: An Essay in the Comparative Anatomy of Human Society*. University of Chicago Press.

Metcalfe, P. and Huntington, R. 1991. *Celebrations of Death: The Anthropology of Mortuary Ritual*, 2nd edn. Cambridge University Press.

Naffine, N. 1990. *Law and the Sexes: Explorations in Feminist Jurisprudence*. Allen & Unwin.

92   Passages

Neidjie, B. 1989. *Story about Feeling*. Magabala Books.

Philippopoulos-Mihalopoulos, A. 2015. *Spatial Justice: Body, Lawscape, Atmosphere*. Routledge.

Plutarch. 1919. *Lives: Sertorius and Eumenes, Phocion and Cato the Younger*, vol. 8. Perrin B. trans. Harvard University Press.

Rose, G. 1996. *Mourning Becomes the Law: Philosophy and Representation*. Cambridge University Press.

Rousseau, J-J. 1979. *Reveries of the Solitary Walker*. Penguin.

Solnit, R. 2001.*Wanderlust: A History of Walking*. Verso.

Sophocles.1947. Antigone. In *The Theban Plays: King Oedipus, Oedipus at Colonus, Antigone*. Watline, E. F. trans. Penguin.

Thoreau, H. D. 1854. *Walden*. Ticnor and Fields.

Thornton, M. 1990. *The Liberal Promise: Anti-Discrimination Legislation in Australia*. Oxford University Press.

Vico, G. 1967.*The New Science of Giambattista Vico*. Bergin T. G. and Fisch M. H. trans. Cornell University Press.

Wordsworth, W. 1793. *Descriptive Sketches: Taken During a Pedestrian Tour in the Italian, Grison, Swiss, and Savoyard Alps*. Joseph Johnson.

Young, A. 1996. *Imagining Crime: Textual Outlaws and Criminal Conversations*. Sage.

Artworks

Long, R. 1967. *A Line Made by Walking*. London: Tate. Available online at www. richardlong.org/Sculptures/2011sculptures/linewalking.html. Accessed 30 March 2016.

Poussin, N. 1648. *The Gathering of the Ashes of Phocion by his Widow*. Liverpool: Walker Art Gallery. Available online at www.liverpoolmuseums.org.uk/picture-of-month/dis-playpicture.aspx?id=370. Accessed 30 March 2016.

Poussin, N. 1648. *Landscape with the Funeral of Phocion*. Paris: Louvre. Available online at www.wga.hu/support/viewer_m/z.html. Accessed 30 March 2016.

Cases

Bayley v Nixon [2015] VSC 744.

Bayley v R [2013] VSCA 295.

Bayley v R (2013) 43 VR 335.

R v Bayley [2013] VSC 313.

Newspaper articles, CCTV footage and other online materials

3AWRadio. 2012. *Jill Meagher CCTV Footage*. Online video. www.youtube.com/watch?v=HiBck13rpcA. Accessed 8 February 2016.

'James Bulger before being kidnapped by Venables and Thompson'. *Wikipedia*, Wikimedia. https://upload.wikimedia.org/wikipedia/en/6/62/Bulger_cctv.jpg. Accessed 8 February 2016.

'Jill Meagher peace march a victory for kindness'. *ABC*, 2 October 2012. www.abc.net.au/local/stories/2012/10/02/3601865.htm. Accessed 8 February 2016.

'Jill Meagher remembered as thousands march down Sydney Road in Melbourne'. *ABC*

News, 30 September 2013. www.abc.net.au/news/2013-09-29/thousands-march-to-remember-jill-meagher/4987756. Accessed 8 February 2016.

jnic0. 2010. *James Bulger Killer Jon Venables Back in Prison*. Online video. https://www.youtube.com/watch?v=e512FdCqjXE. Accessed 8 February 2016.

Lallo, M. 2012. 'Thousands march to reclaim the night'. *The Age*, 20 October 2012. www.theage.com.au/victoria/thousands-march-to-reclaim-the-night-20121020-27yln.html. Accessed 8 February 2016.

McKay, M. 2000. 'Every parent's nightmare'. *BBC News*, 26 October 2000. http://news.bbc.co.uk/2/hi/uk/991562.stm. Accessed 8 February 2016.

'Reclaim the night march for end of violence against women packs road in Melbourne'. *ABC News*, 20 October 2012. www.abc.net.au/news/2013-10-20/reclaim-the-night-march-packs-sydney-road-in-melbourne/5033864. Accessed 8 February 2016.

Shanicee151. 2008. *James Bulger*. Online video. https://www.youtube.com/watch?v=M0XYSgi5f6I. Accessed 8 February 2016.

'Thousands march in honour of Meagher'. *ABC News*, 1 October 2012. www.abc.net.au/news/2012-09-30/community-to-march-in-honour-of-meagher/4287762. Accessed 8 February 2016.

'Thousands march to honour Jill Meagher'. *The Age*, 30 September 2012. www.theage.com.au/victoria/thousands-march-to-honour-jill-meagher-20120930-26t6v.html. Accessed 8 February 2016.

'Thousands take to the streets of Melbourne for peace march following the death of Irish journalist Jill Meagher'. *Daily Mail Australia*, 1 October 2012. www.dailymail.co.uk/news/article-2210838/Thousands-streets-Melbourne-peace-march-following-death-Irish-journalist-Jill-Meagher.html. Accessed 8 February 2016.

Werner, P. 2012a. 'Why I organised what became Melbourne's largest peace march of recent times'. *philip werner foto*. http://philipwernerfoto.com/2012/10/01/peace-march-for-jill-megher-goes-30000-strong. Accessed 8 February 2016.

Werner, P. 2012b. 'The poster I made for the march'. *philip werner foto* http://philipwernerfoto.com/2012/10/01/peace-march-for-jill-megher-goes-30000-strong/. Accessed 8 February 2016.

WordswithMeaning! 2013. *New CCTV Footage of Adrian Ernest Bayley and Jill Meagher Timeline (Raw Original Footage Only)*. Online video. https://www.youtube.com/watch?v=5QbRGBMvk-8. Accessed 8 February 2016.

Zielinski, C. 2013. 'Thousands march to remember Jill Meagher'. *The Age*, 30 September 2013. www.theage.com.au/victoria/thousands-march-to-remember-jill-meagher-20130929-2umj1.html. Accessed 8 February 2016.

Chapter 5

Walking with the dead
Coronial law and spatial justice in the necropolis

Marc Trabsky

> A Coroner of our Lord the King ought to inquire of these Things . . . to the Places where any be slain, or suddenly dead, or wounded.
>
> (Officio Coronatoris 1276)

> [O]ne does not get rid of the dead, one is never finished with them.
>
> (Ricoeur 2009, 9)

The modern history of the coronial institution paints a grim portrait of the plight of the dead. Where the dead were found on a public street, the coroner would carry the corpse from one public house to another, hoping to find a hospitable innkeeper willing to let a room for holding an inquest or at least an outbuilding for storage until a hearing could be held. Where the dead were found in a prison or a hospital without a mortuary, the coroner would transform a cell or a ward into a makeshift morgue. The footprints of the coroner determined the itineraries of the dead. They unravelled a map that bore the traces of legal relations between the living and the dead. In walking through the city, in the performance of his role, the coroner not only carried corpses upon his shoulders, he wrote their histories and biographies, he collected their memories and legacies.[1] In ambulating through alleyways and strolling along promenades, in the routes he walked and the trajectories he followed, the coroner gathered material for a history yet to be written; a history of how techniques of walking cultivated a lawful place for the dead in the modern necropolis.

This chapter explores a spatial history of the office of coroner in the nineteenth century. It examines how the movements of the coroner incorporated the dead into the political life of the city. The proximity of the dead to the living emerged as a particular spatial problem in British colonies in the eighteenth and nineteenth centuries. Corpses not only posed a danger to the physical health of colonists, but

---

1 The use of masculine pronouns in this chapter is employed in their historical sense. Coroners in British colonies were exclusively male throughout the nineteenth century and the early part of the twentieth century.

their presence was also believed to threaten the civilising process of colonial society (Trabsky 2014). The coroner's office assumed greater responsibility for collecting and identifying the dead partially in response to the emergence of this political, technical and spatial problem (Brown-May and Cooke 2004). The manner in which the coroner walked through the city, however, revealed the different ways in which this office formed legal relations with the dead. This chapter outlines how the coroner harnessed techniques of place-making, such as walking, naming and story-telling, to establish a lawful place for the dead in the city. It brings a unique perspective to the question of spaces of justice by offering insight into how justice was administered for the dead through techniques of place-making.

Place-making describes material practices that transform space 'symbolically into a place, that is, a space with a history' (Carter 2010, xxiv). In this chapter I will conceive of place-making as a jurisdictional technique that attaches the law to a place, that encloses and institutes a legal ordering of space, that inaugurates a lawful place (see Dorsett and McVeigh 2012; Barr 2013; 2015). Shaunnagh Dorsett and Shaun McVeigh describe jurisdiction as a 'technique and craft of legal ordering and the art of creating legal relations' (Dorsett and McVeigh 2012, 4). It is a practice, an activity and a technology not simply confined to reading case law or interpreting legislation. The idea that places are historically contingent, that they are formed through spatial practices and legal rituals, highlights how certain features of the role of coroner were important to the colonisation of Australia. The way in which, for example, Melbourne's inaugural coroner, William Byam Wilmot M.D., walked with corpses to and from public houses, suggests that place-making was an essential aspect of performing this role. It was also a jurisdictional technique that in cultivating spatial relations between the living and the dead, furthered the imperial project of civilising colonial society. Techniques of storing and hoarding, carrying and hawking the dead through the streets of the city legitimated the presence of colonial ancestors on what were stolen lands.

The city of Melbourne and its colonial milieu has been offered in this chapter as a fertile site to explore the unfolding of these relations. The primary justification for this choice is that the legal process of incorporating the dead in the political life of the city was contemporaneous with the acceleration of the colonising project. This means that in tracing the movements of the coroner, the chapter is not only able to map the cultivation of legal relations between the living and the dead; it is also able to unravel the complicit role occupied by the coroner in territorialising indigenous lands onto common law jurisdiction. The chapter concludes that the place-making activities of the coroner reveal a history of how the office conducted legal relations with the dead and how it institutionalised the ghosts of ancestors that lingered in the streets of the city.

The place of the dead

Transformations of attitudes to the dead shaped the spatial arrangement of Western cities in the eighteenth and nineteenth centuries. The personalisation of

96 Passages

funerary rituals and tomb inscriptions gained popularity in the eighteenth century, while as Philippe Ariès writes, the nineteenth century witnessed a widespread romanticisation of the cult of the dead. Western cities exhibited a morbid curiosity with the 'death of the other' (*la mort de toi*) (Ariès 1974, 56), apparent in the rapid construction of garden cemeteries, baroque mausoleums and alleyway attractions. The dead were buried in individual tombs in extravagant necropolises, routinely visited by survivors seeking 'a [visible] sign of their presence after death' (Ariès 1974, 70). The urban-dweller in any cosmopolitan city could embrace moribund titillations in arcades and laneways, ranging from penny dreadfuls to macabre theatre, waxworks to the scaffold. Yet, at the same time, the presence of the dead in the city was to be feared. The popular acceptance of miasmatic theories of disease causation depicted the human cadaver as a moral, physical and telluric threat to all human beings.[2] By the end of the nineteenth century the place of the dead was to be respected and dreaded, venerated and segregated from the world of the living.

This attitude to the dead was evident in the decision to appoint a coroner for the periphery of the Colony of New South Wales in the nineteenth century. The superintendent for the district of Port Phillip, Charles La Trobe, appointed William Byam Wilmot M.D. as the first coroner of Melbourne in 1841. Previously, Captain William Lonsdale, the resident magistrate of the district, fulfilled the duties of the office, alongside a rudimentary group of police magistrates and justices of the peace. The historical records of the Melbourne Court Register reveal that from 1836 to 1840 coronial inquests did not formally take place in the district (Jones 1981, ch. 21).[3] The dead were often buried without post mortem examinations, while Lonsdale and his clerks merely recorded witness depositions to either sudden or suspicious deaths (Public Records Office of Victoria 2005). Witnesses testified that they 'were obliged to bury [corpses] immediately' and cited discourses of religion, public health or humanism in support of their decisions ('John Lavender, station cook, drowns in Barwon, 20 December 1836', quoted in Jones 1981, 306).[4] Whether it was due to Christian precepts on the sanctity of the soul, miasmatic theories of disease causation, or simply fear that the unburied dead would become prey to ravenous animals, townsfolk justified burial as in essence 'the best method that could be followed for [the corpse's] preservation until the necessary legal steps could be taken' ('John Buffington, alias Ramsay, shot on Manifold's station, 3 February 1837', quoted in Jones 1981, 307). In a growing populace, colonial burial rituals frustrated the death investigation process, obfuscated the conduct of autopsies and compromised a thorough analysis of death

---

2 For an extended analysis of the reception of miasma theory in colonial society, see Trabsky (2014).

3 Yet according to several anthropological studies, traditional inquiries into death took place in Aboriginal societies prior to the dispossession of their lands by British colonists (Law Reform Commission of Western Australia 2005, 300–317).

4 For an example of the latter, see 'Port Phillip Gazette, 17 April 1839' (quoted in Flannery 2004, 109).

Walking with the dead   97

scenes. They disrupted the effective performance of coronial law to the extent that Lonsdale sought advice as to whether 'the sum of five shillings [be] allowed in each case, for finding a dead body subject to a Coroner's inquest' ('Reward of five shillings for finding bodies subject to inquest, 26 June 1838', quoted in Jones 1981, 310). It was presumed that a monetary reward would discourage townsfolk from immediately burying the dead before contacting the resident magistrate.

The place of the dead re-emerged as a particular kind of spatial problem in Western cities in the eighteenth and nineteenth centuries. Or rather it returned when 'the cemetery once again gained a place in the city – a place both physical and moral – which it had lost in the early Middle Ages, but which it had occupied throughout Antiquity' (Ariès 1974, 74). The dead came to occupy a place, which as Michel Foucault describes in 'Of Other Spaces' (1986), is without a place.[5] What he means here is that the dead became subject to a different kind of spatial arrangement, precisely because of a decline in the religious belief of the resurrection of the immortal spirit. The corpse and the soul reunited during this period in the body of the dead, which demanded to be housed, buried and allotted a place within the city. Foucault employs the term *heterotopia* to denote places that 'neutralize, or invert the set of relations that they happen to designate, mirror, or reflect' (Foucault 1986, 24). In the nineteenth century the cemetery was a heterotopia *par excellence*. It functioned as a counter-site to the city of the living insofar as it inverted, contested and reversed the images of a street, garden and park, while remaining firmly entrenched in them. The graveyard replicated an obverse residential estate with its arrangement of separate dwellings for the dead: charnel houses, mausoleums, crypts, and tombs. But these resting places were only empty facades and absent spaces, where time stood still and yet remained perpetually in motion. The time of the cemetery was incongruous and asynchronous; it marked the end of time as well as its permanence. The problem that troubled this counter-site in the Antipodean frontier was how to fold 'the other city' (Foucault 1986, 25), the under-world, within the civilising process of colonial society. In Melbourne, for example, the transformation of the first cemetery into a thriving marketplace framed the place of the dead as *other* to the economic, social and cultural domains of the living.[6]

The unburied dead, though, posed the most acute threat to the living, and not simply as harbingers of destruction or contagions of miasma. Their indwelling threatened to disrupt this strange equilibrium between the heterotopia of the cemetery and the *topos* of the city. In *The Dominion of the Dead*, Robert Pogue Harrison

---

5 The origins of the concept of heterotopia lie in medical discourse. Heterotopia may designate 'a [medical] phenomenon occurring in an unusual place' (Sohn 2008, 41). Foucault briefly introduced the concept in the preface to *The Order of Things*, but discussed it in more detail in a lecture for architects in 1967, which remained unpublished in English until 1986 (Dehaene and De Cauter 2008, 3).

6 For more information about the transformation of the Old Cemetery into the Queen Victoria Market, see Trabsky (2013).

explains that the activity of burial is crucial for preparing the earth for human habitation and making possible the formation of a place. He writes:

> humans bury not simply to achieve closure and effect a separation from the dead but also and above all to humanize the ground on which they build their worlds and found their histories
>
> (Harrison 2003, xi)

In other words, the practice of burial, which separates the dead from the living, transforms space into place. It historicises the ground, appropriating the land, and founding a city, a nation, an empire on the blood of its ancestors. The sign of the grave, 'here lies', 'effectively opens up the place of the "here", giving it the human foundation without which there would be no places in nature' (Harrison 2003, 20). If the dead were to remain unburied, the heterotopia of the cemetery would spread throughout the city, to the extent that it would be no longer discernible from its inverse, the world of the living. The place of the dead would be at once everywhere and nowhere, and the city would transform into a necropolis, just like the unbounded sea, where the dead float '*like water in water*' (Bataille 1992, 19, italics original).

The decision in 1841 to appoint a coroner, who would establish a lawful place for the newly dead in the district of Port Phillip, can be seen as an integral and more than just incidental part of the imperial project of colonising stolen lands. Melbourne was a contested space in the nineteenth century. The indigenous population that occupied the land prior to the British invasion in 1788 was 'posited as antithetical to the creation and sustainability of an ordered and orderly social space through which the settlement, the colony and the Empire invented and inhabits a place' (Ferguson 2004; see Presland 1994). The colonial project of inhabiting place by burying white settlers on indigenous lands involved forcefully reiterating the fictional doctrine of *terra nullius*. Indeed, burial rituals formed part of a suite of techniques, which included enclosing, surveying and mapping the land, by which the British Empire occupied, inhabited and misappropriated indigenous lands. In a sense such rituals can be viewed as an attempt to eradicate or remove the spirits of the indigenous people that already dwelled within those lands. For if burial practices humanise the ground and imbue in nature the foundations of a place, then settlers burying their dead was nothing other than a violent attempt at re-humanising the ground. While ultimately not obliged to bury the dead – this duty fell to the office of the undertaker – the coroner was responsible for spatially ordering the movements of the dead and facilitating their journey towards their final resting place.

In Lonsdale's request for the appointment of a coroner for the district, he cites the demographic growth of the late 1830s and a concomitant increase in the number of unidentified corpses appearing in the colony. His letter to La Trobe also expressed the concern that 'the public would be better satisfied if these inquiries [into the cause of death] were made in the accustomed manner before a Coroner and jury than before a Magistrate only' ('Increase in sudden deaths requires a coroner, 31 January 1840' quoted in Jones 1981, 311). The absence of coronial inquests in the colony created the impression that the office, insofar as the resident magistrate occupied the role, was derelict in its duties to the dead. However, the public's dissatisfaction with the performance of the office had more to do with the appointment of 'Military men to Civil duties' rather than any dereliction of office (*Port Phillip Gazette* 1841, quoted in Reid 2001, 12). The appointment of a civilian to the role sought to restore public confidence in the civil governance of the dead. The manner in which the coroner occupied this civic role was important in delimiting the boundaries between the domains of the living and dead. His jurisdiction pertained to corpses floating in a river or lying in mud along a street, cadavers prostrate in quasi-public spaces or silent witnesses to suspicious circumstances. His duties involved collecting the dead from where they lay, walking with them through the city, investigating the cause of their death, and issuing burial certificates at the conclusion of his investigations. The office of coroner cultivated spatial relations between the living and the dead, particularly where the presence of the latter threatened to trouble the continuity of the imperial project of civilising colonial society.

The itinerant coroner

Court sittings were peripatetic in Australia in the late eighteenth and early nineteenth centuries (Trabsky 2015, 199). Judicial proceedings took place wherever a magistrate could find temporary accommodation, which included public houses, hotels, churches, schools and hospitals. The first courthouse in Melbourne consisted of 'a wattle and daub hut'; however, the 'police magistrate ... moved around at will, setting up shop wherever whim or duty dictated' (Challinger 2001, 17). By the mid-nineteenth century court sittings had moved from temporary multi-purpose spaces into specially designed courthouses. The history of the movements of the coroner largely followed this trajectory. Prior to the construction of purpose-built courthouses in the late nineteenth century, coroners would travel to wherever the dead lay and hold inquests at the nearest available public house, hotel or brothel.

The movements of the coroner across the English countryside unravelled a narrative of itinerancy. The history of the office of coroner in England depicts an itinerant, who from the twelfth century onwards, travelled across the country keeping the pleas of the Crown, for instance, by collecting death taxes, settling deodands and treasure troves on behalf of the king (Freckleton and Ranson 2006, 35; see also Hunnisett 2008).[7] In *De Republica Anglorum*, which was published in the seventeenth century, Sir Thomas Smith echoed this sentiment when he wrote that '[t]he empanelling of thes enquest, and the viewe of the bodie, and the giving of

---

7 Deodands were things, objects and chattels forfeited to the Crown because they caused a person's death, while treasure troves were coins, gold, silver, found without an owner, that is, where the owner was undiscoverable.

100   Passages

the verdict, is commonly in the streete in an open place' (Smith 1538, quoted in Graham 2003, 239). While deodands, treasure troves and other coronial curiosities were abolished in British colonies by the mid-nineteenth century, the colonial coroner still possessed the character of an itinerant. If the dead lay in a place other than a prison or a hospital, he would 'hawk'[8] the corpse from one public house to another in the hope that a hospitable publican would let a room for holding an inquest, or at least provide an outbuilding for storing the dead body until a hearing could be held. The Coroners Statute 1865 (Vic) obliged publicans in the colony of Victoria to accept any request from an officer to accommodate a corpse on their premises for the purpose of an inquest.[9] If they were to accept the request, they would be financially compensated, while to refuse would result in a fine before a justice of the peace. Only towards the end of the nineteenth century were publicans allowed to refuse entry to a corpse in an offensive state of decomposition.[10]

The role that the public house played in the death investigation process sheds light on how the contingency of place affected the administration of justice for the dead in the nineteenth century. The laws that initially governed the office of coroner were received from England at settlement and only later amended, to reflect not only legislative reforms in England, but also the specific circumstances of the colony (Freckleton and Ranson 2006, 35). Yet no permanent site was ever reserved in Robert Hoddle's rigid survey of the land in 1837 for the purposes of holding coronial inquests or storing dead bodies (Brown-May and Cooke 2004, 6). 'The idea of a central morgue, where bodies would be kept for identification and inquest, was a new one in the urban culture of the nineteenth-century British Empire' (Brown-May 2003, 18). Nor were there any discussions during meetings of the Melbourne City Council of 'the problem of accommodating the dead' until 1852 (Brown-May and Cooke 2004, 6). Hence, when Wilmot assumed the role of city coroner in 1841, the city lacked public buildings or structures of any kind to serve as a central place to inspect, collect and store the dead during the death investigation process.

In a letter addressed to the Colonial Secretary in 1853, Wilmot wrote with much dismay about the emergence of this problem:

> In the present crowded state of the City, the danger attending to the introduction of bodies perhaps in an advanced stage of decomposition into public

---

8 The word 'hawk', which connotes the practices of a commercial traveller, was used by Coroner Wilmot in his correspondence with the Colonial Secretary on 14 January 1853 (Public Record Office Victoria, Correspondence between Coroner Wilmot and the Colonial Secretary, 14 January 1853).

9 Section 11 of the Coroners Statute 1865 (Vic) set out the legal requirement that '[e]very holder of a publican's license', if required by the coroner or constable, must 'receive into [his or her] house . . . any dead body that may be brought to such house for the purpose of an inquest being held thereon'. This section was condemned by members of the licensing board who objected to the obligation on a number of grounds: *The Argus* (Melbourne), 5 May 1858, 6.

10 See, for example, Liquor Act 1898 (NSW) s 100.

houses for the purpose of an inquest must be obvious, and the disgraceful scene which took place on Sunday evening last when a corpse was hawked about the streets before any publican would admit it upon his premises, induces me to urge this matter upon His Excellency. There is great allowance to be made for some publicans in this matter, who have had premises licensed without the compliment of stabling and out offices prescribed by the law.

(Correspondence between Coroner Wilmot and Colonial Secretary, 14 January 1853)[11]

The coroner was clearly enraged by the refusal of publicans to accept a corpse into their dwellings. The reason for this was that taverns provided the only practical solution to the problem of finding a place to hold inquests in a city bereft of a morgue or other adequate facilities. There were several explanations provided as to why public houses emerged as a solution to the spatial problem of accommodating the dead. The 1850s witnessed an exponential growth in the population of Melbourne due to the discovery of gold in the northwestern town of Ballarat, which in turn catalysed an increase in the number of identified corpses appearing in the city. Given the rise in the number of inquests held each year, the use of public houses for such purposes enabled the coroner to avoid, as much as possible, conveying the dead through the 'crowded' streets of the city to, for instance, the mortuary at the hospital. While Wilmot did not specify the 'obvious' dangers of hawking the dead from one public house to another, as I discussed in the previous section, the place of the dead emerged as a political, technical and spatial problem in the nineteenth century. The practice of carrying the dead through the streets of the city troubled the porous boundaries between the realms of the living and the dead.

The reception in the colony of the English custom that an inquest be conducted in full view of the body (*super visum corporis*), a tradition that originated with the first appearance of the coroner in the twelfth century, and which was practised to verify the existence of a dead body before an inquest, meant that conducting the ceremony in hotels, brothels or public houses conveniently provided the coroner with a steady stream of available, though often intoxicated, jurors willing to sit in front of a corpse for a small fee.[12] In other words, public houses were opportune places to round up a jury of peers. The unbearable heat of the Antipodean

---

11 The 'disgraceful scene' alluded to in his letter was summarised by *The Argus* (Melbourne), 11 January 1853. In short, on Sunday 9 January 1853, Wilmot 'hawked [a corpse] from house to house' until 'it was accepted by the Friend-In-Hand'.

12 The requirement that an inquest be held before a jury was enshrined in the Coroners Statute 1865 (Vic) s 5 and the Coroners Act 1890 (Vic) s 6. The Coroners' Juries Act 1887 (Vic) s 4 and the Coroners Act 1890 s 9 also set out a scheme for paying jurors a small fee for attending coronial inquests. However, section 2 of the Coroners Act 1903 (Vic), which amended the Coroners Act 1890, granted coroners the power to hold an inquest without a jury, unless required by another legal institution. Note that the custom of recruiting jurors in public houses incidentally led to accusations that the coroner's inquest was a farce. Several prominent members of the community

102 Passages

summer also situated public houses as the most convenient place to conduct an inquest or their outbuildings as the most suitable place to store dead bodies until a hearing could take place. The reason for this was that heat increased the acceleration of decomposition and threatened to compromise evidence of the death scene, and the only way to avoid the horrid sensory experience of holding an inquest before a jury in full view of a partially decomposing body was to hold the inquest as soon as possible after death took place. The alternative option of storing dead bodies in the outhouses or stables of taverns was especially pertinent given that the city coroner lived in a rural seaside town (Reid 2001, 15). The languor of his stride and the delays that ensued from the long horse ride into the city led to his admonishment at the time by *The Argus* newspaper as a lazy coroner ('The Lame, the Halt and the Blind', *The Argus* (Melbourne), 12 October 1855).[13]

Wilmot did not simply complain about the behaviour of publicans in his letter to the Colonial Secretary. He also proposed a site for his office and a morgue near the embankment of the Yarra River, which was later described as 'a kind of catacomb, which will be marked with shrubs' (*The Argus* (Melbourne), 13 May 1854, 5). He even sketched designs for the building that would eventually house the coroner's office – a neat low building with a fence in which to remove any offence to the public (Correspondence between Coroner Wilmot and Colonial Secretary, 29 March 1853) – and he urged La Trobe to promptly comply with his requests (Correspondence between Coroner Wilmot and Colonial Secretary, 2 March 1853).[14] In fact, Wilmot linked the construction of a proper office to the effective performance of his institutional role:

> [A]n increasing need arises for an office for my department, its duties now absorb my undivided attention and I feel it requisite to be completely identified with the offence in order to seem [sic] me from the constant interruptions to which my professional position [require].
>
> (Correspondence between Coroner Wilmot and Colonial Secretary, 2 March 1853)

Building, dwelling, place-making

The coroner's petition for the construction of an office, but also his insistence on participating in the design process, reveals how he conceived of the role of

---

chided the coroner for relying on drunk patrons in summoning a jury for the purposes of an inquest (Freckleton and Ranson 2006, 49).

13 It is important to note here that corpses were sometimes stored for days on end, for only following the completion of an investigation would the coroner grant a death certificate and call upon the undertaker to carry the dead to one of the city's cemeteries.

14 The Mayor of Melbourne likewise informed La Trobe of the hardship of licensed owners being required to accommodate dead bodies awaiting inquests in crowded public houses. He requested the erection of a morgue or dead house along the Yarra River (Correspondence between Mayor of Melbourne and Colonial Secretary, 23 September 1853).

coroner. The place in which he dwelled was integral to the way he performed the duties, obligations and responsibilities that attached to his role. Martin Heidegger investigates the etymological origins of the concept of dwelling in a short essay titled 'Building, Dwelling, Thinking'. He contends that the ineluctable relationship between building and dwelling derives from the etymology of the former:

> The Old English and High German word for building, *buan*, means to dwell. This signifies: to remain, to stay in a place. The real meaning of the verb *bauen*, namely, to dwell, has been lost to us.
>
> (Heidegger 1971, 146)

The word *bauen*, which in the modern German language means 'to build', also signifies according to Heidegger, not only the practice of dwelling, but the manner of being, the manner of dwelling. 'To be a human being means to be on the earth as a mortal. It means to dwell' (Heidegger 1971, 147). The notion that building is dwelling and dwelling implies an ethos is furthered by Heidegger's assertion that cultivating constitutes the means by which to dwell. To cultivate signifies to produce, to 'bring forth' not only buildings, but to nurture the growth of oneself. It is in this sense that Heidegger draws links between the Latin term for cultivating and the Greek word for 'bringing forth' (*techne*). Cultivation is a technique of making 'something appear, within what is present, as this or that, in this way or that way. The Greeks conceive of *techne*, producing, in terms of letting appear' (Heidegger 1971, 159). Dwelling is thus a technique that cultivates, produces a set of relations between places, persons and things. Building an office for the work of the coroner and a morgue for housing the dead involves letting the dead dwell, letting them appear, allowing them to remain in place.

Building on the writings of Heidegger, Robert Pogue Harrison suggests that language is the ultimate expression of dwelling. He argues that before dwelling in place, humans dwell in *logos* (Harrison 1992, 200). *Logos*, as Harrison understands it, is something irreducible to language. While the word undoubtedly denoted language in Ancient Greek, it also signified 'relation':

> *Logos* is that which binds, gathers, or relates. It binds humans to nature in the mode of openness and difference. It is that wherein we dwell and by which we relate ourselves to this or that place.
>
> (Harrison 1992, 200)

The ineluctability of *logos* and dwelling is precisely what Paul Carter gestures towards in his historical account of the spatial constitution of Australia in *The Road to Botany Bay*. Place-making functions for Carter as an activity of dwelling. The manner of this dwelling makes use of techniques of place-naming and story-telling in addition to spatial practices of walking, tracing and mapping. The making of a spatial history, the inhabitation of a place, the discovery of lands, begins in language. The purpose of place-naming 'was to preserve the means by which [names] came to be known, the occasion of places, the sense in which places are means, not of settling, but of travelling on' (Carter 2010, 32). In other words, both language and walking, naming and travelling were techniques of place-making by which colonists moved across, dwelled within and formed relations with indigenous people on their lands. Place-making was not simply a means of settling lands, but of transforming space into a place with an imperial history, a colony of the British Empire.

Wilmot's insistence on a proper place and a proper name for his office revealed the importance of techniques of place-making for performing the role of coroner. Historians have long argued that the effective administration of justice in British colonies was contingent upon the construction of public buildings to house court sittings (see for example Mulcahy 2011; Bennett 1987). Russell Hogg pursues this idea further by suggesting that purpose-built structures were necessary in the colony in order to position legal institutions 'in relation to those it seeks to rule, as separate from and above them' (Hogg 2002, 35). In Melbourne, the absence of a specially designed courthouse did not so much render the coronial inquest ineffectual, but rather exposed techniques of place-making as integral to the administration of coronial justice. In walking with the dead through the streets of the city, the world of the living collided with the domain of the dead. The activities of the coroner were not 'removed from private homes and the streets into the purpose designed, functionally specific, ritually demarcated and ostensibly socially neutral spaces of the courtroom' (Hogg 2002, 37). Yet, precisely through such techniques of walking, naming and story-telling, the coroner cultivated intimate, spatial and legal relations between the living and the dead.

The coroner of Melbourne from 1841 to 1857 was only partially successful in petitioning the first lieutenant governor of the colony of Victoria, Charles La Trobe, for the construction of a central office for the institutional home of the coroner. While everyone agreed with Wilmot that '[d]ead bodies in varying states of decomposition should be seen as little as possible', La Trobe and the Colonial Architect disagreed with Wilmot on the proposed central location of the morgue (Correspondence between Coroner Wilmot and Colonial Secretary, 2 March 1853).[15] La Trobe found the mooted site 'horrible' (Correspondence from Lieutenant General, 26 April 1854). Despite such criticisms, the coroner's office was built in 1854 on the corner of a main thoroughfare, which *The Argus* chided as infringing upon the 'busy street-life of a bustling city', while the morgue was added to the site in 1871 (Correspondence from Lieutenant General, 26 April 1854).[16] The city coroner from 1857 to 1897, Dr Richard Youl, was more successful in

15 Note that the initial plans for the office included a room for the coroner, a room for the registrar of births, deaths and marriages and a post mortem examination room. See Correspondence between the Colonial Engineer and Colonial Secretary, 26 May 1854 and Correspondence between Auditor General and Colonial Engineer, 18 December 1854.

16 Both buildings were acquired by the Railway Department in 1883. The Melbourne Fish Market stood opposite the coroner's office from 1865 to 1892, which was demolished in 1900 to make way for the new Flinders Street train station.

lobbying the government for a purpose-built structure for conducting inquests and storing dead bodies. His tenure as coroner oversaw the passing of the Morgue Site Act 1886 (Vic) and the construction of a specially designed coroner's courthouse in 1888 (see Trabsky 2015).

The persistent lobbying for an office and a morgue in the city were not simply idiosyncrasies of piqued coroners. Such concerns were equally shared by jurors, councillors, undertakers, journalists and other officers of the colony. When Youl, as acting city coroner, sent a report in 1855 to a committee investigating 'the condition and accommodation of Government Offices', and implored the surveyor general and colonial engineer of 'the absolute necessity which exists for the erection of a morgue, in connection with the office of the coroner', he was not simply speaking on behalf of a disgruntled government department (*The Argus* (Melbourne), 27 January 1855, 6).[17] He was also voicing the chagrin of the public who were compelled by the absence of a morgue to share their dwellings with the dead. Particularly in the scorching summer days of January, when decomposing corpses lay in public houses awaiting coronial inquests, which as one journalist intimated was 'an intolerable nuisance, at this season of the year especially' (*The Argus* (Melbourne), 3 January 1855, 5), the plea for a dead house could be heard alike from the coroner, the publican and the drunkard.[18] Wilmot and Youl exposed a technical problem inherent in the imperial project of colonising foreign lands, that is to say, the problem of how the living should live lawfully with the dead.

In the mid-nineteenth century the coroner would travel to where the dead lay and carry them from one public house to another hoping to find a hospitable innkeeper willing to accommodate them for the purpose of an inquest or at least provide storage until a hearing could be held. He would continue to carry the dead through legal procedure towards the place of burial. What this means is that the itineraries of the dead and the movements of the coroner emerged as spatial problems in the colonial city. While the initial construction of the coroner's office and later the erection of a morgue sought to resolve this problem, the role of the coroner was imbued with the responsibility to walk with the dead. Wherever the

17 The medically trained Youl was appointed the district coroner for Bourke in 1853. His jurisdiction included the surrounding suburbs of Melbourne, but not the city itself. He was then appointed the acting coroner of Melbourne in 1854. He succeeded William Byam Wilmot as city coroner in 1857 (Mitchell 1976).

18 On 3 January 1855, Coroner Youl, believing that the erection of a morgue was imminent, arranged with Mr Crofts, the undertaker, to store any dead bodies found in the city at his premises in Queensberry Street, North Melbourne. Each corpse would be stored with the undertaker until an inquest could be held at the Queensberry Hotel. It seems that the scorching temperatures during December 1854 precipitated this arrangement, as evident by a report in *The Argus*, that Alexander McQueen, who drowned in the Yarra River, was 'deposited in a fowl-house' while awaiting an inquest, and in turn, his decomposing body was 'exposed to the heat of the atmosphere', which caused not only great distress for his friends, but also for the newspaper: *The Argus* (Melbourne), 1 December 1854. See also, *The Argus* (Melbourne), 3 January 1855 and Brown-May and Cooke (2004).

coroner travelled, the itineraries he followed and the routes he took constituted activities of place-making, which had as their aim the cultivation of a lawful place for the dead in the city. The coroner's movements, especially when recorded in the inquest dispositions he sent to the colonial government, unravelled a spatial history of the dead. The places he visited were re-signified by the indwelling of the dead, the lingering of the ghosts of colonial ancestors. But his movements were also crucial in the successful lobbying for the erection of a morgue and integral to the institutionalisation of the office in the administration of colonial government.

Conclusion

It would not have been surprising to read in *The Argus* newspaper on 11 November 1852 about the arduous journey that an unidentified corpse suffered under the jurisdiction of the office of coroner. When the corpse was found on Monday it was hawked from one public house to another, and refused entry by a number of innkeepers, before finally being accepted by the landlord of the Queen's Arms on Swanston Street. The partially decomposing body was stored in a cramped tavern for two days, awaiting a coroners' inquest in full view of the body. While the jury returned an enigmatic verdict of 'Found Dead', what was more important for *The Argus* were calls made by the Mayor for the incident to be investigated:

> Some great dereliction of duty has occurred somewhere which demands an inquiry, how a dead body should be allowed to remain from Monday until Wednesday before an inquest could be held and in a house crowded with lodgers.
>
> (*The Argus* (Melbourne), 11 November 1852, 5)

It is unclear whether *The Argus* was suggesting in this passage that the 'dereliction of duty' lay with the coroner himself, who often took a couple of days to reach the city, or whether it lay with the failure of the government to provide a proper structure for interring the dead until an inquest could take place. In any case, what these accusations revealed was the ineluctable connection between the duties that pertain to the performance of an institutional role and the places in which those performances materialise. My intention in this chapter has been to show that in writing a spatial history of the office of the coroner, it is imperative to account for how the office became materially placed and in turn made possible a lawful place for the dead in the city.

In chapter 4 of *Jurisdiction*, Dorsett and McVeigh examine how practices of writing, mapping, precedent and taxonomy are techniques capable of creating and representing lawful relations. They also analyse how rituals, such as the making of oaths, 'mark the existence of legal institutions and give shape to lawful relations [and] the institutional forms of the authorisation of law' (Dorsett and McVeigh 2012, 34). In this chapter I have presented place-making as a jurisdictional technique of the office of coroner. The way in which he travelled to the place where the dead lay, hawked their corpse from one public house to another, and conducted inquests in taverns, hotels or brothels, cultivated technical, spatial and legal relations between the living and the dead. Techniques of place-making attached the dead to the land and bound them to the practices of coronial law and procedure. The way in which the coroner walked with the dead made possible a place for their presence in the political life of the city.

This chapter has shown how techniques of place-making were an important aspect of the character of the office of coroner in the nineteenth century. The coroner performed his institutional role by assuming the attribute of an itinerant. In the absence of a dedicated office and a central morgue, the coroner's movements were determined by where the dead lay and where they could be accommodated for the purpose of an inquest hearing. In walking with the dead through the streets of the city, the coroner could not shield their presence from the living. Indeed, the coroner's role was not to bury the dead, but rather to carry them, in full view of the public, through coronial law and procedure. Both Wilmot and Youl embraced such responsibilities to administer a spatial justice for the dead. Here, justice meant restoring a tradition of honouring the dead; learning to live with the dead in the city. In the contested space of nineteenth-century Melbourne, a spatial history of the coroner thus reveals how important relations between the living and the dead were, and how important the continuity between the present and the past was in furthering the imperial project of colonising stolen lands.

References

The Argus (Melbourne) 11 November 1852, 11 January 1853, 13 May 1854, 1 December 1854, 3 January 1855, 27 January 1855, 12 October 1855.

Ariès, P. 1974. *Western Attitudes Toward Death: From the Middle Ages to the Present.* Ranum, P. M. trans. Johns Hopkins University Press.

Barr, O. 2013. Walking with empire. *Australian Feminist Law Journal* 38: 59–74.

Barr, O. 2015. A jurisprudential tale of a road, an office and a triangle. *Law and Literature* 27(2): 199–216.

Bataille, G. 1992. *Theory of Religion.* Hurley, R. trans. Zone Books.

Bennett, J. M. 1987. The evolution of court houses in New South Wales. In *Places of Judgment: New South Wales*, ed. Naughton, T., 1–13. Law Book Co.

Brown-May, A. 2003. History and development of the site. In *Federation Square*, eds Brown-May, A. and Day, N., 1–22. Hardie Grant Books.

Brown-May, A. and Cooke, S. 2004. Death, decency and the dead-house: The city morgue in colonial Melbourne. *Provenance: The Journal of Public Record Office Victoria* 3. http://prov. vic.gov.au/publications/provenance/provenance2004/death-decency-and-the-dead-house. Accessed 18 November 2015.

Carter, P. 2010. *The Road to Botany Bay: An Exploration of Landscape and History.* University of Minnesota Press.

Challinger, M. 2001. *Historic Court Houses of Victoria.* Palisade Press.

Dehaene, M. and De Cauter, L. 2008. Heterotopia in a postcivil society. In *Heterotopia and the City: Public Space in a Postcivil Society*, eds Dehaene, M. and De Cauter, L., 3–9. Routledge.

108 Passages

Dorsett, S. and McVeigh, S. 2012. *Jurisdiction*. Routledge.

Ferguson, K. 2004. Imagining early Melbourne. *Postcolonial Text* 1(1). http://postcolonial.org/index.php/pct/article/view/294/780. Accessed 18 November 2015.

Flannery, T. ed. 2004. *The Birth of Melbourne*. Text Publishing.

Foucault, M. 1986. Of Other Spaces. Miskowiec, J. trans. *Diacritics* 16(1): 22–27.

Freckleton, I. and Ranson, D. 2006. *Death Investigation and the Coroner's Inquest*. Oxford University Press.

Graham, C. 2003. *Ordering Law: The Architectural and Social History of the English Law Court*. Ashgate.

Harrison, R. P. 1992. *Forests: The Shadow of Civilization*. University of Chicago Press.

Harrison, R. P. 2003. *The Dominion of the Dead*. University of Chicago Press.

Heidegger, M. 1971. Building, dwelling, thinking. Hofstadter, A. trans. In *Poetry, Language, Thought*, 141–160. Harper and Row.

Hogg, R. 2002. Law's other spaces. *Law Text Culture* 6(1): 29–38.

Hunnisett, R. F. 2008. *The Medieval Coroner*. Cambridge University Press.

Jones, P., ed. 1981. *Historical Records of Victoria: Volume 1: Beginnings of Permanent Government*. Victorian Government Printing Office.

Law Reform Commission of Western Australia. 2005. *Aboriginal Customary Laws, Project 94, Discussion Paper*. State Solicitor's Office.

Mitchell, A. 1976. 'Youl, Richard (1821–1897)'. *Australian Dictionary of Biography*, National Centre of Biography, Australian National University, http://adb.anu.edu.au/biography/youl-richard-4900/text8201. Accessed 18 November 2015.

Mulcahy, L. 2011. *Legal Architecture: Justice, Due Process and the Place of Law*. Routledge.

Officio Coronatoris: The Office of the Coroner 4 Edward 1 AD 1275, 1276.

Presland, G. 1994. *Aboriginal Melbourne: The Lost Land of the Kulin People*. McPhee Gribble.

Public Record Office Victoria. Correspondence between Coroner Wilmot and the Colonial Secretary, 14 January 1853. VPRS 1189, P0, Unit 128, Item 53/446.

Public Record Office Victoria. Correspondence between Coroner Wilmot and Colonial Secretary, 2 March 1853. VPRS 1189, P0, Unit 128, Item A53/2203.

Public Record Office Victoria. Correspondence between Coroner Wilmot and Colonial Secretary, 29 March 1853. VPRS 1189, P0, Unit 128, Item A53/3173.

Public Record Office Victoria. Correspondence between Mayor of Melbourne and Colonial Secretary, 23 September 1853. VPRS 1189, P0, UNIT 128, Item C53/8470.

Public Record Office Victoria. Correspondence from Lieutenant General, 26 April 1854. VPRS 1189, P0, UNIT 128, Item E54/5695.

Public Record Office Victoria. Correspondence between Colonial Engineer and Colonial Secretary, 26 May 1854. VPRS 1189, P0, UNIT 128, Item E54/5695.

Public Record Office Victoria. Correspondence between Auditor General and Colonial Engineer, 18 December 1854. VPRS 1189, P0, UNIT 128, Item 54/14059.

Public Record Office Victoria. 2005. *Agency VA 2263 Coroners Courts: History of Coroner's Courts*. Public Records Office of Victoria. www.access.prov.vic.gov.au/public/component/daPublicBaseContainer?component=daViewAgency&breadcrumbPath=Home/Access%20the%20Collection/Browse%20The%20Collection/Agency%20Details&entityId=2263

Reid, J. 2001. *The Life of Dr William Byam Wilmot M.D. (1805–1874)*. Unpublished: Victorian Institute of Forensic Medicine Library.

Ricoeur, P. 2009. *Living Up to Death*. Pellauer, D. trans. University of Chicago Press.

Sohn, H. 2008. Heterotopia: Anamnesis of a medical term. In *Heterotopia and the City: Public Space in a Postcivil Society*, eds Dehaene, M. and De Cauter, L., 41–50. Routledge.

Trabsky, M. 2013. Law in the marketplace. In *Law and the Question of the Animal: A Critical Jurisprudence*, eds Otomo, Y. and Mussawir, E., 133–148. Routledge.

Trabsky, M. 2014. Institutionalising the public abattoir in nineteenth century colonial society. *Australian Feminist Law Journal* 40(2): 169–184.

Trabsky, M. 2015. The custodian of memories: Coronial architecture in nineteenth century Melbourne. *Griffith Law Review* 24(2): 199–220.

Part III

Appropriations

Chapter 6

Space, politics, justice

Chris Butler[1]

The contours of spatial justice

In recent years, the physical and cultural usage of space has been widely acknowledged as a crucial element in the strategic armoury of radical politics. The explosive challenges to state power that marked the rebellions of the Arab Spring, the challenges to capital in movements such as Occupy and the massive demonstrations against the neoliberal constitutionalisation of austerity by the *Aganaktismenoi* in Greece, the Spanish *Indignados* and the *Nuit Debout* movement across France, are all prominent examples of this phenomenon (Douzinas 2012; Guardiola-Rivera 2012). The use of public space by each of these 'occupying' movements has been materially and symbolically central to their challenges to existing political and legal orders (Wall 2012). Of course the political uses of space have also been intrinsic to the emergence of innumerable social movements which extend beyond these instances of public assembly. A classic Australian example is the Aboriginal Tent Embassy, established in 1972 on the lawn in front of Old Parliament House in Canberra. This extended campsite on land at the centre of the national capital has not only operated as a public demand for the formal recognition of Aboriginal land rights, but is in itself an open-ended assertion of 'the authority of a sovereign people to use their land' without seeking permission (Iveson 2014, 253). Another example of the politicisation of the inhabitance of space can be seen in the struggles against evictions and campaigns for the provision of public housing by the South African shack dwellers' movement Abahlali baseMjondolo (Pithouse 2009; 2010).

In pitching themselves against the exclusions, abstractions and manifestations of instrumental violence that are intrinsic to the exercise of sovereign power, each of these contemporary struggles is also defined by a certain spatiality – a set of spatial relations which they have produced and which, in turn, enframes their

---

1 I would like to express my thanks to Ed Mussawir, Andreas Philippopoulos-Mihalopoulos, Illan Wall, Zanny Begg, Olivia Barr, Marc Trabsky, Anne Bottomley, Lee Stickells and Amelia Thorpe, who collectively formed the generous and attentive audience for my presentation of an earlier version of this chapter at the *Spaces of Justice* symposium in December 2013.

practices and possibilities. An acknowledgement of the importance of addressing the spatial dimensions of these sites of struggle is no longer a controversial or particularly remarkable position within contemporary critical geography. Indeed it has become a guiding premise throughout the last three decades in writing which has explored the relationships between space and juridico-political concepts such as law, power and rights (Blomley 1994; Blomley et al. 2001; Delaney 2010; Harvey 2008). One noticeable recent development in this scholarship has been a discursive shift towards a consideration of the concept of 'spatial justice'. As highlighted in the introductory chapter to this volume, expositions of this idea have been dominated by the academic and practical concerns of those working in spatial disciplines such as geography, planning and urban studies. First popularised for an international audience in the form of 'territorial spatial justice' through the early work of the Marxist geographer and social theorist David Harvey, there has been a progressive revival of interest in the concept, particularly following the publication of Edward Soja's book *Seeking Spatial Justice* (Harvey 1973; Soja 2010).

But despite this increased attention, there have been few attempts to trace the theoretical contours of spatial justice, and within much of this literature the concept has ultimately been assimilated within a liberal account of distributive justice, which is presumed to be seamlessly operationalised 'in space'.[2] As a consequence, it has largely been left to critical legal scholars to investigate the ways in which it might be possible to theorise an explicitly *spatial* interpretation of justice. An excellent example of this can be seen in the work of Andreas Philippopoulos-Mihalopoulos, who provides a sophisticated critique of the way spatial justice has been theoretically circumscribed as a subset of Rawlsian distributive justice (Philippopoulos-Mihalopoulos 2010; 2011; 2015). Drawing on the theoretical resources of Deleuze and Guattari, object-oriented ontologies and writing on new materialisms, Philippopoulos-Mihalopoulos presents spatial justice as premised on an ontological *withdrawal*, which mediates between the abstractions of law and space.

> This is perhaps the crux of the concept of spatial justice – and indeed the answer to the kind of justice that spatiality dictates: that the only way in which its demands can be met is through a *withdrawal*, through the departure of the one who occupies the contested space, and the simultaneous conceding of priority to the other's claim.
>
> (Philippopoulos-Mihalopoulos 2011, 200)

This chapter is also a contribution to the broader challenge of reimagining spatial justice, but my ambitions are slightly different to those pursued by

---

2 One important exception to this trend was the early work of Mustafa Dikeç, who was the first scholar to seriously explore the contribution of Henri Lefebvre's writings to an understanding spatial justice: see Dikeç 2001; 2009).

Philippopoulos-Mihalopoulos. In particular, I want to focus in more detail on the inescapably political dimensions of spatial justice. Philippopoulos-Mihalopoulos is wary of the well-established tendency within critical geography to use politics as a discursive means for representing law and justice, when it is but one of many influences, including economics, history, gender, sexuality, aesthetics and corpo-reality (Philippopoulos-Mihalopoulos 2010, 208; 2011, 189; 2015, 19). While I am conscious of the dangers of reductionism or the introduction of 'grand-narrative aspirations', my argument here is that an indispensable aspect of any attempt to bring 'space' and 'justice' together is an awareness of how each are linked through the political. One of my aims in doing so is prompted by the need to respond to a certain strand of writing about spatial justice which conflates it with the functional preoccupations of institutionalised policy formation, and thereby empties it of its radical potential. Such approaches tend to reduce spatial justice to a slogan concerned with tactical proposals for the delivery of urban services and the dis-tribution of resources, which obscures the meaningful contribution it might make to critical spatial politics. As an alternative, I will approach the question of how spatial justice emerges from the politics of space by bringing three aspects of the social theory of Henri Lefebvre into dialogue with Walter Benjamin's fragmentary early writings on the relationship between law and justice.

Lefebvre's writing has played a central role in the rise of critical and radical geography throughout the last four decades, but the importance of his contribu-tion is less prominent within critical legal scholarship, and even in the interdisci-plinary literature on spatial justice his work is generally referenced in a cursory manner. So it is worthwhile to begin with his theoretical orientation towards space, which he defines in terms of relations between inhabiting and producing bodies. Lefebvre's approach here is directly influenced by Leibniz's critique of the Newtonian 'absolute' theory of space, which he develops most comprehensively in his 1974 book *The Production of Space* (Lefebvre 1991). In that work, Lefebvre premises his argument about the relationality of bodily inhabitance on the idea of the 'appropriation of space' as the radical other to institutional, technological and political forms of spatial dominance and control. Amidst the whirl of theoretical innovation and conceptual challenge that has been generated in recent years by influences such as actor-network theory, non-representational theory and assem-blage thinking, I want to reassert the continued importance of Lefebvre's theory of space, particularly for the task of articulating the possibility of spatial justice.

This highlights a second aspect of Lefebvre's work that is central to the argument presented here – the ways in which space and politics are inherently entwined. Bodily inhabitance is not only premised on the aesthetic and creative appropriation of space, but it is also inherently defined by political struggles over the design of spatial form and the uses to which it is employed. There is a widespread recogni-tion of Lefebvre's interventions on the political character of space within critical geography and, to a certain extent, they have provided the foundations for the emergence of a 'radical' orthodoxy within the spatial disciplines. However, a less commonly discussed element of his account is the association he draws between

116 Appropriations

inhabitance and the explicitly utopian character of struggles over the production of space. These two elements of the politics of inhabitance, appropriation and utopian impulses, are most often explored through Lefebvre's understanding of the right to the city. Whether this demand is understood in terms of de-radicalised tactical interventions into official policy development or as driven by extra-institutional activism, in this chapter I will stress the importance of extending on the right to the city, in order to deepen our understanding of spatial justice.

In approaching this task, I will draw on a final element of Lefebvre's thought which is influenced by Leibniz's monadology – his 'theory of moments' (Lefebvre 2002, 340–358). Lefebvre defines the 'moment' as a gesture towards the possibility of the impossible, and I will argue that the moment of justice can be best understood as a rupture, which punctures and resonates through the existing constellation of spatial relations. As a way of pursuing this idea further, I will draw an analogy between Lefebvre's understanding of the moment of justice and the intimate connections between justice and the politics of transformation that can be read into the political philosophy of Walter Benjamin (Benjamin 1978). Through this method, my aim is to present spatial justice as a moment of intersection between spatial relations, the politics of inhabitance and the potentiality for a rupture, which breaches the artificial boundaries between the possible and the impossible. While this approach differs in some important respects from the ontology of immanence that drives Philippopoulos-Mihalopoulos's work, the argument pursued here highlights a shared interest in exploring the radical potential that a deep understanding of spatiality may offer for a revitalised conceptualisation of spatial justice.

Spatial relations and bodily inhabitance

One of the central themes in Philippopoulos-Mihalopoulos's extensive work on spatial justice is the need to challenge the inadequate ways in which space is theorised in much of the contemporary scholarship which invokes this concept. For many of these accounts 'the spatial remains an adjectival context' in which pre-existing social determinants, such as 'identity, community, demos, popular will and consensus' retain their privileged status and continue to be understood in a relatively aspatial manner (Philippopoulos-Mihalopoulos 2010, 204). While this remains a curious state of affairs, given how much of this work has been generated from within spatial disciplines such as human geography and urban studies, it is not an entirely new criticism. Even Gordon Pirie in his tentative early essay explicitly recognises the importance of providing an adequate theorisation of space in any inquiry into spatial justice:

> what is left from which to form a concept of spatial justice? One avenue which remains open to exploration is formulation of the concept in relation to an alternative conception of space itself. Conceptualising spatial justice in terms of a view of space as process, and perhaps in terms of radical notions of

Space, politics, justice 117

justice, stands as an exacting challenge and, not unlikely, as the single occasion there might be for requiring and constructing a concept of spatial justice.

(Pirie 1983, 471)

In taking this issue seriously, my conceptual point of departure in this chapter is to outline the theory of space that structures my investigation of spatial justice. The most immediate influence on my thinking in this regard is the theory of space that Lefebvre articulates in greatest detail in his 1974 book *The Production of Space*. In this work, Lefebvre attempts to theoretically engage the physical, mental and social dimensions of space and, in doing so, he approvingly cites Leibniz's relational conception of space (Lefebvre 1991, 296–297). Leibniz developed this account through a critique of Newton's 'absolute' theory of space and time, in a famous extended correspondence with the theologian Samuel Clarke between 1715 and Leibniz's death in 1716 (Alexander 1956). In this exchange, Clarke defended Newton's claim that space is logically prior to and exists independently of matter. In Newton's own words: '(a)bsolute space, in its own nature, without relation to anything external, remains always similar and immovable' (Newton 1968, 6–9).[3] By contrast, Leibniz argued that space does not have substance in itself but is best understood as 'the order of *coexistence* . . . among the mutually contemporaneous states of things' (Rescher 1979, 86).[4] While Newton's theory implied that space is a passive receptacle for material objects, Leibniz conceived of space as a set of relations determined by the objects and processes that constitute it (Leibniz 1969, 675–721).[5]

Lefebvre recounts the difference between the spatial perspectives of the two philosophers in the following terms:

For the most part, philosophers have taken the existence of an absolute space as a given, along with whatever it might contain: figures, relations and proportions, numbers and so on. Against this posture, Leibniz maintains that space 'in itself' . . . is neither 'nothing' nor 'something' – and even less the totality of things or the form of their sum; for Leibniz space was, indeed, the indiscernible.

(Lefebvre 1991, 169)

In *The Production of Space*, Lefebvre invokes Leibniz's attack on the idea of a universal or absolute space as a central strand in his attempt to critique a widely accepted philosophy of space which in ontological terms, treats it as an empty vessel waiting to be filled by matter. But he also rejects the idealist epistemological

---

3 See also Cassirer 1943.

4 Conversely, 'time is the order of *succession* – that is the order among the various different mutually coexisting states of things which [because they are] mutually coexisting . . . must . . . have some sort of "spatial" structure' (Rescher 1979, 86–87). See also Rescher 1981, 86–87.

5 See also Harvey 1996, 250–251; Ballard 1960; Barbour 1982; Hartz and Cover 1988.

premises guiding many contemporary philosophical accounts which, he argues, derive from Kant's depiction of space as a transcendental, *a priori* category (Lefebvre 1991, 1–2; Elden 2004, 187). Lefebvre argues that these two orientations have generated an impoverished treatment of space which reinforces the fragmentation of the physical, mental and lived fields. As an alternative to this approach, Lefebvre argues that these aspects of space can only be brought together in a coherent manner by understanding space as a social product. Indeed, it can only be properly described as the product of a particular society – and, therefore, a particular mode of production (Lefebvre 1991, 31). For Lefebvre, this 'production of space' is the outcome of the dialectical interrelationship between the physical, mental and lived dimensions of space, which he expresses through the following conceptual triad:

i.   *Spatial practices*: composed of daily rhythms, rituals and routines, through which a coherent *perception* of one's orientation in space is established;
ii. *Representations of space*: forms of knowledge and abstract discourse which emanate from the institutions which organise and dominate spatial relations; and
iii. *Spaces of representation*: 'space as directly lived', imagined and symbolised by the 'inhabitants and users' of space, which opens up possibilities for the generation of non-hegemonic forms of spatial practice and representations of space.

(Lefebvre 1991, 33, 39)[6]

In presenting this conceptual delineation of the three dimensions of space – the physical, the mental and the lived – Lefebvre proceeds to argue that they are dialectically bound together through the production and social use of space. This provides a counter-move to dominant tendencies that treat space as a mere container for matter, and subsume the social and physical aspects of space into abstract mental categories. Lefebvre's relational account of space is one of a number of similar theoretical moves within human geography in the decades following the publication of *The Production of Space* in 1974. David Harvey's work is an obvious example, and he too draws on Leibniz as an intellectual support, both in developing a philosophy of internal relations appropriate to dialectical thinking, and as an important influence in the development of a 'historical-geographical materialism' that avoids the limitations of conceptualising space solely in absolute terms (Harvey 1973, 13–14; 1996, 69–76, 249–255; 2000, 90; 2006, 271–274). Aiming to subvert the reactionary implications of Leibniz's theism, Harvey argues that it is possible to draw out a secular interpretation of his thought, which allows us to understand space and time 'as ordering systems inherent within social practices and activities', which are not pre-given, but are 'chosen' or 'arrived at' (Harvey

6 Harvey identifies the similarity of this 'tripartite division of modes of human spatial experience' to that of Cassirer's delineation of *organic, perceptual* and *symbolic* spaces (Harvey 2006, 278).

1996, 253). For Harvey, Leibniz provides a theoretical framework for envisaging and realising the social and cultural production of alternative spatio-temporalities.

Another distinctive and original influence on the development of relational theories of space has been the work of Doreen Massey, who defines space as 'the product of interrelations', 'the sphere of coexisting heterogeneity', and an open process of becoming (Massey 2005: 9). In doing so, Massey pursues a confrontation with thinkers such as Henri Bergson and Ernesto Laclau, who are charged with denigrating space by associating it with forms of representation and stasis (Massey 2005, 9; 1992; 1999). Her response is to propose that space be understood as 'the simultaneous coexistence of social relations that cannot be conceptualized as other than dynamic' (Massey 1992, 81). Importantly for Massey, 'simultaneity is absolutely not stasis'.

> Seeing space as a moment in the intersection of configured social relations (rather than as an absolute dimension) means that it cannot be seen as static. There is no choice between flow (time) and a flat surface of instantaneous relations (space). Space is not a 'flat surface' in that sense because the social relations which create it are themselves dynamic by their very nature. . . . [A]s a result of the fact that it is conceptualized as created out of social relations, space is by its very nature full of power and symbolism, a complex web of relations of domination and subordination, of solidarity and cooperation.
>
> (Massey 1992, 81)[7]

In addition to the influences of Lefebvre, Harvey and Massey on the proliferation of variations on the theme of 'thinking space relationally' within Marxist and critical geography, in recent years there has also been an explosion of interest in a variety of relational accounts of space which have drawn on influences such as actor-network theory, non-representational theory and assemblage thinking.[8] While some of these approaches to space adopt immanent or flat ontologies which conflict in some respects with the theoretical orientations of Massey, Harvey and Lefebvre, what is common to all these positions is an understanding of space as constituted by a multitude of relational entities and processes. This means that an

---

7 In particular, Massey takes issue with Laclau's identification of space as 'any repetition that is governed by a structural law of successions' (Laclau 1990, 41). For Massey this means that 'any postulated causal structure which is complete and self-determining is labelled spatial' (Massey 1992, 68). More sympathetic interpretations of Bergson's rejection of the 'spatialization of time' can be found in Fraser 2008 and Seigworth 2000.

8 It is not possible here to detail all the commonalities and contradictions that appear across the range of relational approaches to space that include Sarah Whatmore's hybrid approach to human/non-human relations; Nigel Thrift's non-representational geography; Sally Marston's 'flat ontology'; and the Deleuzian-inspired geography of Marcus Doel (see Whatmore 2002; Thrift 2008; Marston et al. 2005; Doel 1999). For overviews of this work see Graham and Healey 1999; Murdoch 2006; Sheppard 2008, 2608–2609. For more sanguine assessments of the efficacy of relational approaches to space see Jones 2009; 2010; and Malpas 2012: 239.

120 Appropriations

important consequence of a relational conception of space is that the apparent permanence of any given spatial formation or entity is always a provisional stabilisation of the relations that produce it – or in Lefebvrean terminology, always subject to the inherently contested and political character of the production of space (Anderson 2008, 231; Harvey 1996, 261–262).

Here I am particularly interested in the implications that flow from a second aspect of Lefebvre's relational theory of space which also draws on Leibniz's philosophy. This is his insistence on the necessity of space to be '*occupied*' by the body (Lefebvre 1991, 169–170). While an absolute conception of space encourages a separation between spatial form and material content, the Leibnizian position adopted by Lefebvre presupposes 'an immediate relationship between the body and its space, between the body's deployment in space and its occupation of space' (Lefebvre 1991, 170). Here Lefebvre is not talking of corporeality in general, but inhabitance by

> a specific body ... capable of ... demarcating and orienting space. ... Before *producing* effects in the material realm (tools and objects), before *producing itself* by drawing nourishment from that realm, and before *reproducing itself* by generating other bodies, each living body *is* space and *has* its space: it produces itself in space and it also produces that space.
>
> (Lefebvre 1991, 170)

For Lefebvre, bodies can be understood as 'deployments of energy'. It is through their movements, rhythms and expenditure of energy that they produce their own spaces while reproducing themselves. However, they do so subject to the 'laws' and 'properties' of space which are not the product of the mind or a 'transcendent spirit', but derive from the 'actual "occupation" of space' (Lefebvre 1991, 171). This notion of bodily inhabitance is a recurring theme in Lefebvre's social theory and it is clear that it is at least partly influenced by his reading of both Martin Heidegger on the intimate connections between dwelling and 'Being' and Gaston Bachelard's depiction of the poetic force of the domestic realm in his book, *The Poetics of Space* (Heidegger 1971; Bachelard 1969). Lefebvre is indebted to both these writers for drawing out the degree to which remnants of archaic spaces of representation linger on – even within the abstract spatial fabric of the contemporary metropolis. However, he is not content to retrace the steps taken by these thinkers and he resists both the elegy for a pre-industrial idyll that many have read into Heidegger's writings on dwelling, and the style of poetic remembrance that characterises Bachelard's work on the traditional bourgeois home. Instead, Lefebvre looks beyond the false dichotomy between nostalgia for a past era and the technological modernism that characterises the 'abstract space' of contemporary capitalism, towards a politics of inhabitance through which the body engages in the creative 'appropriation' of its own space. In this sense, appropriation encompasses the 'full and complete *usage*' of space by its inhabitants in their daily routines, work practices and forms of play (Lefebvre 1996, 179). Lefebvre argues that any potential transformation of spatial relations relies upon the body's inhabitance of space through the remaking of spatial practices, representations and symbolic codes. It is through such a politics of inhabitance that it becomes possible to glimpse the spatiality of justice.

Inhabiting the moment of justice

An important element of Lefebvre's account is that bodily inhabitance is not only concerned with the aesthetic and creative appropriation of space, but is also deeply bound up with the political dimensions of struggles over spatial production. In other words, there is an inherent connection between aesthetic fulfilment, the restoration of the body's full range of gestures and a political orientation towards the self-management or *autogestion* of space (Lefebvre 1991, 166–167; 2009, 138–152; Maycroft 2001). The central way in which Lefebvre explores this politics of inhabitance is via the concept of the 'right to the city' – perhaps his most well-known contribution to contemporary transdisciplinary debates within geography, law and urban studies (Lefebvre 1996; Attoh 2011; Butler 2009; 2012; Fernandes 2007; Gilbert and Dikeç 2008; Harvey 2008; Mitchell 2003; Purcell 2002; 2008). Originally proposed as a radical challenge to positivist and technocratic forms of urbanism during the late 1960s, Lefebvre depicts the right to the city as a 'transformed and renewed *right to urban life*', which can be distinguished from presumed entitlements to enjoy commodified spaces of leisure or the tourist's visitation licence to indulge in 'authentic' experiences of the historical city. In an often-quoted passage, Lefebvre states that 'the right to the city is like a cry and a demand', which is grounded in the physical occupation and appropriation of urban space (Lefebvre 1996: 158).

While the right to the city emerges from the essential spatial qualities of the urban as a site of 'centrality', 'gathering' and 'encounter' (Lefebvre 1996: 195; cf. Merrifield 2013), it is perhaps more accurate to understand it in Brenner's terms as a generalised right to inhabit space, the pursuit of which lies at the heart of contemporary spatial politics (Brenner 2000: 375). In the context of expanding processes of planetary urbanisation, such an approach avoids methodologically fetishising the city as a privileged scale for the enactment of spatial autogestion (Angelo and Wachsmuth 2015; Brenner and Schmid 2011; Merrifield 2013). As Purcell argues,

> The right to the city then becomes not just a claim to the concrete space of the city as a scale and settlement pattern, but a strategic claim in a broader movement for the right to inhabit not just urban space, but space in general.
> (Purcell 2008: 103)

Just as it is crucial not to fall into the trap of focusing unduly on the city in defining the politics of space, it is also important to remember that Lefebvre's formulation of the right to the city is premised on a radical opposition to the

122 Appropriations

destructive violence of abstract space, alongside a demand for the self-managed transformation of urban spaces. However, in recent years, the idea of the right to the city has increasingly been redefined and constricted by scholars, activists and policy-makers interested in the promotion of social justice, effective governance and sustainability in an urban context. This widespread interest in the concept has led to attempts to co-opt, institutionalise and, in some cases, to juridify the right to the city, as it is positioned as yet one more addition to a long list of orthodox liberal human rights claims (Brown and Kristiansen 2009; Coggin and Pieterse 2012). While these associations of the right to the city with a broadly social liberal, distributive agenda have gained strength within mainstream scholarship and policy discourse, they have largely sidestepped the radical implications of Lefebvre's original idea. Such de-radicalised caricatures of the right to the city have also had an impact on the ways in which spatial justice has been conceptualised, particularly where the two concepts have been conflated.

A prominent example of this can been seen in Edward Soja's *Seeking Spatial Justice*, where he states that the 'two concepts, spatial justice and the right to the city, have become so interwoven in their contemporary usage that it has become increasingly difficult to tell them apart' (Soja 2010: 95). While Soja laments the degree to which Lefebvre's explicitly spatial orientation and his radical political objectives have been absorbed into a weakly defined, policy-oriented, liberal version of municipal rights, Soja's own formulation of spatial justice is open to similar criticisms. As Cunningham points out, popular usage of the right to the city 'oscillates between . . . reformist or even essentially conservative/nostalgic modalities, and . . . futurally oriented, "progressive" ones', and this leaves Soja's attempt to link a 'justice politics' to a loosely defined notion of the right to the city always in danger of lapsing into a nebulous, left-liberal reformism (Cunningham 2010: 604–605; Souza 2011). But even if the right to the city is not constrained within the limits of institutionalised urban policy and is presented as a simultaneously strategic and utopian demand for the appropriation of space, it is misplaced to collapse all distinctions between it and the idea of spatial justice. While it emerges from the politics of inhabitance, spatial justice exceeds the right to the city, and here I would like to propose a more promising way of conceptualising it as a rupture which breaches the artificial divide between the possible and the impossible.

In order to pursue this interpretation of spatial justice further, I will introduce Lefebvre's 'theory of moments', as a third and final aspect of his work which draws on the influence of Leibniz. Lefebvre originally presented this theory in his autobiography *La Somme et le Reste* in 1959 and reprised it in the second volume of the *Critique of Everyday Life* as a crucial methodological tool for an 'immanent critique of the everyday' (Lefebvre 1959a, 233–238; 1959b, 637–655; 2002, 340–358). Lefebvre defines the moment as a 'modality of presence' which arises from the spatiality of everyday life and links it to a range of temporal potentialities 'embedded in the totality of being' (Lefebvre 2002, 345; 1959a, 234–235; Gardiner 2004, 243). In emphasising this relationship between moments and totality, Michael Gardiner explains how 'moments are themselves partial totalities that reflect and refract larger wholes' and draw out 'the rich and manifold possibilities that are presented to us at given historical conjunctures' (Gardiner 2004, 243). As fleeting, sensate irruptions from the routine of everyday life, moments open up opportunities to 'attempt to achieve the total realisation of a possibility':

> Possibility offers itself; and it reveals itself. It is determined and consequently it is limited and partial. Therefore to wish to live it as a totality is to exhaust it as well as to fulfil it. The Moment wants to be freely total; it exhausts itself in the act of being lived.
>
> (Lefebvre 2002, 348)

Lefebvre resists an exhaustive catalogue or typology of these forms of everyday epiphany, but in addition to 'play, love, work, rest, struggle . . . [and] . . . "poetry"', he positions the 'moment of justice' as opening up possibilities that continually present themselves through each act of judgement (Lefebvre 2003, 170; 2002, 344, 354). In Lefebvre's account, moments puncture the repetition and banality of the everyday and provide a source of both spatial and temporal discontinuity (Shields 1999, 60). A central influence here is Leibniz's controversial late doctrine of the 'substantial link (*vinculum substantiale*) between monads', which Lefebvre enthusiastically embraces as a counter to Bergson's understanding of time as linear duration (*durée*) (Lefebvre 2002, 370 n. 2). At one point, he even states that the theory of moments

> is the product of a violent protest against Bergsonism and the formless psychological continuum advocated by Bergsonian philosophy. Its wish is to reinstate discontinuity, grasping it in the very fabric of the 'lived' . . .
>
> (Lefebvre 2002, 342)[9]

Moving beyond such polemical justifications, Lefebvre's endorsement of the doctrine of the *vinculum substantiale* can be better explained by the fact that it allows him to embed the theory of moments within a relational understanding of the spaces of the everyday. While the substantial bond has often been dismissed as a 'diplomatic' attempt by Leibniz to account for the possibility of transubstantiation in his correspondence with the Jesuit scholar Des Bosses, Brandon Look describes how the development of this concept was the result of a much more thorough investigation by Leibniz into the nature and unity of composite substance (Look 1999; 2000). In this sense, the bond acts as a 'unifying linkage', enabling a body to become more than an 'aggregation of monads' and establish its own 'substantial form' (Rescher 1979, 115). One prominent example of the reception of this concept within contemporary continental philosophy appears in Deleuze's

---

9 A critique of Bergson's thought in similar terms can be found in Bachelard 2000. However, Fraser challenges the characterisation of Bergson's notion of time as linear and suggests that Lefebvre is indebted to Bergson much more than is usually acknowledged (Fraser 2008, 340).

124 Appropriations

discussion of the significance of Leibniz for the study of baroque space, time and aesthetics in *The Fold*. In that work, Deleuze presents the vinculum thesis as aiding an understanding of the necessary but incomplete unity of bodies, always open to possibilities for 'mutations, explosions, abrupt associations and dissociations, or reconcatenations' (Deleuze 2006, 132).[10] For Lefebvre, the substantial bond can be used to explore the relational connections between separate moments, not as embedded in a world of permanent monadic entities, but as interacting and combining with each other through complex and continuously transforming socio-spatial processes.[11]

A crucial aspect of Lefebvre's portrayal of 'moments' is their inherent capacity to rupture the continuum of the everyday. For example, whether we are thinking of justice pursued 'as a virtue' through the practices of everyday life or as an aspiration for institutional decision-making, the moment of justice aspires to be an 'absolute'. In this sense it is a source of utopian impulses that lie within the everyday and work to destabilise juridical and administrative strategies for imposing regulative order (Lefebvre 2002, 346, 355). In Gardiner's words, the theory of moments is an attempt to 'grasp the complex skein of negative and positive forces embedded in the dense textures and rhythms of everyday life', and to explore how these forces suggest 'the possibility of alternative modes of being' (Gardiner 2004, 245). Alongside the promise of such transformative potentialities, moments also rupture the banality of the everyday through failure and tragic loss. Indeed, Lefebvre situates the moment as lying at the intersection of the utopian and the tragic. This means that attempts to attain justice in the human world, in the absence of a 'Supreme Judge', are destined to follow a tragic trajectory towards failure (Lefebvre 2002, 354–355).

> Precisely because it proclaims itself to be an absolute, [the moment] provokes and defines a determined alienation . . . In so far as it is alienating and alienated, the moment has its specific negativity. It is destined to fail, it runs headlong towards failure. . . . In our view, the link between the tragic and the everyday is profound; the tragic takes shape within the everyday, comes into being in the everyday, and always returns to the everyday . . .
>
> (Lefebvre 2002, 347)

---

10 More recently, Kyle McGee has described the *vinculum substantiale* 'as a fully real, dynamically productive association between monads', in an attempt to recuperate Leibniz's monadology for the analysis of contemporary forms of power (McGee 2011, 41).

11 Lefebvre's situating of moments within a relational account of space in this way gains the support of Harvey, who elaborates on it using an example from the field of political economy. Harvey argues that the economic reductionism of orthodox Marxist thought can be attributed to its lopsided emphasis on the foundational status of production, which fails to recognise it as merely one moment in the reproduction of capitalism (alongside the moments of exchange, distribution and consumption). In making this argument, Harvey also draws on Leibniz, along with David Bohm's discussion of moments, in *Wholeness and the Implicate Order* (Harvey 1996, 73–74).

Understood in this way, the moment of justice takes up a quasi-spectral status as an 'impossible possibility', which nevertheless generates perennial hopes that 'what is impossible in the everyday' may indeed become possible (Lefebvre 2002, 347). As Lefebvre describes in *La Somme et le Reste*,

> Justice is not of this world, and there is no other world. . . . Justice is an absolute, around which we become dizzy. Like every absolute, this one makes demands and alienates. There is an absolute of justice, just as ungraspable as others, as compelling, as urgent; however as a moment, justice is necessary.
>
> (Lefebvre 2003, 169)

The possibility of spatial justice

This account of the ruptural character of justice can be deepened by exploring some important connections with Walter Benjamin's juxtaposition of the mythical violence of legal power and the pure immediacy of 'divine violence' (Benjamin 1978, 294–297). For Benjamin, all law is founded on an original positing violence, which 'impedes, denies and compromises itself', as it inevitably degenerates into a law-preserving violence (Hamacher 1994, 110). The oscillation between 'lawmaking and law-preserving' forms of mythical violence can never provide a foundation for justice (Benjamin 1978, 300). By contrast, Benjamin associates justice with the rejection of myth and the totalising fetishism of idols that it generates. The vehicle for this challenge to the idolatry of mythical violence is what Benjamin refers to as divine violence – the very antithesis of mythical lawmaking.

> Lawmaking is power making, and, to that extent, an immediate manifestation of violence. Justice is the principle of all divine end making, power the principle of all mythical lawmaking.
>
> (Benjamin 1978, 295)

In a discussion of the implications of Benjamin's argument for understanding the tensions between right and justice, Massimiliano Tomba argues that the monopoly on the exercise of (mythical) violence held by the sovereignty of the modern state effectively establishes a Hobbesian '*foreclosure* of justice' in which 'no law can be unjust'. As a consequence, political struggle is necessarily concerned with 'how to realise the possibility of the impossible'.

> To pose the question of justice within this conceptual constellation means to consider *the possibility of the impossible*, to 'puncture' this constellation in order to uncover new political possibilities.
>
> (Tomba 2009, 129–130)

This interpretation of Benjamin's 'weak messianism' has an affinity with Lefebvre's understanding of the moment of justice as a puncturing of the conceptual field

126 Appropriations

of possibilities of the everyday, and in doing so, reconstituting the relationship between the possible and the impossible (Benjamin 1992, 246).

But it is important to recognise that this connection is not one that is universally accepted in all expositions of Benjamin's account of justice. For example, in one of the most influential interpretations of Benjamin's violence essay, Werner Hamacher presents justice as a form of pure means – untainted by the degrading 'powers of imposition' and the positing of ends that accompanies legal and 'administrative violence'. He states that 'justice must therefore belong to a sphere equally distant from the law on the one hand, and from the violence of its imposition and enforcement on the other' (Hamacher 1994, 110). In order to ensure that justice is insulated from the effects of mythical power, Hamacher argues that divine violence must be understood as remaining within the realm of language as pure mediacy (Hamacher 1994, 116). However, this burying of divine violence and justice within 'an amorphous conception of language' is a questionable way to analyse Benjamin's account. As Alison Ross explains, by binding divine violence to a notion of 'the "pure mediacy" of open-ended communication without content', Hamacher reinstates 'the type of totalizing form of mythic semblance' that Benjamin tries to challenge in the essay on violence (Ross 2014, 109).[12] While Hamacher aims to situate justice within a 'politics of pure mediacy', his interpretation actually leads to a depoliticised form of justice which fails to connect divine violence with

> concrete political acts that are able to interrupt the history of oppression in the here and now. Because of this, . . . divine violence [is seen] as an esoteric and spectral violence or a pure event that will never take place.
>
> (Hirvonen 2011, 112)

In a similar way, Jacques Derrida's ambivalent reading of Benjamin's essay leads him to characterise justice as an 'experience of the impossible', which is always yet 'to come' – lying beyond any accessible presence (Derrida 1990, 947). Reflecting his mistrust of Benjamin's messianism, Derrida constantly circles around the possibility and operability of justice. He initially asserts that justice does not wait, but is 'always required immediately', and he eventually positions it on the 'boundary between the divine and the human', where it haunts us, but fails to 'enter directly in the world' (Martel 2012, 79).

> Justice remains, is yet, to come, *à venir*, it has an, it is à-venir, the very dimension of events irreducibly to come. It will always have it, this *à venir*, and always has. Perhaps it is for this reason that justice, insofar as it is not only a juridical or political concept, opens up for *L'avenir* the transformation, the

---

12 Ross provides a detailed critique of the tendency of deconstructive readings of Benjamin's essay to collapse divine violence into language as a 'single' but 'unending space of communication' (Ross 2014, 102, 106).

recasting or refounding of law and politics. 'Perhaps', one must always say perhaps for justice.

(Derrida 1990, 969)

Both Derrida's paradoxical reading of Benjamin's essay and Hamacher's search for 'pure mediacy' appear unprepared to acknowledge the inextricable relationship between the pursuit of justice and a politics of transformation of the impossible into the possible. It is in this context that the recent work of James Martel helpfully reminds us that for Benjamin, justice is not primarily a question of waiting, deferral or pure, linguistic non-violence, but is better understood as simultaneously 'in the world', while remaining unknowable and beyond our senses (Martel 2012, 78–79).[13] As Andrew Benjamin explains, the essay on violence presents 'justice is a potentiality within life itself', which is 'neither an external regulative ideal nor there as that which is necessarily unconditioned. Justice is defined in terms of the actualisation of a potentiality' (Benjamin 2013, 98).

It is this intense connection between messianic disruption and human action that makes Benjamin's messianism a force in the world that is not purely 'to come', not just perhaps but one that continues to erupt in the world, in the here and in the now in a very tangible, actual way.

(Martel 2012, 78; 2011, 165)

This interpretation provides a way of understanding the moment of justice as emerging from within the given constellation of spatial relations that constitute everyday life. Such moments not only temporarily explode the linearity of duration – they also reconfigure the spatial relations between the bodies caught up within it. Accordingly, spatial justice must be understood, not as some pure and harmonious smoothing of difference and disquiet, not as a 'negation of the everyday', but as a moment that is both already here within the materiality of everyday life, while simultaneously opening towards transformative possibilities. This places spatial justice at the intersection of appropriation, tragedy and utopia and provides a demonstration of what Gardiner describes as Lefebvre's 'concrete utopianism' (Gardiner 2004, 245). As Lefebvre declares,

The moment is passion and the inexorable destruction and self-destruction of that passion. The moment is an impossible possibility, aimed at, desired and chosen as such. Then what is impossible in the everyday becomes what is possible, even the rule of impossibility.

(Lefebvre 2002, 347)

13 In the essay on violence, Benjamin states: 'This divine power is attested not only by religious tradition but is also found in present-day life . . .' (Benjamin 1978, 297).

Conceptualising spatial justice in this way allows us to interpret the many recent examples of mass urban uprisings against war, capitalist globalisation, political corruption and neoliberal austerity as ruptures of the imposed division between the possible and the impossible. As Ari Hirvonen argues, in these revolts 'everything is valued and contained in the event itself . . . and justice is always already present in the moment of the event and not merely present as its justifying goal' (Hirvonen 2011, 115). But as has been argued in this chapter, the politics of inhabitance extends beyond mass occupations of public space and can be understood more broadly as the creative appropriation of the physical, intellectual and lived dimensions of space. By foregrounding a theorisation of space based on relations between inhabiting bodies, it has been possible to identify the inherent connections between space and politics. Through a triangulation of the three terms – space, politics and justice – I have argued that we can best understand spatial justice as a moment of rupture, which carries with it possibilities that arise from the utopian impulses that are latent, both within and beyond the spatial relations of everyday life. It is only through exploring the relations surrounding the bodily inhabitance of specific spaces, the conflicts that emerge from them and the everyday rhythms that pass through them, that we will be able to fully comprehend the possibilities of spatial justice.

References

Alexander, H. G., ed. 1956. *The Leibniz–Clarke Correspondence*. Manchester University Press.
Anderson, B. 2008. Doreen Massey, *For Space* (2005). In *Key Texts in Human Geography*, eds Hubbard, P., Valentine, G. and Kitchin, R., 227–235. Sage.
Angelo, H. and Wachsmuth, D. 2015. Urbanizing urban political ecology: A critique of methodological cityism. *International Journal of Urban and Regional Research* 39(1): 16–27.
Attoh, K. A. 2011. What kind of right is the right to the city? *Progress in Human Geography* 35(5): 669–685.
Bachelard, G. 1969. *The Poetics of Space*. Beacon Press.
Bachelard, G. 2000. *The Dialectic of Duration*. Clinamen Press.
Ballard, K. 1960. Leibniz's theory of space and time. *Journal of the History of Ideas* 21(1): 49–65.
Barbour, J. 1982. Relational concepts of space and time. *British Journal for the Philosophy of Science* 33(3): 251–274.
Benjamin, A. 2013. *Working with Walter Benjamin: Recovering a Political Philosophy*. Edinburgh University Press.
Benjamin, W. 1978. Critique of violence. Jephcott, E. trans. In *Reflections*, 277–300. Schocken Books.
Benjamin, W. 1992. Theses on the philosophy of history. Zohn, H. trans. In *Illuminations*, 245–255. Fontana Press.
Blomley, N. 1994. *Law, Space, and the Geographies of Power*. Guilford Press.
Blomley, N., Delaney, D. and Ford, R. T., eds. 2001. *The Legal Geographies Reader: Law, Power and Space*. Blackwell.
Brenner, N. 2000. The urban question as a scale question: Reflections on Henri Lefebvre,

urban theory and the politics of scale. *International Journal of Urban and Regional Research* 24(2): 361–378.

Brenner, N. and Schmid, C. 2011. Planetary urbanization. In *Urban Constellations*, ed. Gandy, M., 10–13. Jovis.

Brown, A. and Kristiansen, A. 2009. *Urban Policies and the Right to the City: Rights, Responsibilities and Citizenship.* UNESCO.

Butler, C. 2009. Critical legal studies and the right to the city. *Social and Legal Studies* 18(3): 313–332.

Butler, C. 2012. *Henri Lefebvre: Spatial Politics, Everyday Life and the Right to the City.* Routledge.

Cassirer, E. 1943. Newton and Leibniz. *The Philosophical Review* 52(4): 366–391.

Coggin, T. and Pieterse, M. (2012) Rights and the city: An exploration of the interaction between socio-economic rights and the city. *Urban Forum* 23(3): 257–278.

Cunningham, D. 2010. Rights, politics and strategy: A response to *Seeking Spatial Justice.* *City* 14(6): 604–606.

Delaney, D. 2010. *The Spatial, the Legal and the Pragmatics of World-Making: Nomospheric Investigations.* Routledge.

Deleuze, G. 2006. *The Fold: Leibniz and the Baroque.* Continuum.

Derrida, J. 1990. Force of law: the 'mystical foundation of authority'. *Cardozo Law Review* 11: 919–1045.

Dikeç, M. 2001. Justice and the spatial imagination. *Environment and Planning A* 33(10): 1785–1805.

Dikeç, M. 2009. Space, politics and (in)justice. *Justice Spatiale/Spatial Justice*, 1, available at: www.jssj.org

Doel, M. 1999. *Poststructuralist Geographies: The Diabolical Art of Spatial Science.* Rowman and Littlefield.

Douzinas, C. 2012. Athens rising. *European Urban and Regional Studies* 20(1): 134–138.

Elden, S. 2004. *Understanding Henri Lefebvre: Theory and the Possible.* Continuum.

Fernandes, E. 2007. Constructing the 'right to the city' in Brazil. *Social and Legal Studies* 16(2): 210–219.

Fraser, B. 2008. Toward a philosophy of the urban: Henri Lefebvre's uncomfortable application of Bergsonism. *Environment and Planning D: Society and Space* 26(2): 338–358.

Gardiner, M. 2004. Everyday utopianism: Lefebvre and his critics. *Cultural Studies* 2/3: 228–254.

Gilbert, L. and Dikeç, M. 2008. Right to the city: Politics of citizenship. In *Space, Difference, Everyday life: Reading Henri Lefebvre*, eds Goonewardena, K., Kipfer, S., Milgrom, R. and Schmid, C., 250–263. Routledge.

Graham, S. and Healey, P. 1999. Relational concepts of space and place: Issues for planning theory and practice. *European Planning Studies* 7(5): 623–646.

Guardiola-Rivera, O. 2012. A jurisprudence of indignation. *Law and Critique* 23(3): 253–270.

Hamacher, W. 1994. Afformative, strike: Benjamin's critique of violence. Hollander, D. trans. In *Walter Benjamin's Philosophy: Destruction and Experience*, eds Benjamin, A. and Osborne, P., 110–138. Routledge.

Hartz, G. and Cover, J. 1988. Space and time in the Leibnizian metaphysic. *Noûs* 22(4): 493–519.

Harvey, D. 1973. *Social Justice and the City.* Johns Hopkins University Press.

Harvey, D. 1996. *Justice, Nature and the Geography of Difference.* Blackwell.

Harvey, D. 2000. Reinventing geography. *New Left Review* 4: 75–97.

Harvey, D. 2006. Space as a keyword. In *David Harvey: A Critical Reader*, eds Castree, N. and Gregory, D., 270–293. Blackwell.

Harvey, D. 2008. The right to the city. *New Left Review* 53: 23–40.

Heidegger, M. 1971. Building, dwelling, thinking. Hofstadter A. trans. In *Poetry, Language, Thought*, 143–161. Harper Colophon.

Hirvonen, A. 2011. The politics of revolt: On Benjamin and critique of law. *Law and Critique* 22: 101–118.

Iveson, K. 2014. The spatial politics of the Aboriginal Tent Embassy, Canberra. In *The Aboriginal Tent Embassy: Sovereignty, Black Power, Land Rights and the State*, eds Foley, G., Schaap, A. and Howell, E., 251–266. Routledge.

Jones, M. 2009. Phase space: geography, relational thinking, and beyond. *Progress in Human Geography* 33(4): 487–506.

Jones, M. 2010. Limits to 'thinking space relationally'. *International Journal of Law in Context* 6(3): 243–255.

Laclau, E. 1990. *New Reflections on the Revolution of Our Time*, Verso.

Lefebvre, H. 1959a. *La Somme et le Reste: Tome I*. La Nef De Paris Editions.

Lefebvre, H. 1959b. *La Somme et le Reste: Tome II*. La Nef De Paris Editions.

Lefebvre, H. 1991. *The Production of Space*. Blackwell.

Lefebvre, H. 1996. *Writings on Cities*, eds Kofman, E. and Lebas, E., Blackwell.

Lefebvre, H. 2002. *Critique of Everyday Life II: Foundations for a Sociology of the Everyday*. Verso.

Lefebvre, H. 2003. The inventory. In *Key Writings*, 166–176. Continuum.

Lefebvre, H. 2009. Theoretical problems of *autogestion*. In *State, Space, World: Selected Essays*, eds Brenner, N. and Elden, S., 138–152. University of Minnesota Press.

Leibniz, G. 1969. *Philosophical Papers and Letters*, 675–721. Reidel.

Look, B. 1999. *Leibniz and the 'Vinculum Substantiale'*. Steiner.

Look, B. 2000. Leibniz and the substance of the vinculum substantiale. *Journal of the History of Philosophy* 38(2): 203–220.

Malpas, J. 2012. Putting space in place: Philosophical topography and relational geography. *Environment and Planning D: Society and Space* 30(2): 226–242.

Marston, S., Jones, J. P. and Woodward, K. 2005. Human geography without scale. *Transactions of the Institute of British Geographers*, n.s., 30: 416–432.

Martel, J. 2011. Waiting for justice: Benjamin and Derrida on sovereignty and immanence. *Republics of Letters* 2(2): 158–172.

Martel, J. 2012. *Divine Violence: Walter Benjamin and the Eschatology of Sovereignty*. Routledge.

Massey, D. 1992. Politics and space/time. *New Left Review* I/196: 65–84.

Massey, D. 1999. Philosophy and politics of spatiality: some considerations. The Hettner-Lecture in Human Geography. *Geographische Zeitschrift* 87(H1): 1–12.

Massey, D. 2005. *For Space*. Sage.

Maycroft, N. 2001. Henri Lefebvre: Alienation and the ethics of bodily reappropriation. In *Marxism's Ethical Thinkers*, ed. Wilde, L., 116–143. Palgrave.

McGee, K. 2011. Demononics: Leibniz and the antinomy of modern power. *Radical Philosophy* 168: 33–45.

Merrifield, A. 2013. *The Politics of the Encounter: Urban Theory and Protest under Planetary Urbanization*. Athens, GA: University of Georgia Press.

Mitchell, D. 2003. *The Right to the City: Social Justice and the Fight for Public Space*. Guilford Press.

Murdoch, J. 2006. *Post-Structuralist Geography: A Guide to Relational Space*. Sage.

Newton, I. 1968. *The Mathematical Principles of Natural Philosophy Vol 1*. Motte, A. trans. Dawson.

Philippopoulos-Mihalopoulos, A. 2010. Spatial justice: Law and the geography of withdrawal. *International Journal of Law in Context* 6(3): 201–216.

Philippopoulos-Mihalopoulos, A. 2011. Law's spatial turn: Geography, justice and a certain fear of space. *Law, Culture and the Humanities* 7(2): 187–202.

Philippopoulos-Mihalopoulos, A. 2015. *Spatial Justice: Body, Lawscape, Atmosphere*. Routledge.

Pirie, G. 1983. On spatial justice. *Environment and Planning A*. 15: 465–473.

Pithouse, R. 2009. Abahlali baseMjondolo and the struggle for the city in Durban, South Africa. *Cidades* 6(9): 241–270

Pithouse, R. 2010. Abahlali baseMjondolo and the popular struggle for the right to the city in Durban, South Africa. In *Cities For All: Proposals and Experiences Towards the Right to the City*, eds Sugranyes, A. and Mathivet C., 133–140. Habitat International Coalition.

Purcell, M. 2002. Excavating Lefebvre: The right to the city and its urban politics of the inhabitant. *GeoJournal* 58: 99–108.

Purcell, M. 2008. *Recapturing Democracy: Neoliberalization and the Struggle for Alternative Urban Futures*. Routledge.

Rescher, N. 1979. *Leibniz: An Introduction to His Philosophy*. Blackwell.

Rescher, N. 1981. *Leibniz's Metaphysics of Nature: A Group of Essays*. Reidel.

Ross, A. 2014. The distinction between mythic and divine violence: Walter Benjamin's 'Critique of Violence' from the perspective of Goethe's *Elective Affinities*. *New German Critique* 41(1): 93–120.

Seigworth, G. 2000. Banality for cultural studies. *Cultural Studies* 14(2): 227–268.

Sheppard, E. 2008. Geographic dialectics. *Environment and Planning A* 40: 2603–2612.

Shields, R. 1999. *Lefebvre, Love and Struggle: Spatial Dialectics*. Routledge.

Soja, E. 2010. *Seeking Spatial Justice*. University of Minnesota Press.

Souza, M. L. 2011. The words and the things. *City* 15(1): 73–77.

Thrift, N. 2008. *Non-Representational Theory: Space/Politics/Affect*. Routledge

Tomba, M. 2009. Another kind of *Gewalt*: Beyond law, re-reading Walter Benjamin. *Historical Materialism* 17: 126–144.

Wall, I. 2012. Tunisia and the critical legal theory of dissensus. *Law and Critique* 23(3): 219–236.

Whatmore, S. 2002. *Hybrid Geographies*. Sage.

Chapter 7

Immersing, comprehending and reappropriating

Milan, unreformed, in the alternative architectures of Ugo La Pietra

Alexandra Brown

Ugo La Pietra's 1977 short film, *La riappropriazione della città* (The Reappropriation of the City), is concerned neither with the design of an architectural object, nor the analysis of buildings and streets that make up Milan's city centre. In fact, throughout the film, La Pietra's understanding of the role of the architect and architectural production within the late capitalist city appear completely disconnected from the realisation of physical structures within the urban environment. Instead, in *La riappropriazione della città*, architecture has become a toolkit for the individual city dweller – a series of representational techniques for understanding their own everyday experiences and behaviours. In this sense, the 'reappropriation' for which La Pietra argues is based on the individual citizen's capacity to see their environment primarily in terms of their own patterns of use and experience. The city of Milan remains physically unaltered at the end of La Pietra's film, but a series of maps and drawings made by the architect reveals multiple new cities consisting of the routes and monuments unique to the architect's exploration of the urban environment.

Although not primarily seen as a film-maker, the Milanese architect, artist and designer La Pietra made a number of short films during the 1960s and 1970s, of which *La riappropriazione della città* remains both the longest and the most ambitious. Viewed alongside a number of La Pietra's earlier projects and installations from the preceding decade, *La riappropriazione della città* can be read as an extension of the anti-reformist, critical architectural thinking evident in the architect's earlier *sistema disequilibrante* (Unbalancing System) experiments. Across these works, La Pietra remained focused on questions of individual agency and freedom within the so-called public spaces of his home city of Milan – particularly the street.

Much of the current literature on La Pietra written in English has focused on his association with the *architettura radicale* (radical architecture) tendency and his role as editor of the magazines *In* and *Inpiù*.[1] While, broadly speaking, his work

---

1 See, for example Colomina and Buckley (2010). There has also been recent interest in La Pietra's contribution to the Counter-environments section of the 1972 'Italy: The New Domestic Landscape' exhibition at the Museum of Modern Art, alongside other so-called 'radical' architects: see Lobsinger (2012).

sits within the anti-capitalist alternative architectural practices that characterised *architettura radicale*, La Pietra's output can also be distinguished from many of the collectives and individuals associated with that tendency through his insistence on local experimentation within the public streets of his home city of Milan. In this respect, the influence of the writings of the Situationist International and the Viennese radical scene on La Pietra's work marked what he saw as a clear point of difference between his architectural thinking and the more Pop-inspired production of radical Florentine collectives such as Archizoom and Superstudio.

> I feel closer to the Viennese culture than to the Florentine, my design approach, in fact, had its roots in a series of aesthetic experiences that I developed in the late fifties and early sixties, experiences related to some of the painting methods of Fontana, the material works of Milani and the brutalism of Viganò. To these matrices I should add a set of ideas that I absorbed in those years through some writings of the Situationist International, and a climate ripe for challenge (my first job in the Faculty of Architecture dates back to 1963).
>
> (La Pietra 1983, 15)[2]

Acknowledging the specificity of his position, the following discussion does not seek to further position La Pietra in relation to the Italian radical project. Rather, it explores La Pietra's architectural tools for 'the recovery of the citizen' during this period, in order to further understand the ways in which his non-traditional architectural practices intersect with concepts of spatial justice and the agency of the individual within the city (Dorfles 1983). The articulation of a growing distance between the totalising forces that shape the physical urban environment and the highly subjective experiences of the individual within this work mirrors distinctions and tensions registered between the concepts of law and justice in the work of Jacques Derrida. By exploring La Pietra's work through these points of tension between the individual and the public in the city, the discussion seeks to further understand how a concept of architecture without buildings or objects might be seen to expose or disrupt the city's tendency to physically, politically and legally homogenise its inhabitants. In this sense, La Pietra's particular interest in exposing the ideology of so-called public space on the streets of Milan through alternative forms of architectural production during the 1960s and 1970s, challenged the limitations of traditional practice and, with it, the idea that the priorities of the individual and those of the city could be easily reconciled through structural interventions.

The chapter begins with a brief introduction to the Italian radical project and its uptake of autonomist-Marxist ideas (notably those of *operaismo* and Mario Tronti) as a way of understanding La Pietra's anti-reformist position and his rejection of buildings in relation to architecture and the city. Following this, the study traces a

---

2 Translation by author.

134 Appropriations

line from the single-user devices that were constructed and deployed on the streets of Milan as part of La Pietra's *il sistema disequilibrante* research, through to the drawing and mapping activities framed as architectural tools for reclaiming the city by the mid-to-late 1970s. When questions of justice and power are considered from within architecture, these notions are more typically read through realised buildings and the history of established building types associated with the law – for example, the courthouse or the prison (Tobe et al. 2013). La Pietra's architecture, actively divorced from the formal planning and construction processes of the city, attempted to articulate an architecture of the individual, concerned with identity and singular experience over the expression of the political and institutional structures of the city.

Architecture against the capitalist city

As noted earlier, Ugo La Pietra's work during the 1960s and 1970s is often framed as part of the Italian *architettura radicale* (radical architecture) project and the anti-capitalist alternative architectural production of the individuals and collectives associated with this tendency. This is a useful way to outline the broader terms of La Pietra's critique of the post-war Italian city (and Milan in particular), while also helping to underline some of the more distinctive ideas embedded in his work. Broadly speaking, the Italian radical architecture project consisted of a series of experiments with non-traditional architectural production. In as much as the term can be thought of as one retrospectively applied to the diverse output of a loosely associated group of architects and designers during this time, the tendency can nevertheless be understood as attaining a sense of coherence through a shared refusal to adhere to client-driven traditional modes of practice that might result in a realised building, alongside a critique of capitalism through architecture.

In this sense, the radicals took quite seriously the Italian historian and critic Manfredo Tafuri's claim that architecture had become complicit with late capitalism, placing them (to varying degrees) within a spectrum of architecturally trained individuals and collectives who sought to understand the critical capacity of architecture during the mid-to-late twentieth century. In Italy in particular, these attitudes were crystallised not only through the events of 1968 and the 'hot autumn' *(autunno caldo)*, but also the worker and student protests and occupations in the years leading up to these events. This culture of protest, coupled with the visibility of the country's extra-parliamentary Left across the decade, provided fertile conditions for the formation of a 'radical' architectural response.

Recent interest in connections between *architettura radicale* and Italian autonomist-Marxism (notably *operaismo*) has shed further light on the political ambitions of many of those associated with the tendency. Pier Vittorio Aureli has been largely responsible for identifying and describing the ways in which the *operaista* theory of Mario Tronti informed the work of the Florentine collective Archizoom during the late 1960s (Aureli 2008; 2013a; 2013b). Although a number of architects and designers who are identified with the Italian radical project did not necessarily share this more direct connection to Tronti's writings, generally speaking, *architettura radicale* was aligned with the anti-reformist strategy of refusal. As Aureli has observed, this alignment excluded the possibility of operating outside prevailing systems, prompting the uptake of a position 'within and against' capitalism that also characterised *operaista* thought.

Bound up in the anti-reformist thinking of much of the alternative architectures of *architettura radicale* was a rejection of the utopian thinking that underpinned modernism during the early twentieth century. Reformism was generally undesirable for both these tendencies because it continued the logic of prevailing conditions under capitalism by striving to improve them without being able to alter the fundamental conditions of capitalist control. For the Italian radicals then, buildings or planning schemes could only reinforce the oppressive conditions of the capitalist city through the conditions of their realisation. Those who could afford to commission architecture, as well as the authorities and companies charged with the approval and construction of these projects, were largely those who benefitted from the prevailing economic and political conditions of the city. According to this logic, a truly critical architectural project could only challenge these conditions through exposing the reality of capitalist control and its restrictive and negative effects on the majority of the city's inhabitants.

Il sistema disequilibrante: immersing and comprehending

Within La Pietra's work, exposing the city as an expression of capitalist production and consumption meant demonstrating the lack of freedom and control for the individual within even the most public spaces of the urban environment. During the late 1960s, La Pietra used the concept of *il sistema disequilibrante* (The Unbalancing System) as a theoretical framework for his installations and interventions. The system consisted of a series of 'ruptures' within the city that could offer moments of freedom and play to an individual, thereby highlighting the absence of these conditions within what had become, for La Pietra, highly programmed and ideologically driven public spaces.

Through this work, La Pietra sought to avoid more typical approaches to architectural design that 'attempt to restructure and transform the current conditions that exist within urban settings' (La Pietra 1983, 12),[3] without simply retreating into the imaginary alternatives of utopian schemes. As he noted in 1967:

> To talk of a city-wide unbalancing system means not accepting either of these attitudes, but through the invention of 'signals' (freed from urban systems), to highlight the contradictions that exist between the actual needs of social groups and the intervention of decision-making structures, providing a quick definition for areas within which (through free behaviour) an autonomous decision-making framework could be located. Places that do not reduce but

3 Translation by author.

136 Appropriations

increase choices on the part of individuals, and serve to promote intervention in the process of setting up an environment.

(La Pietra 1983, 12)[4]

The *immersioni* (immersions) and *modelli di comprehensione* (models of comprehension) devices designed and realised around the beginning of the 1970s were carefully chosen strategies for exposing this lack of freedom for the individual within the city. Their aim was not to attempt to 'fix' the dominant capitalist ideology of the city, but to critique and expose it by making the city's inhabitants more aware of their own loss of individual freedom within the urban streetscape.

For La Pietra, the street and sidewalks of the city provided only the illusion of freedom for its inhabitants. Despite the accessibility of these spaces, he viewed the street as completely dominated by the trading system – a network designed primarily for the efficient distribution of goods with little regard for non-commercial activity and the experience of the pedestrian.[5] Because of this, the movements and actions of the pedestrian were shaped to a considerable degree by the trading system of the street. For example, where and when one might walk or wait could be thought of as substantially determined by signs and signals relating to both vehicular traffic, as well as commercial storefronts. The notion of the street as 'public' space within the city seemed problematic for La Pietra, because it worked to obscure the level of control asserted over the individual and their behaviour.

Within the *immersioni* series, the earliest installations tended to focus on audio-visual effects and the user's ability to control artificial interior environments through this technology. Two interior multi-user, audio-visual installations were also realised and exhibited during the late 1960s. The first was *'Self service' audio-visivo* for the occupied XIV Triennale di Milano in 1968, while the second was *Ambiente audio-visivo* at the 'Al di là della pittura' exhibition in San Benedetto del Tronto the following year. The Triennale installation was completed in collaboration with designer Paolo Rizzato and consisted of a highly interactive space constructed predominantly from opaque and transparent acrylics. Within *'Self service' audio-visivo*, visitors were encouraged to step into suspended acrylic helmets and select from different musical arrangements in order to view a coloured light show associated with these sounds. The installation allowed a number of users to experience a degree of control over their individual environments, as well as the overall appearance of the space. *Ambiente audio-visivo* continued to explore this idea of user-controlled sound and lighting environments, using two long tunnels containing 'micro-instruments' that allowed users to control the installation. These tunnels defined a clear path and direction for experiencing the work and, according to La Pietra, referenced the highly prescribed, axial logic of the urban

---

4 Translation by author.

5 Discussing a 1969 intervention in the streets of Como, La Pietra noted 'the absolute subjugation of the road to the trading system' (La Pietra 1983, 82). Translation by author.

street (La Pietra 1983). Following these audio-visual installations and their references to the street, La Pietra moved his work to the streets of Milan and began to create a series of single-user structures that both altered the user's view of their urban context, while offering an aspect of control over the conditions within the device. These smaller devices used forms of sensory isolation to direct attention to microenvironments that could be (to some degree) shaped or controlled by a user.

Nell'acqua (1970) consisted of a black steel cylindrical tank, elevated on three legs to sit at head height. At the centre of the base of the tank was a clear acrylic dome that created a viewing area, allowing a user to inhabit the interior of the structure by moving their head into place when standing underneath the tank. The device contained a body of water that could be filled and drained by the user through a closed-circuit hydraulic hose system. *Nel turbine* (1970) used the same elevated tank structure, but within this device the tank walls were constructed of clear acrylic and the structure contained polystyrene beads. These lightweight beads could be moved around the tank by controlling a compressor connected to air jets around the tank perimeter. Air was also the focus of the *Nel vento* (1970) device, which used an oxygen tank controlled by a trigger mechanism to direct air directly towards the user though a long horizontal cylinder mounted at head height. Or, as La Pietra put it: 'For every gun shot (action) there is a corresponding strong jet of wind (counter-action)' (La Pietra 1983, 72).[6]

These *immersioni*, designed and realised within a relatively short time period, each used a similar strategy of partially enclosing the user's head and field of vision with a micro environment over which they could demonstrate and experience some degree of control. The act of 'immersing' the user within this single-occupant structure was used here as a method for temporarily disrupting (unbalancing) the conditioned behaviours imposed on the individual within the supposedly public space of the city. This disruption occurred both through entering a new environment and modifying it, while simultaneously drawing attention to the lack of control or agency outside of this moment.

Writing in the catalogue for the 1972 Museum of Modern Art exhibition, 'Italy: The New Domestic Landscape', La Pietra explained further the contradictions that engagement with the *immersioni* would expose:

> The result is a crisis between the user's desire to isolate himself from the context, and his aspiration for an unbalancing inclusion in the system. But this very ambiguity, which is a clash between the aspiration for freedom and the limitation that every choice imposes on freedom itself, is seen as an 'awareness' that the liberation from the social and psychological conditioning by the context proceeds through personal immersion in a space that offers itself as a point for critical and imaginative reflection on the context itself.
>
> (La Pietra 1972, 226)

6 Translation by author.

138 Appropriations

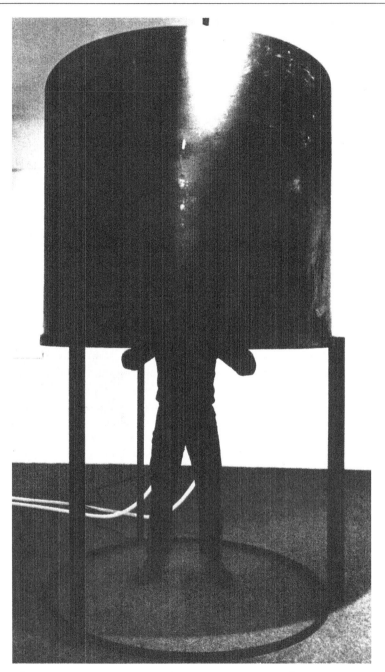

Figure 7.1 Ugo La Pietra, *Immersione nell'acqua (Water immersion)* from *Il sistema disequilibrante*.

Courtesy Archivio Ugo La Pietra, Milano.

In this sense, the *immersioni* set out to construct a spatial moment within which the impossibility of reconciling individual freedom with the systems that generate and control the city can be made clear. While La Pietra is not explicitly focused on a concept of justice within this structure, a question can be asked about how this kind of architectural proposition can be read in relation to a notion of justice connected to individual agency in the city. This is to suggest that, within the *immersioni*, the drive to expose the ideology of the city through the individual can also be seen to implicate structures of power within the urban environment more generally. The distance that La Pietra observed between the formal construction and planning systems of the city and the needs and desires of the individual is, in this sense, also an architectural articulation of the distance between the law and a concept of justice.

In particular, the moment of crisis generated through the individual's experience of the *immersioni* calls to mind Derrida's exposition of the relationship between justice and law in relation to wider decision-making processes. In his 'Force of Law' essay, Derrida argued that the destabilisation of authority that underpins a political critique of the law promotes an awareness of legal decisions as part of an interface with justice as an irrational (and somewhat unknowable) concept (Derrida 1990). As William Sokoloff observed in relation to Derrida's destabilised notion of authority, 'Set into motion by justice, drawing attention to the mystical foundation of authority is therefore an act of political resistance that affirms a conception of justice over and beyond law and manifests itself as political critique' (Sokoloff 2005, 344).

The 'crisis' of decisions and desires that La Pietra sought to induce through the experience of the *immersioni* relies on the same mode of destabilisation to create awareness around the specificity and difficulty of decision-making. Decision, framed through the interactive, user-controlled aspects of the *immersioni*, is presented to the user as a form of action not governed by the totalising systems of the city (whether political, legal or economic). Instead, the experience of the *immersioni* is individual, temporary and thus does not lend itself to reproduction. As such, this ephemeral, 'singular' interaction held up against the more static, generic structures of the city is broadly consistent with Derrida's account of the distinction between justice and law.[7]

At around the same time as La Pietra was constructing the immersion devices for the streets of Milan, he was also developing what he referred to as *modelli di comprehensione*. Like the *immersioni*, these included a number of single-user structures

---

7 Derrida's distinction between justice and law relies on the irreconcilable needs of the individual and the norm:

How are we to reconcile the act of justice that must always concern singularity, individuals, irreplaceable groups and lives, the other or myself as other, in a unique situation, with rule, norm, value or the imperative of justice which necessarily have a general form, even if this generality prescribes a singular application in each case?

(Derrida 1990, 949)

140 Appropriations

that were tested on the city street. La Pietra remained committed to the idea of exposing the oppressive conditions of the city through the *modelli di comprehensione*, but instead of a form of isolation, these devices offered an altered, and thus somehow more authentic view of the context.

During 1970 and coinciding with the *immersioni*, La Pietra constructed *Il commutatore* (The Switch), an A-frame structure with a small foot support that placed the user on an incline and altered their view of street facades. Within the retrospective publication *Abitare la città: ricerche, interventi, progetti nello spazio urbano dal 1962 al 1982* (1983), La Pietra describes using *Il commutatore* on the via Santi Filippo e Giacomo in Genoa as part of a 1971 exhibition, but we also see the device in use in Milan throughout the 1974 short film *Per oggi basta!* (Enough for Today!) (La Pietra and Livietti 1974). Rather than occupying the sidewalk, the device sits in the middle of the street, with the user facing adjacent building facades. As the angle to the A-frame decreases, the user's gaze is directed to the upper levels of the buildings, and finally towards the sky. According to La Pietra, this action allowed the user to overcome conditions 'in which our eyes see . . . nothing but signals that automatically inform our behaviour' (La Pietra 1983, 88).[8] Unlike the *immersioni* series, with structures that seemed to possess a clear interior and exterior, the *modelli di comprehension* such as *Il commutatore* began to break down any sense of enclosure. These devices mostly appeared as structural elements that prompted either direct occupation by a user or, as with *il ciceron elettronico* (1971), supported forms of audio-visual communication.

The speculative and constructed street devices of the *immersioni* and *modelli di comprehensione* series both sought to raise awareness about the prevailing conditions of the city through temporarily altering an individual's understanding of their context. At the heart of these interventions was a change in the user's understanding of their immediate environment, rather than a change in the physical conditions of the city. As part of this position, La Pietra maintained a rigorously utilitarian approach to the design of these works in order to distinguish them from 'status-symbol objects' and their 'superexpressive mediating materials' (La Pietra 1972). Further, these works reinforced the irreconcilability of the individual's experiences of the urban environment with the totalising systems that structured and governed the city as at large.

Reappropriating the city without building/s

Throughout the early and mid-1970s, La Pietra continued to design a wide variety of architectural works, including furniture items, as part of his practice. Nevertheless, in terms of his analytical work around Milan, La Pietra moved much more decisively away from realised structures and towards drawings, collage and writing throughout the 1970s, following the *immersioni* and *modelli di comprehensione*

8 Translation by author.

Alternative architectures of Ugo La Pietra   141

devices.[9] Coinciding with this move away from physical interventions within Milan was also the execution of more ambitious film projects by La Pietra, including *La riappropriazione della città*, the film with which I began this discussion. Within this study, *La riappropriazione della città* is revealing in terms of its behavioural focus and rejection of the physical structure of the city. In this sense, this work can be understood as an extension of some of the ideas embedded within La Pietra's *il sistema disequilibrante* research discussed earlier.

La riappropriazione della città opens on Ugo la Pietra standing at the mirror in his robe, applying shaving cream to his face while being careful to work around his impressive moustache. The sounds of peak hour traffic in Milan provide a rather intrusive soundtrack to the architect and artist's morning bathroom ritual. After a few moments he turns to the camera and says, rather matter-of-factly, 'Abitare è essero ovunque a casa proprio' – or, 'to inhabit is to be at home everywhere'. The camera then pans out to reveal that he is conducting his shaving routine on the footpath of a busy Milan street. We return to La Pietra's morning street shave and this observation from Frederick Kiesler a number of times across the film.

La riappropriazione is a film of three parts, which La Pietra described as analysis, reverse engineering and design. In a somewhat romanticised fashion, the first section of the film draws attention to the perceived freedom of the self-build processes and conditions of Milan's informal settlements at the edge of the city. In examining these conditions, La Pietra attempted to draw attention to the perceived freedom of these slum settlements in allowing inhabitants to manipulate their environment.

Made from found and repurposed materials, the film documents the settlement's functional, hand-made structures, including enclosed shelters, tools, fences and trellises. We also see workers in the process of salvaging found materials and fixings, while being made aware of the extensive working gardens across the settlement, as well as the process of harvesting food from these areas. Within *La riappropriazione*, La Pietra puts to one side the difficult conditions experienced by those who inhabit these settlements, recasting the slum not as a place for the disenfranchised, but as an example of reclaimed territory, where the overarching system of the city has been rejected in favour of individual moments of creation, improvisation and modification.

The second part of the film sees La Pietra present a series of 'encoded' and 'decoded' spaces. Using a series of postcards depicting iconic buildings in Milan as examples of encoded spaces, La Pietra contrasts these with places that he experiences in his own activities within the city. The images that the city projects are thus contrasted with what La Pietra sees as 'places connected to the everyday experience of the individual' (La Pietra 1983; 1977).[10] Among other landmarks,

---

9 La Pietra did return to some forms of physical interventions within Milan in 1979 with the 'Paleti e catene' (*Stakes and Chains*) proposals that were also included in the film *Interventi pubblici per la città di Milano* that was made for the Triennale di Milano the same year.

10 Translation by author.

142 Appropriations

La Pietra contrasts a postcard of Milan's central station ('la stazione centrale') with footage of him entering his car in the driveway to his own apartment building ('la mia stazione'), and the Milan cathedral ('la cattedrale') with the cultural workshop space – previously the St Carpoforo – in which he worked as an animator ('la mia cattedrale'). As La Pietra observes:

> The places in which we live are constantly imposed on us, when actually the space in which we work can only exist as a mental model that is continuously modified by our experience. We must look for the form that arises from our experiences rather than by imposed schemes.
>
> (La Pietra 1977)[11]

This leads La Pietra, within the third section of the film, to propose a set of processes for representing individual experience, instead of the highly regulated conditions of the city and its built form. He demonstrates the mapping process by taking a tourist map of the city and overlaying it with successive pieces of tracing paper. On each of these sheets, La Pietra maps (and instructs his audience to map) a series of activities and experiences. Each sheet, and therefore map, creates a city: 'the city of your sights', 'the city of your information', 'the city of your routes' and even 'the city of your mind'. La Pietra demonstrates these mapping processes by recording visual 'signs' and markers noticed throughout the city, points of engagement with different kinds of audio-visual technology and communication devices, transportation routes, as well as emotional experiences. The resultant maps are a series of nodes and connections, and with each layer of tracing paper, the original and permanent forms of the city begin to disappear.

Both the architectural object and the notion of the domestic interior almost completely disappear from the city as it is represented and reclaimed through these individual maps. La Pietra's Milan, and the city that he encourages the individual to create through mapping and re-mapping their urban environment, is a series of connected nodes of activity that ignore the private and wholeheartedly embrace the public. Architecture is no longer connected to the creation of buildings – the existing structures of Milan serve only as a backdrop to the idea of architecture that he presents as a set of tools and modes of thinking to understand one's behaviour and activities. The city is reclaimed for the citizen by virtue of being created by each individual as a series of moments. This is what La Pietra's maps represent and, as a result, this is the city that one can reclaim, own, create, have control over.

La Pietra's radical architecture project, 1969–77

From his *il sistema disequilibrante* street structures at the beginning of the 1970s, through to *la riappropriazione della città* in 1977, La Pietra's turn away from the

11 Translation by author.

Alternative architectures of Ugo La Pietra 143

architectural object, towards an architecture of 'tools' was broadly consistent with the trajectory of the *architettura radicale* tendency across this time and in the lead up to the formation of the Global Tools initiative in 1973.[12] Nevertheless, this association does not help to explain La Pietra's fixation with the notion of public space in the city and the agency of the individual within it. The realised experimental structures of *il sistema disequilibrante* and La Pietra's detailed studies of Milan clearly set his work apart from a number of the figures whose work might be considered 'radical' within Italy during this period.

In order to begin to understand La Pietra's architectural thinking with works like the street structures of *il sistema disequilibrante* and *la riappropriazione della città*, then, we should move past the more obvious association with *architettura radicale*. La Pietra's output during the 1970s can be understood as a sustained critique of the politics of the city's 'public space' – one informed in no small part by the work of Hans Hollein and the writings of the Situationists. Arguably more so than many of his contemporaries within this tendency, La Pietra's work also approached a spatial articulation of justice connected to the experience of the individual and their agency within the urban environment.

In this final section I will examine La Pietra's individually oriented alternative urban architectural practices of the 1970s with a brief discussion of three broad ideas: the rejection of the object, the disappearance of the interior and the map as architecture. These ideas are held up here against more direct architectural influences (Hollein and the Situationists), as well as thinking on the relationship between justice and law that is implicitly referenced in La Pietra's critical architectural practices during this time.

As previously discussed, the experiential focus of the urban experiments from *il sistema disequilibrante* was based on a rejection of the look of the designed object, referred to earlier and by La Pietra as 'status-symbol objects'.[13] The black, rigidly utilitarian structures built as *immersioni* and *modelli di comprehensione* were made to

12 Global Tools brought together the major architecturally trained figures and collectives associated with the radical project, and it was through this initiative that they announced a new direction for their work. *Casabella* director Alessandro Mendini and others from the magazine were joined by Florentine collectives Archizoom, 9999, UFO and Superstudio, as well as Remo Buti, Ugo la Pietra, Gaetano Pesce, Riccardo Dalisi, Gianni Pettena, Zziggurat, Ettore Sottsass Jnr. and Adalberto Dal Lago from *Rassegna*. Appearing in May of the same year, *Casabella* 377 featured the Global Tools participants on a cover designed by Adolfo Natalini. The issue opened with the initiative's first published output, 'Documento 1', alongside articles by regular *Casabella* contributors and Global Tools members Mendini, Sottsass and Branzi (Global Tools 1973). See also Branzi (1973); Sottsass (1973); Mendini (1973). As 'Documento 1' explained, Global Tools was to function as an alternative educational facility for the teaching of craft-based construction techniques and activities.

13 It should be noted that, while La Pietra was also engaged with a number of diverse activities as a furniture and product designer and artist during this period, his investigation of the urban environment remained consistent in its rejection of the architectural object and its commodity status. For examples of La Pietra's industrial design objects, see his furniture and lighting developed for Poggi: Ambasz 1972.

144 Appropriations

resist being read as a design or art.[14] The devices reinforced their destabilising function on one level simply by presenting as blank instruments read against the context of the message and signal-laden spaces of the city streets. An inherent contradiction in this work, however, was that these devices existed primarily as non-functional microenvironments and structures for user-controlled experimentation, or play.

With the release of *La riappropriazione della città* later, both the design of the architectural object, as well as the attention paid to the existing architecture of the city disappeared more completely. La Pietra literally substituted the buildings of Milan with experience-driven places and interactions within the second part of the film, before erasing the buildings completely through the overlay of successive sheets of tracing paper towards the conclusion of the film. An important consequence of this manoeuvre is the related erasure of interior private space and, through the completely individualised mapping process, the erasure of the architect.

If, as Hans Hollein stated in his 1968 photo essay, 'everything is architecture', La Pietra's work leading up to and within *La riappropriazione della città* played this argument out (Hollein 1968). Hollein's essay, as Craig Buckley observed more recently, is inclusive in its definition of architecture while actively sidelining the idea of architecture as building and architecture's connection to form.

> The injunction that returns at several points in the manifesto – 'architects must cease to think only in terms of buildings' – finds its analog not only in the montage's ban on showing objects traditionally understood as buildings but in the move to subordinate formal similarities. With this disabling of relationships of visual likeness, the emphasis falls upon the creation of significance through the organization of relations of contiguity.
>
> (Buckley 2007, 112)

This approach to architecture as no longer connected to buildings or questions of form is evident in La Pietra's focus on the scale of the individual and his subsequent turn towards mapping. Whether exposing relations of power through the earlier device-driven work of *il sistema disequilibrante*, or reclaiming a purely experiential version of the city in *la riappropriazione della città*, La Pietra's architecture remained committed to the scale of the individual and their activities on the city streets. He routinely ignored any notion of buildings beyond acknowledging their facades in relation to the street, with the mapping language that he developed doing away with the physical presence of built form in the city altogether.

In his turn to mapping as architecture, La Pietra seemed to reference the psychogeographies of the Situationists and their process of *dérive* (drift), while creating, in the end, a very different end result. Guy Debord described the *dérive* in 'Theory of the Dérive', first published in 1956, as 'a technique of rapid passage

---

14 La Pietra described the *immersioni* series specifically as '[e]nvironmental objects that were most often read as tools, not so much art' (La Pietra 1983, 46).

through varied ambiances' (Debord 2006b, 69).[15] The process involved quite literally 'drifting' through the city and experiencing the terrain of the city. In this sense, and unlike La Pietra's mapping, the *dérive* sits outside of everyday activities as specialised experience of the city. Further, while for the Situationists, the *dérive* could exist as an autonomous activity, the end product of La Pietra's (and the individual citizen's) experiences and activities was always a series of maps. Layered, incomplete maps that progressively erased the standard city street map, replacing it with a city of completely constructed connections experienced by the individual. The *dérive* could be used to generate data for psychogeographic maps, but these documents were not, strictly speaking, records of any one *dérive* experience.

Debord's 'Naked City' map of Paris from 1957 further exposes some key differences between La Pietra's mapping and that of the Situationists. Notably, Debord's map is fragmented, privileging a series of distinct 'atmospheres' through collaging pieces of an existing street map of Paris, with thick arrows moving between them. As noted, La Pietra also made use of a standard city map ('the kind you can buy at a kiosk') within *la riappropriazione della città*; however, his process involved working over this existing document. By working over an existing city map, a completely new document is created—one that subscribes to the scale and proportions of the original tourist map. In addition, through the trace layers we see the original map of the city, but it becomes more faint as more experiences and patterns of use are mapped, until a completely user-generated understanding of the urban environment is created. As a result, the focus is on connections and pathways over fragments and distinct entities.

The *dérive* informed and, in turn, was informed by psychogeographic mapping and the existing forms of maps that formed the basis of these new documents. This is an important distinction between this process and that of La Pietra – perhaps one that speaks to more fundamental political differences between each work. Namely, for the Situationists, activities and processes such as the *dérive* and related psychogeographies were part of a series of provocations that would lead to changes in the city. Debord was clear about this in the opening paragraph of his 'Report on the Construction of Situations and on the International Situationist Tendency's Conditions of Organization and Action' (1957) when he stated that, 'We want the most liberating change of the society and life in which we find ourselves confined. We know that such a change is possible through appropriate actions' (Debord 2006a, 35).

Perhaps it was in part through the dramatic events of 1968, or a loose connection to the *operaista* theory that became infused in the mentality of so many Italian radical architects, but within La Pietra's decidedly post-*autunno caldo* works we see no such idea of structural change. The maps produced in *La riappropriazione della città*, the maps that La Pietra encouraged the individual to make and continue to make, are the reappropriated city – the bricks and mortar of Milan and the

---

15 Originally published as Debord 1958.

146　Appropriations

Figure 7.2 Film still, Ugo La Pietra, *La riappropriazione della città* (ed. Centre George Pompidou, Paris, 1977)

Courtesy Archivio Ugo La Pietra, Milano.

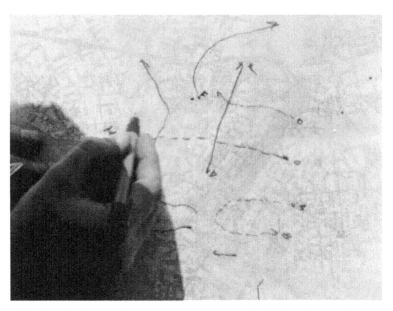

Figure 7.3 Film still, Ugo La Pietra, *La riappropriazione della città* (ed. Centre George Pompidou, Paris, 1977)

Courtesy Archivio Ugo La Pietra, Milano.

logic of capitalist production and consumption to which it complies, will remain unreformed.[16]

Returning briefly once more to Derrida's understanding of the relation between justice and law, the tension in La Pietra's works between the individual and the public in these mapping processes continues to share some important common ground with this later writing. As La Pietra's explorations demonstrate, the problem of acknowledging, or even empowering, the individual within the public spaces of the city is not simply one of reconciliation. The city and the 'public' that the city can account for is fundamentally incompatible with the experiences of the individual. In this respect, the truthfulness of La Pietra's mapping processes cannot necessarily be agreed upon. Instead, it is a unique set of documents that does not retain a consistent meaning at the level of the city and its public at large.[17] The kiosk map from which La Pietra begins his mapping processes perhaps constitutes a more accurate representation of Milan for the generic user, but the individual's nodes and lines can only be the Milan of a specific individual during a specific point in time – these are not paths to be followed.

Can we think of La Pietra's devices and mapping processes of the 1970s as, among other things, a kind of alternative architectural articulation of justice in relation to law? A discussion of his work in these terms has highlighted some of the ways in which the experience of the individual citizen might function as a critical tool for exposing the totalising structures of the city. Furthermore, exploring La Pietra's architectural practice outside of the immediate context of *architettura radicale* might also contribute to an expanded understanding of the relationship between spatial justice and architecture, beyond building typologies associated with the law and legal procedures.

It was La Pietra's anti-reformist position of the city as an expression of capitalist processes that helped to focus the scale of his alternative architectural production during this period on the individual and their experience. In this respect, the street structures of *il sistema disequilibrante* and the mapping processes highlighted in *la riappropriazione della città* should not be read as a retreat from the reality of the city, but rather, a steadfast commitment to exposing this reality. As we have seen, for La Pietra, traditional architectural practice could only continue to perpetuate the existing conditions of the city. His architectural engagement with the city of Milan, freed from the realisation of buildings, became a tool for the individual to comprehend their urban environment as distinct from the generic city of the 'public'.

16 Wollen discusses the impact of 1968 on our understanding of Situationist thought: 'The main activity of May 68, however, was the promotion of occupations and, most celebrated of all, the painting of graffiti. Occupations changed the relations of power, temporarily, but didn't change the architecture' (Wollen 2001, 134).

17 This tension around truth that is also characteristic of the postmodern conceptualisation of justice for Derrida, as it is for Costas Douzinas and Ronnie Warrington. As Douzinas and Warrington note with respect to justice, the concept 'is not about theories and truth; it does not derive from a true representation of just society' (Douzinas and Warrington 1994, 179)

References

Books and articles

Ambasz, E. ed. 1972. *Italy: The New Domestic Landscape: Achievements and Problems of Italian Design*. Museum of Modern Art in collaboration with Centro Di, Florence.

Aureli, P. V. 2008. *The Project of Autonomy: Politics and Architecture Within and Against Capitalism*. Princeton Architectural Press.

Aureli, P. V. 2013a. Manfredo Tafuri, Archizoom, Superstudio and the critique of architectural ideology. In *Architecture and Capitalism: 1845 to the Present*, ed. Deamer, P., 217–238. Routledge.

Aureli, P. V. 2013b. More money/less work: Archizoom. In *EP Vol. 1, The Italian Avant-garde: 1968–76*, ed. Rossi, C. and Coles, A. Sternberg Press.

Branzi, A. 1973. Radical notes: Global tools. *Casabella* 377 (May): 8.

Buckley, C. 2007. Absolute to everything: Taking possession in 'Alles Ist Architektur'. *Grey Room* 28: 108–22.

Colomina, B. and Buckley, C., eds. 2010. *Clip, Stamp, Fold: The Radical Architecture of Little Magazines, 196X to 197X*. Actar.

Debord, G. 1958. Théorie de la dérive. *Internationale Situationniste* 2.

Debord, G. 2006a. Report on the construction of situations and on the International Situationist Tendency's conditions of organization and action. Knabb, K. trans. In *Situationist International Anthology*, ed. Knabb K., 25–43. Bureau of Public Secrets.

Debord, G. 2006b. Theory of the dérive. Knabb, K. trans. In *Situationist International Anthology*, ed. Knabb, K., 50–55. Bureau of Public Secrets.

Derrida, J. 1990. Force of law: The 'mystical foundation of authority'. *Cardozo Law Review* 11(5–6): 920–1045.

Dorfles, G. 1983. Introduction. In La Pietra, U. *Abitare la città : ricerche, interventi, progetti nello spazio urbano dal 1962 al 1982*, 7–8. Alinea.

Douzinas, C. and Warrington, R. 1994. *Justice Miscarried: Ethics, Aesthetics and the Law*. Harvester Wheatsheaf.

Global Tools. 1973. Documento 1. *Casabella* 377 (May): 4.

Hollein, H. 1968. Alles ist architektur. *Bau: Schrift für Architektur und Städtebau* 20(½): 1-28.

La Pietra, U. 1972. The domicile cell: A microstructure within the information and communication systems. In *Italy : The New Domestic Landscape: Achievements and Problems of Italian Design*, ed. Ambasz. E., 226–231. Museum of Modern Art in collaboration with Centro Di, Florence.

La Pietra, U. 1983. *Abitare la città: ricerche, interventi, progetti nello spazio urbano dal 1962 al 1982*. Alinea.

Lobsinger, M. L. 2012. Domestic environments: Italian neo-avant-garde design and the politics of post-materialism. In *Atomic Dwelling: Anxiety, Domesticity, and Postwar Architecture*, ed. Schuldenfrei, R., 186–204. Routledge.

Mendini, A. 1973. Didattica dei mestieri/The teaching of crafts. *Casabella* 377 (May): 7.

Sokoloff, W. 2005. Between justice and legality: Derrida on decision. *Political Research Quarterly* 58(2): 341–352.

Sottsass, E. 1973. Per ritardato arrivo dell'aeromobile (Because of the late arrival of the aircraft): C'è un posto dove provare? (Can it be tried somewhere?). *Casabella* 377 (May): 7.

Tobe, R., Simon, J. and Temple, N., eds. 2013. *Architecture and Justice: Judicial Meanings in the Public Realm*. Ashgate.

Wollen, P. 2001. Situationists and architecture. *New Left Review* 8: 123–39.

Films

La Pietra, U. and Livietti, M. 1974. *Per oggi basta!* Jabik & Colophon, Milan.

La Pietra, U. 1977. *La riappropriazione della città*. Centre Georges Pompidou, Paris.

Chapter 8

This agitated veil
A spatial justice of the crowd?

Illan rua Wall[1]

This agitated veil

Benjamin writes in 'On Some Motifs in Baudelaire' that the crowd 'was the agitated veil' through which Baudelaire saw the city (Benjamin 2009, 43). The city and the crowd were entwined. Baudelaire's genius was to live and write the city *through* the crowd. Benjamin explains that despite this, the crowd is rarely to be found explicitly in his work precisely because the crowd was his manner of framing the city. The city, in its very urbanity, gathers crowds of all sorts. We might say in a very non-Benjaminian vein that the crowd is proper to the modern city, it is *a property* (in the sense of an attribute or characteristic) of the city. Crowds are typical of an urban environment, from the rush hour crush on public transport to the frenzy of 'retail' sites on any major Saturday, or worse a 'black Friday'. But because of its quotidian status, this crowd which is proper to the post-Fordist city becomes all but invisible to us. At the same time, the urban environment that we inhabit seems to take on a 'natural' or 'obvious' character: as though it is as it should be, or it is as it must be. The solidity of the old stone buildings alongside the sparkling new (and increasingly not-so-new) glass infrastructure, denote an always already built environment; constructed and completed. The city seems to bustle with life, flowing past the solidity of its walls, through the channelling streets, all the time made safe by the policed and regulated nature of its 'public' spaces of shopping centres, streets and parks. The productivity, movement and life of the denizens is thus to be contrasted with the apparently stable sense of the built environment.

Increasingly over recent years, a different crowd has entered this everyday urban stage, a crowd that rejects the stability and fixity of the 'given' urban environment. Spatial justice has been one of its catch cries. Anyone who has followed movements like Occupy Wall Street, the Greek *aganaktismenoi* or Spanish *indignados*

---

1 I would like to thank Brid Spillane and Jayan Nayar, whose insightful comments I have too often ignored, Andreas Philippopoulos-Mihalopoulos for sending me down the rabbit hole of atmospheric analysis, and Chris Butler and Edward Mussawir as organisers of the *Spaces of Justice* event at Stradbroke Island and editors of this volume.

will appreciate that there is a direct connection between the practices and claims associated with spatial justice – often framed in the language of the right to the city – and crowd formations. But these are not just any crowds. They are not simply the crowds out shopping in the post-Fordist city or the crowds that attend a sporting or cultural occasion (Passavant 2009). These are occupation crowds, who begin to shift the urban environment by their act of staying beyond their allotted time, by an act of impropriety. There remains a popular nervousness around the question of 'the crowd' – particularly when we move away from Baudelaire's everyday street crowds towards a more directed and political mode of action. These crowds are often associated with irrational anger or hatred, turbulent volatility and gender violence. This chapter aims to make the simple point that the crowd is a (discursive) formation that can be recovered, particularly from the discourse associated with crowds that emerged in the late nineteenth and early twentieth century. I will suggest that instead of a question of 'de-individuation' and demagoguery, the crowd should be thought of as a *genus of modes* of action that has spatial, temporal and affective dimensions. In this it provides an important site for spatial justice claims, by marking spatial *injustice*, de-propriating it, and in a protean sense, beginning the reassembly of environments.

The denigration of the crowd

'The crowd' has long been a problem for rulers. It is unsettled and explosive in its dynamics, it is a fluid process which constantly changes state, an emergent thing.

> Theories of sovereignty are particularly concerned with the control of the crowd and preoccupied with fear of what a crowd *can do*. Crowd is not a *demos* . . . It can be with or without a leader, where a leaderless crowd is a crowd that the sovereign fears the most.
>
> (Zevnik 2014, 106)

The crowd manifests or creates a political instability or uncertainty, signifying that all is not well with the political settlement of a state. It signifies a legal disquiet, a seething roughness before the law and at its hands. To write of the crowd seems to require liquid terms, it is to think about the sea and storm: the crowd's surge and churn, it is tempestuous, wild, angry, raging, boiling, seething, agitated. The American crowd psychologist Boris Sidis captures this sense when he describes this turbulence as the 'savage fury of a hurricane' which rises to the surface from crowds (Sidis 1898, 17). Nobel laureate for literature and crowd theorist Elias Canetti talked about a wave that surges over the city (Canetti 1999, 488); Hippolyte Taine referred to the crowd as growing from a stream to a torrent and then to a cataract,[2] which hurled itself against the dyke of the forces of law and order (Taine 1876, 227). Rancière tells us that the post-platonic Western project

---

2 A cataract here is a large waterfall rather than an eye condition.

152 Appropriations

of founding a politics is an attempt to escape this maritime instability. 'The whole political project of Platonism can be conceived as an anti-maritime polemic. The *Gorgias* insists on this: Athens has a disease that comes from its port' (Rancière 1995, 1). The project of political foundation must be grounded, it must escape the *almuron* ('the tang of brine'). Rancière explains: 'The sea smells bad. This is not because of the mud, however. The sea smells of sailors, it smells of democracy. The task of philosophy is to found a different politics, a politics of conversion which turns its back on the sea' (Rancière 1995, 2). If the problem for Platonism is that of creating the just city, it is also then a matter of generating particular forms of crowding. This is also a matter of determining those best suited to democracy (Rancière 2004), because as McClelland notes 'the democratic constitution of Athens made [the crowd and democracy] the same thing' (McClelland 1989, 37). For Plato, there is a crowding which is proper to the well-founded city, and many which are not.

There are many long and difficult histories of the shifting relations and characterisations of the crowd, from questions of turbulence, morality, labour value and poverty, to internal affective or identificatory coherence, but this is not the place to recount them. So let us simply shift our ground to industrial modernity, where we find the intensification of many current strands of crowd thinking. This is because the modern industrial and subsequently the post-industrial city, gathers crowds with growing intensity, and in the anonymity of large numbers. It presents sites of great wealth and power in close proximity to a mass of those in poverty and deprivation. Industrial modernity intensifies the relation between the crowd and the city, and so it should not surprise us that so-called 'crowd theory' emerges from the end of the nineteenth century, with its great crowded political effervescence. After the Paris Commune, there was a growing sense among the reactionary thinkers of France that the crowd had become the object which posed a threat to European 'civilisation'. For Tarde or Le Bon, the crowd presents irrationality which is ultimately connected with the fear of demagoguery and of the leadership of the crowd.[3] The crowd becomes the exercise of power of the demagogue, 'a crowd without a demagogue was either a contradiction in terms, or nothing, not a crowd at all in any sense that was worth worrying about' (McClelland 1989, 32). Le Bon's most significant addition was the idea that the crowd shared a mind – an unconscious mind – which became closely related to that of the demagogue:

> The group mind was at once the leader's creation and his source of power, because he could fill it with any content that he wished; it became his mind, to do with as he pleased . . . the leader knew instinctively what the crowd wanted because the crowd, being his crowd, and its mind being his mind, would always want what he wanted . . . [This] is the equality of equal slavishness.
>
> (McClelland 1989, 295)

---

3 This view was conceived precisely against the idealist tradition so prevalent at that point. Borch argues convincingly that Le Bon is a paradigmatic biopolitical thinker (Borch 2009, 271).

The question for the early crowd theorists is of the transmission of the ideas of the leader through the mass and ultimately through the nation. For example, in Freud, the crowd forms part of his *Massenpsychologie*, although this never falls into the type of 'super-individuality' that we see in Le Bon or Jung's collective unconscious. McClelland is absolutely correct to detect the latent Hobbesian view of the early crowd theorists (McClelland 1989, 297). They argued that the crowd is incomplete without its head, which is its unification in the mind of the leader. Cacciari reports Le Bon repeating that certain classes had a 'mass thirst for submission' (Cacciari 2009, 166), or Tarde says that 'Every mob, like every family, has a head and obeys him scrupulously' (Tarde 1968, 325). The flipside of this hierarchical structuring is that the crowd itself is instrumentalised as the leader's *means* to power. The crowd is a standing reserve, an army of irrationality, always subject to the desires of the demagogue.

Le Bon's crowd is a savage entity. But savagery does not simply equate to condemnation – although that comes as well. To begin, Le Bon's crowd is not an aggregation of individuals. It is not made up of a collection of single entities, but rather in this gathering a new subject is born. This is why his collective unconsciousness is so important, it allows him to deal specifically with the crowd as an entity in itself. When men enter the heaving mass of the crowd they descend the levels of civilisation, losing their individuality and regressing to their common unconscious nature, Le Bon says. In this sense, Man's [sic] most base instincts are released.

> A crowd is not merely impulsive and mobile [in its sentiments]. Like a savage, it is not prepared to admit anything can come between its desire and the realization of its desire. It is the less capable of understanding such interventions, in consequence of the feeling of irresistible power given it by its numerical strength. The notion of impossibility disappears for the individual in a crowd. An individual knows well enough that alone he cannot set fire to a palace or loot a shop, and should he be tempted to do so, he will easily resist the temptation. Making part of a crowd, he is conscious of the power given to him by number, and it is sufficient to suggest to him the ideas of murder and pillage for him to yield immediately to temptation.
>
> (Le Bon 1903, 42–43)

The crowd, 'like a savage' will not allow any interruption between that which it desires and the realisation of this desire. The *individual* can quickly repress any desire he might have had to overthrow, loot or pillage. His civilisation depends precisely upon his ability to suspend the realisation of his desire. In fact, the extent to which he is civilised is determined by the extent to which this thought even enters his head. Someone who has to consciously repress the urge to transgress has not sufficiently interiorised this civilisation.

The suspension of individuality in the crowd is identical to the suspension of the restraint of civilisation. Man is torn between the primal elements of

154 Appropriations

sentiment and reason, the latter having emerged only recently in human evolution and seldom exercising real influence on human affairs ... All emotions, fear, hate and sexual passions, were survivals of savagery, and, according to Le Bon, especially dominant in those who lacked the opposite principle, reason.

(Nye 1975, 42)

The crowd is savage, unreasoned. With the suspension of individuality, comes suggestibility. The crowd is a collective subject capable of being infinitely directed from above. This sounds like the crowd is being framed as a pure instrument, but the leader's own psychology is not the rational Machiavellian. Leaders:

are especially recruited from the ranks of those morbidly nervous, excitable, half-deranged persons who are bordering on madness ... They sacrifice their personal interest, their family – everything. The very instinct for self-preservation is entirely obliterated in them, and so much so that often the only recompense they solicit is that of martyrdom ... The multitude is always ready to listen to the strong-willed man, who knows how to impose himself upon it. Men gathered in a crowd lose all force of will and turn instinctively to the person who possesses the quality they lack.

(Le Bon 1903, 134–135)

These leaders start from the mass, but break away by their fixation upon an idea. They are possessed by the idea. 'It has taken possession of him to such a degree that everything outside it vanishes, and that every contrary opinion appears to him an error or a superstition' (Le Bon 1903, 134). The leader uses the crowd instrumentally, certainly, but they are not in control of their use, their desires. Instead it is the idea which possesses them that has become sovereign. Their madness, their possession by the idea, generates a crowd that is rabid. But Le Bon's idea throughout, is not simply that we can eliminate crowds, but rather that they should be put to use and controlled by elites through the very mechanisms that he describes. The savagery can be put to effect – and indeed was put to use in elements of the French military strategy in the First World War. His agenda is in the demand that crowds be channelled.

It is certainly not correct to equate Le Bon with all crowd theory of the time. Nor is he the most nuanced, developed or coherent theoretician of crowds in the period. Far from it in fact; McClelland is scathing of Le Bon's plagiarism, not to mention the contradictions that appear throughout his oeuvre. But he insists that Le Bon's *The Crowd* is not so much a 'book *about* mass psychology, but an exercise *in* mass psychology' (McClelland 1989, 203). This is important because McClelland argues that it accounts for the 'Le Bon phenomenon' – that is, the astounding success and popular effect that *The Crowd* had at the beginning of the twentieth century.

The secret of Le Bon's success was to use science to frighten the public, and then to claim that what science could understand it could also control. His advice to public men about how to deal with crowds, or at least how not to be dominated by them, was put before a public that was quick to make heroes of great engineers ...

(McClelland 1989, 196)

McClelland convincingly suggests that Le Bon's retelling of crowd theory quickly became 'a widespread ideology, and . . . a prevailing theory of social explanation' (McClelland 1989, 282). I have already mentioned the effects Le Bon's ideas had on French military strategy in the First World War, but it is also helpful to mention Bendersky's research, which traces his impact on US military thinking in the Second World War (Bendersky 2007). At the same time, Brighenti insists that Le Bon's thought was imbibed by '*both* Nazi-fascist *and* democratic leaders; Mussolini, Hitler and Goebbels, on the one hand; F.D. Roosevelt, De Gaulle, and Giscard d'Estaing on the other hand' (Brighenti 2010, 293). The problem for any attempt to think about questions of crowds today is that this late nineteenth-century theoretical framework remains generally operative, despite the fact that decades of social psychology and political theory have raised serious doubts about its plausibility.[4]

One example of this will suffice. In the preparation material for the 2006 UK police's Public Order Commanders Course, there is regular reference to crowd behaviour being 'a kind of temporary insanity' where 'all go crazy together'. It says

all psychologists seem to agree, that membership of a crowd results in a lessening of an individual's ability to think rationally, whilst at the same time his/her more primitive impulses are elicited in a harmonious fashion with the emerging primitive impulses of the other crowd members. The result being the establishment of a collective mind.

(Quoted in Stott 2009)

As already noted, social psychologists and political theorists make the point repeatedly that this is not the case. This model of crowds is outdated and problematic. However, the Le Bon effect is even more pernicious and effective than

---

4 In social psychology, from the late 1920s there was a major reaction against the conception of the crowd's transcendent collective unconsciousness. One important strand of this response was the Elaborated Social Identity Model theorists, who refuse the deindividuation thesis and instead propose processes of social identity formation which do not destroy other social identities (or indeed modes of rationality), but add to them. So, for instance see: Cocking (2013); Drury et al. (2003); Drury and Reicher (2000); Reicher et al. (2004). In political theory, the critiques of de-individuation come from many different directions, particularly from within different limbs of critical theory, for instance: Blackman (2012); Borch (2012); Brennan (2004); Brighenti (2010); Douzinas (2013); Laclau (2005); McClelland (1989).

156 Appropriations

simply providing a theoretical framework for those who claim expertise in crowd control. Instead of being isolated to the confines of academia or policy expertise, Le Bon's ideas seem to reach the level of a 'common sense'. The point here is that when we think about the crowd we begin with a series of preconceptions and misunderstandings of the processes involved. These need to be identified and examined closely before we can begin to think about the relation between a number of recent crowd formations and the question of spatial justice.

Not to put too fine a point on it, the crowd is at once proper to the city, in the sense that streets, buses, trains, theatres, or slums are all crowded. The problem of *over*-crowding reveals precisely that crowding is a normalcy in the city. What the intense myth-making of the crowd theorists sought to do was underline the impropriety of certain crowds, to make the 'agitated veil' visible as a generator of worry and terror for the establishment. The message from Le Bon is almost simple – the crowd presents a danger to civilisation. I say it is *almost* simple, because he quickly adds that the solution to this problem of the socialist and syndicalist crowds is the crowd itself (but now in the hands of a suitable elite). Parallel to this dynamic of im/proper crowds, is a similar story about the city, about the proper comportment of reasonable subjects (propriety), and about the right order of property and possession, which I will return to in the concluding section.

Rethinking crowds

Le Bon and the other early crowd theorists all agree that deindividuation in crowds is something that happens to even the most stable and calm persona. What is more, they seem to also agree that it happens almost automatically in crowds. However, anyone who has taken part in today's political crowds will find it difficult to identify their own moment of deindividuation. I would suggest that the most common affect of a modern protest will be boredom. A long slow walk around a major city; stopping and starting constantly; barely heard speeches; shouted slogans and perhaps some witty posters. Rarely does any form of deindividuation take place, and when it does it tends to be only in the most extreme moments. The deindividuation thesis is challenged strongly in current models of social psychology. Today, the Elaborated Social Identity Model (ESIM) holds that individuals do not lose themselves in a group, but rather, under certain conditions they begin to gain a common social identity. In a submission to the review of the policing of public order, Stott explains that where the police use forceful tactics like dispersal charges (with batons or on horseback) or heavy handed collective containment (kettling), and the crowd perceive themselves as not being a threat to public order, it is plausible for the crowd to believe in the illegitimacy of the actions of the police. This

> would then lead directly to a change in the nature of the crowd's social identity (their shared sense of categorisation of 'us' and 'them') along two critically important dimensions . . . On the one hand, the indiscriminate use of force

would create a redefined sense of unity in the crowd in terms of the illegitimacy of and opposition to the actions of the police. Consequently, there would be an increase in the numbers within the crowd who would perceive conflict against the police as acceptable or legitimate behavior. On the other, this sense of unity and legitimacy in opposition to the police would subsequently increase the influence of and empower those prepared to engage in physical confrontation with the police. Such processes could then draw the crowd into conflict even though the vast majority had no prior intention of engaging in disorder.

(Stott 2009, 7)

Crucially here, to the police, it appears as though a strategic decision has been made in response to a real or perceived threat to public order. As the crowd reacts violently, initial suspicions are then confirmed (Drury et al. 2003, 1480). But to the protestors in the crowd, they have been unfairly targeted, and an increasing number are willing to confront the police directly. Thus, instead of a linear causality, we find a sort of spiral causality, where the actions of one group impact on the other, intensifying their preconceptions and resolve, and accelerating their response.

In this model there is no real sense of deindividuation. There is no release of a savage, unconscious energy, that will tear apart 'civilisation'. Instead of 'losing yourself' in a crowd, you actually gain a new and different sense of yourself. Vaughan Bell explains through a different example. He asks his readers to imagine themselves sharing a public bus with various other city dwellers – there are teenagers listening to music on their phone, an earnest old couple, etc.:

You feel nothing in common with anyone on the bus and, to be honest, those teenagers are really pissing you off. Suddenly, two of the windows smash and you realise that a group of people are attacking the bus and trying to steal bags through the broken windows. Equally as quickly, you begin to feel like one of a group. A make-shift social identity is formed ('the passengers') and you all begin to work together to fend off the thieves and keep each other safe. You didn't lose your identity, you gained a new one in reaction to a threat.

(Bell 2011)

Bell's example makes it clear. We might imagine people forgetting the differences between themselves while they bend to their task of defending the bus. They might share a certain equality of purpose, a social identity defined in opposition to the attackers. But they do not lose themselves completely in their task.

The elaborated social identity model has many great advantages. Rather than focusing a crowd's essence such as violence or irrationality, which is simply expressed on the streets through protest, it allows us to think about crowds as dynamic and shifting modes of identification and attachment. But the problem with this social psychological model is its reliance upon a representational analysis

158   Appropriations

of crowds as social identity producers. Identity thinking in relation to individuals has long been critiqued ontologically, epistemologically and politically (Brown 1995; Butler 1990; 1993; Connolly 1991; Derrida 1978; Fraser 1997; Young 1997). But in crowds it must be rendered even more problematic; this is particularly so in the sort of flat organisation and communication that you get in protest crowds. Identity thinking, even if produced contextually and from below, still falls into the trap of reifying (even momentarily) a dynamic and changing pattern of singular and plural identifications into the meta-identity of a group of individuals. It reduces crowds to the process of in-group and out-group formation, before investigating the contextual, social and cultural factors involved in this process. In the face of the longstanding prevalence of early crowd theory, the ESIM is a major step forward, but we must not get stuck within it.

Elias Canetti's account in *Crowds and Power* opens a different avenue (1962). Initially the book looks like it is undertaking a full taxonomy of crowds: there are the open and closed, rhythmic, stagnating, slow, invisible, baiting, flight, prohibition, reversal, feast and double crowds. But as you read on, you begin to see Canetti's cunning, because with each new dynamic, the possibility of a complete taxonomy seems to drift ever further from reach so that by the time you have completed the first part of the book on crowds, you have understood the impossibility of the task. What emerges instead is that the crowd is determined by its spatial, temporal and affective relations. As an instantiation of this, the first type of crowd that he thinks about is the 'open crowd'. The open crowd is open in the sense that it is un-boundaried. There is no point of division where the crowd could repel new-comers, no boundary where a sovereign could exclude. The simple rule of this crowd is growth, or at least the possibility of growth. The crowd has a mass, a density and a gravity; and this gravity draws people in. It is to be distinguished, Canetti tells us, from the closed crowd which is determined by its boundary.

> The closed crowd renounces growth and puts its stress on permanence. The first thing to be noticed about it is that it has a boundary. It establishes itself by accepting its limitation. It creates a space for itself which it will fill. This space can be compared to a vessel into which liquid is being poured and whose capacity is known. The entrances to this space are limited in number, and only these entrances can be used; the boundary is respected whether it consists of stone, of solid wall, or of some special act of acceptance, or entrance fee. Once the space is completely filled, no one else is allowed in.
>
> (Canetti 1962, 17)

The boundary – usually a building – remains even when the crowd disperses. As such, the closed crowd maintains a different transcendence to that of its open variant. The open crowd's transcendence happens in the sharing out of the equality of its happening. The building or walls of the closed crowd, however, allow the crowd to continue even when it is not actually taking place. Canetti says:

The building is waiting for them; it exists for their sake and, so long as it is there, they will be able to meet in the same manner. The space is theirs, even during the ebb, and in its emptiness it reminds them of the flood.

(Canetti 1962, 17)

The closed crowd has a duration which extends beyond the crowded moment. Canetti imagines crowds in theatres, in stadia and in churches; and each of these has its own dynamics. But the open crowd, as it flows through the streets or gathers in public squares, is never boundaried. There is no edifice which would stand in for it when the crowd dissipates. While the theatre or church stand for their audience-crowd in their absence, there is nothing to function like this for the open crowd. Now this is a radically different mode of analysis from the ESIM, in the sense that it displaces the collective identification of the participants from the determination of the sense of the crowd. The crowd is not simply determined by those that take part in it, but by the spaces that it inhabits. The possibilities of a crowd shift, indeed the crowd itself changes as it moves through space. The spaces that it inhabits become a determining feature of its possibilities. Temporality too is essential, with different crowds holding out different ways of occupying time. The open crowd cannot be held together beyond its material manifestation, but the closed crowd has a more permanent, haunting presence.

The point of focusing on Canetti is not to simply stick to this dichotomy between open and closed crowds; as mentioned previously, his crowds escape taxonomical categories. Rather I am interested in using Canetti to begin a reorientation of our analysis and a different type of questioning to that of the ESIM or the deindividuation thesis. Just as Canetti foregrounds temporal and spatial dynamics, so too is the affective significance of crowd dynamics examined. The 'war crowd' for instance, is the manner in which one crowd is matched by a second, against whom war is declared. Canetti sees the crowd as an affective dynamic as well as a set of spatial and temporal relations. The war crowd is doubled by its enemy, they face off against one another, becoming the principle of permanence for each other (Canetti 1962, 68). Each side will do anything to maintain its unity; it must not lose. Canetti suggests:

The fact that wars can last so long, and may be carried on well after they have been lost, arises from the deep urge of the crowd to maintain itself in the acute stage; not to disintegrate; to remain a crowd. This feeling is sometimes so strong that people prefer to perish together with open eyes, rather than acknowledge defeat and thus experience the disintegration of their own crowd.

(Canetti 1962, 71)

The point here is not simply to adopt this account of crowds, nor to open the question of whether more ethereal collectives like 'nation' or 'people' should be

160 Appropriations

thought of as crowds.[5] Rather the point is to underline the affective nexus that Canetti is drawing. The gravity that draws people into the crowd can also at times hold the crowd together. In a sense, theatre and cinema crowds operate in this way – as the feature begins the crowd starts to cohere around the performance or screening. They cohere in the sense that they are bound in their attentiveness. There are crowds without *this* affective bind: crowds in shopping centres, streets, at bad films or plays, but the point remains that there are other affects in operation there. We must resist the temptation to talk of 'individual' and 'collective' affects, in that even the most isolated singular affect is exuded. Teresa Brennan insists that the *transmission* of affects 'undermines the dichotomy between the individual and the environment and the related opposition between the biological and the social' (Brennan 2004, 7). It does not remain contained, but rather wafts and disperses. As Andreas Philippopoulos-Mihalopoulos says, affect spreads 'through and in-between a multiplicity of bodies like a sticky substance' (Philippopoulos-Mihalopoulos 2015, 122). In this sense, all affects are collective or common, but that does not mean that there is a simple identity between the affective experience of a person, and the atmosphere(s) that they inhabit. Sara Ahmed argues that affects stick to us, but they are never simply prior to the mood that we are in (Ahmed 2010). Thus, for instance, the atmosphere of anxiety in an exam hall will stick differently to a candidate about to sit the exam and an examiner about to invigilate. As Brennan says: 'If I walk . . . into the atmospheric room . . . and it is rank with the smell of anxiety, I breathe this in' (Brennan 2004, 68).

Andrea Brighenti suggests that we should neither focus upon the individual subject which is either lost (de-individuation) or added to (social identity) in the crowd, nor think about the crowd as the whole entity irreducible to its constituent parts. Instead, he suggests, we should think through a third position – where the crowd becomes a mode. Brighenti explains by referring to Durkheim's theory of rituals, where 'the effects of the physical co-presence of the members of a group congregated in a religious assembly in terms of an "avalanche" that grows bigger and bigger as a sort of "electricity" passes among the participants tightly packed together' (Brighenti 2010, 295). He asks:

> What is the proper object of sociological analysis: the parts, the whole, or 'electricity' itself? Durkheim famously opts for the idea that the whole is irreducible to its constituent parts. But the subsequent debate between methodological holists and methodological individualists seemed to forget electricity.
>
> (Brighenti 2010, 296)

---

5 Here I would agree more with Tarde, who argued that a crowd was 'a collection of psychic connections produced essentially by physical contacts' (Tarde 1969, 278). Canetti's war crowd strays from the sense of a crowd as a material thronging. Instead, it is capable at once of being an ephemeral sense of nation or people, as well as the throngs of an army as they line up in trenches or bases.

A spatial justice of the crowd? 161

Brighenti suggests that the key is to think neither about the unity nor the constitutive parts, but of the different types of irreducible multiplicity. In this, the crowd is neither a subject nor an object, but a *mode*. He suggests that thinking about crowds as modes leads us away from the questions posed above, and begins to get us thinking through the manifest potentiality of particular formations.

The danger with Brighenti's modal analysis, however, is that it tends to produce categorisations of crowds which then seem to have a singular mode (even if the singular mode is understood in its complexity). We might contrast this with a more nuanced account of crowded affects. In particular, the recent work on atmospheres is useful here. An atmospheric analysis would resist Brighenti and Canetti's tendency to deploy a more uni-modal analysis of crowds – where a crowd's particular potentiality could be discovered in its typification. Instead it tries to think about the complex flows and ripples of affect. Crowds generate a multitude of affects. As I have said, boredom is a familiar shared sentiment, as is attraction to or curiosity about crowds. Near the point of police force (either in the form of baton charges or kettling/containment) one finds ripples of fear, anger, terror, passion, shock, outrage, exhaustion and exhilaration. But the difficulty is of method – how can we begin to understand the sheer complexity of the atmospheric production and transmission? This is resolved in the ESIM by reliance on in/out group identification, but atmospheric analysis goes much further into the complexity of the situation.

Atmospheres can be multiple, uncertain and ambiguous. They are 'both ontologically and spatially discrete from one another, but they can also coexist within the same space or environment without necessarily affecting one another' (Anderson and Ash 2015, 49). Anderson and Ash provide a beautiful and nuanced account of a public hospital waiting room. This has the significant advantage (over Vaughan Bell's spectacular example above of a bus being attacked) of being a very quotidian moment. They draw out the problems of non-representational methods through the various waves of urgency, hush, anxiety, or suspense, as they mutate. Atmospheres may be heavy, bearing down on those within, or light and airy and barely noticeable. But crucial is the causality that Anderson and Ash identify:

> It's around 2:40 a.m., and the room is quiet. People appear in pain. Some are worried; others doze more or less quietly. Doctors come and go; people arrive and leave. Two parents are tired, awake. Our daughter sleeps nestled into her mother's shoulder. Suddenly, she cries out. It's not a noise we've heard before. It startles and scares us . . . The noise jolts other people, and they turn to us, some stealing glances at our daughter. One man says quietly, 'Poor thing.' . . . On the one hand, the atmosphere of the room conditions how waiting happens. An atmosphere appears to have a quasi-autonomous existence, shaping actions that are themselves part of how an atmosphere settles and shifts a little, but continues to stay a while. Perhaps lacking the sense of solidity we give to other more obvious material conditions, atmospheres

162 Appropriations

condition by becoming part of how situations and events happen. On the other hand, atmospheres are conditioned by the ensemble of bits and pieces from which they emanate.

(Anderson and Ash 2015, 42–43)

This double causality is important; atmospheres are created by the ensemble of entities in the situation, but they have real effects. They change comportment and bearing, they leave some people untouched, but others cower or are emboldened. Crowd atmospheres can be *particularly* intense – a point that seems to me to be precisely at the heart of all of crowd theory – and this makes it all the more important that we understand their role in the process of occupation.

While it is important to understand crowded atmospheres, what is perhaps more interesting is that sometimes the atmosphere begins to escape the crowd. From the square or park the atmosphere begins to seep outwards, gradually settling upon the city or even the state (as a sense of crisis or urgency). In this new atmosphere, there is a revision of the type of political organisation and politico-legal settlement that is realistic and possible. And with this new city-atmosphere, the crowd process is intensified. In Paris in late 1935, Georges Bataille seemed to identify precisely this moment. He addressed the group *Contre-Attaque* during the period of the 'popular front', where fascism seemed to menace the Third Republic, and the communists and socialists sought to take power together electorally, with the aid of a general strike and popular mobilisation. Thinking about the atmosphere in Paris in this moment, Bataille argued:

What drives the crowds into the street is the emotion directly aroused by striking events *in the atmosphere of a storm*, it is the contagious emotion that, from house to house, from suburb to suburb, suddenly turns a hesitating man into a frenzied being.

(Bataille 1985, 162)

In other words, the crowd produces an atmosphere which escapes it, before settling on the city, where it continues to excite further crowds and turbulence.

Conclusion: occupation crowds and spatial justice

These atmospherics bring us back to the fluidity of the crowd that began this chapter. The occupation crowd is a *turba*; a churning, crashing, turbulent mode of politics (Zevnik 2014). It becomes essential for political philosophers to develop the politics of the 'proper' crowd, that is, a politics in which the crowd knows or is shown its place. We have seen the intensity of this production with the late nineteenth-century crowd theorists discussed in the first section above. But in a sense, Western political philosophy has never stopped asking the question of how to discipline its crowds by distinguishing between the rabble and the good property owning citizens, or between the mob and

A spatial justice of the crowd? 163

the people.[6] It is important to note that I am not trying to simply valorise the crowd as though we could identify its destiny as the essential agent of spatial justice. The crowd has *no fundamental political* character. Crowds can be turned to most political ends: from Trump and the Tea Party to Tahrir Square. But my purpose here is *not* to recover the crowd as some sort of *guaranteed* subject – the crowd is *not* the 'multitude' with its ontological warranty (Fitzpatrick 2004; Mazzarella 2010). The promise of political crowds is that they embolden and valorise, generating an energy. They might even constitute this energy, transmitting it into a different form of political activity as with 15-M and *Podemos*. Today's occupation crowds in Zucotti Park, Puerto del Sol or Syntagma Square, do more than simply reject our late capitalist distribution of power and resources. They perform a refusal of the space provided in the post-Fordist city, taking up Lefebvre's insistent demand that the city was a form of making, an *oeuvre* (Lefebvre 1996; Butler 2012). The city is not just a series of zones of consumption. It is not a theme park for consumers and tourists (Passavant 2009; Sorkin 1992). These 'improper' occupation crowds challenge the 'proper' construction of the crowd, and in so doing they 'de-propriate' the city. This de-propriation may be the object – as in a prefigurative politics – or it may be translated into other political forms such as a party (see Dean 2016), or it may dissipate.

The sense of de-propriation, however, I suggest is the key connection to the right to the city and spatial justice. In conventional jurisprudence, law deals with the question of a just distribution of space by way of various modes of measuring. Each party does (or does not) get a parcel of land, the use of a plot, access to some amenity or resource. In this, the metaphysics of property, contract and measure, along with their attendant temporality (permanence, predictability, span, etc.) are placed at the heart of the question of the spatial order and the justice-claims made of it. Yet justice, like freedom and equality, always escapes attempts to fix or freeze it. It is always to-come, there is always something which escapes. The crowd is one way that we can identify the momentary flash of justice in the present, that moment as Benjamin describes it, when 'divine violence' settles and destroys (Benjamin 1978; Martel 2012). 'Spatial justice' as it has developed in the last few decades has been used as a way of problematising the established modes of spatial distribution, whether that is by way of Soja's (2010) and Philippopoulos-Mihalopoulos's (2015) versions of spatial justice, or Harvey's (2013) and Marcuse's (2009) versions of the right to the city. So it should not surprise us that the crowd plays at least some role in each of their accounts. The crowd is one mode of this other spatial politics. It operates to spatially, temporally and affectively *de-propriate* the city. The occupation crowd, in its 'impropriety', underlines the plasticity of space. Working in shorter spells, it de-propriates the extant measure of just and

6 While there is much yet to be written on this history of crowds, there is already a well-developed set of reflections from various different angles, for instance: Hobsbawm 1959; McClelland 1989; Borch 2012; Linebaugh and Rediker 2002.

References

Ahmed, S. 2010. Happy objects. In *The Affect Reader*, eds Gregg, M. and Seigworth, G., 29–51. Duke University Press.

Anderson, B. and Ash, J. 2015. Atmospheric methods. In *Non-Representational Methodologies*, ed. Vannini, P., 34–51. Routledge.

Bataille, G. 1985. *Visions of Excess*. University of Minnesota Press.

Bell, V. 2011. Riot psychology, published on 10/08/2011. Available at http://mindhacks.com/2011/08/10/riot-psychology/. Accessed 7 July 2016.

Bendersky, J. W. 2007. Panic: The impact of Le Bon's crowd psychology on US military thought. *Journal of the History of the Behavioral Sciences* 43(3): 257–283.

Benjamin, W. 1978. Critique of violence. Jephcott, E. trans. In *Reflections*, ed. Demetz, P., 277–300. Schocken Books.

Benjamin, W. 2009. On some motifs in Baudelaire. In *Poetry and Cultural Studies: A Reader*, eds Damon, M. and Livingston, I., 37–55. University of Chicago Press.

Blackman, L. 2012. *Immaterial Bodies*. Sage.

Borch, C. 2009. Body to body: On the political anatomy of crowds. *Sociological Theory* 27(3): 271–290.

Borch, C. 2012. *The Politics of Crowds*. Cambridge University Press.

Brennan, T. 2004. *Transmission of Affect*. Cornell University Press.

Brighenti, A. M. 2010. Tarde, Canetti and Deleuze on crowds and packs. *Journal of Classical Sociology* 10(4): 291–314.

Brown, W. 1995. *States of Injury*. Princeton University Press.

Butler, C. 2012. *Henri Lefebvre: Spatial Politics, Everyday Life and the Right to the City*. Routledge.

Butler, J. 1990. *Gender Trouble*. Routledge.

Butler, J. 1993. *Bodies That Matter*. Routledge.

Cacciari, M. 2009. *The Unpolitical*. Fordham University Press.

Canetti, E. 1962. *Crowds and Power*. Viking Press.

Canetti, E. 1978. *The Human Province*. Farrar, Straus and Giroux.

Canetti, E. 1999. *Memoirs: The Play of the Eyes, A Torch in the Ear, The Tongue Set Free*. Farrar, Straus and Giroux.

Cocking, C. 2013. Crowd flight in response to police dispersal techniques: A momentary lapse of reason? *Journal of Investigative Psychology and Offender Profiling* 10(2): 219–236.

Connolly, W. 1991. *Identity/Difference*. Cornell University Press.

Dean, J. 2016. *Crowds and Party*. Verso.

Derrida, J. 1978. *Of Grammatology*. Johns Hopkins University Press.

Douzinas, C. 2013. *Philosophy and Resistance in the Crisis*. Polity.

Drury, J. and Reicher, S. 2000. Collective action and psychological change: The emergence of new social identities. *British Journal of Social Psychology* 39(4): 579–604.

Drury, J., Stott, C. and Farsides, T. 2003. The role of police perceptions and practices in the development of 'public disorder'. *Journal of Applied Social Psychology* 33(7): 1480–1500.

Fitzpatrick, P. 2004. The immanence of *Empire*. In *Empire's New Clothes*, eds Passavant, P. and Dean, J., 31–56. Routledge.

Fraser, N. 1997. *Justice Interruptus*. Routledge.

Harvey, D. 2013. *Rebel Cities: From the Right to the City to the Urban Revolution*. Verso.

Hobsbawm, E. 1959. *Primitive Rebels*. Norton.

Laclau, E. 2005. *On Populist Reason*. Verso.

Le Bon, G. 1903. *The Crowd: A Study of the Popular Mind*. Fisher Unwin.

Lefebvre, H. 1996. The right to the city. In *Writings on Cities*, eds Kofman, E. and Lebas, E., 61–181. Blackwell.

Linebagh, P. and Rediker, M. 2002. *The Many Headed Hydra*. Verso.

Marcuse, P. 2009. From critical urban theory to the right to the city. *City* 13(2–3): 185–196.

Martel, J. 2012. *Divine Violence: Walter Benjamin and the Eschatology of Sovereignty*. Routledge.

Mazzarella, W. 2010. The myth of the multitude, or, who's afraid of the crowd? *Critical Inquiry* 36(4): 697–727.

McClelland, J. S. 1989. *The Crowd and the Mob*. Unwin Hyman.

Nye, R. 1975. *Origins of Crowd Psychology*. Sage.

Passavant, P. 2009. Policing protest in the post-Fordist city. *Amsterdam Law Forum* 2(1): 91–114.

Philippopoulos-Mihalopoulos, A. 2015. *Spatial Justice: Body, Lawscape, Atmosphere*. Routledge.

Rancière, J. 1995. *On the Shores of Politics*. Verso.

Rancière, J. 2004. The order of the city. *Critical Enquiry* 30: 267–291.

Reicher, S., Stott, C. Cronin, P. and Adang, O. 2004. An integrated approach to crowd psychology and public order policing. *Policing: International Journal of Police Strategy and Management* 27(4): 558–572.

Sidis, B. 1898. *The Psychology of Suggestion*. Appleton & Co. Available at: www.sidis.net/ps2. htm. Accessed 21 March 2016.

Soja, E. 2010. *Seeking Spatial Justice*. University of Minnesota Press.

Sorkin, M., ed. 1992. *Variations on a Theme Park: The New American City and the End of Public Space*. Hill and Wang.

Stott, C. 2009. Crowd psychology and public order policing: Submission to Her Majesty's Inspectorate of Constabularies, Policing of Public Order Review Team. Available at: http://content.yudu.com/Library/A1vpaw/HMCICSubmissionCrowd/resources/1. htm. Accessed 21 March 2016.

Taine, H. 1876. *The Origins of Contemporary France*. Available at Project Gutenberg: www. gutenberg.org/files/2577/2577-h/2577-h.htm. Accessed 21 March 2016.

Tarde, G. 1968. *Penal Philosophy*. Little, Brown.

Tarde, G. 1969. The public and the crowd. In Tarde, G., *On Communication and Social Influence*, ed. Clark, T. N. Chicago University Press.

Young, I. M. 1997. *Intersecting Voices*. Princeton University Press.

Zevnik, A. 2014. Maze of resistance: Crowd, space and the politics of resisting subjectivity. *Globalizations* 12(1): 101–115.

Index

Abahlali baseMjondolo 113
Aboriginal Housing Company (AHC) 57
Aboriginal land rights 57, 113
Aboriginal people 57–8
Aboriginal Tent Embassy 57, 113
absolute space 9, 117
abstraction, loss of 85–7, 90
actor-network theory 115, 119
advertising 30–1
affect: and immaterial labour 62; excess of 30, 31; transmission of 160–1
Agamben, Giorgio 50–1
Aganaktismenoi 113, 150
agency: lack of 137; 'postcode lottery' of the distribution 64; within public spaces 14, 132, 143; within the city 14, 133, 139, 143
AHC *see* Aboriginal Housing Company
Ahmed, Sara 160
Alienation 13
Anderson, B. 161–2
anteriority 25
Antigone 88–9
Antiquity 97
Ant-Optic 25
appropriation 116: defined 13; of space 13, 115, 120–2, 127-8
Arab Spring 113
Arcades Project 26
architecture 47; and capitalism 134–6; and legal procedure 47–8; without buildings 133–4, 140–2, 144, 147; *see also architettura radicale* movement

architettura radicale movement 14, 132–5, 143, 147
Archizoom 14, 133, 134
Argus, The 106
Ariès, Philippe 96
art: and consumption 11, 63, 65; and spatial justice 11, 54; in the public interest 54–7; *see also* artists; public art
artists 54–67; and gentrification 56, 58–60, 67; and middle class 60; income of 60
Ash, J. 161–2
assemblage thinking 115, 119
atmosphere 28–33; and surveillance 31; and the crowd 161–2; captured in photography 28–32; engineered 30, 34; withdrawal from 34–5
audio-visual installations 136–7
Aureli, Pier Vittorio 134–5
austerity 113, 128
authority 139
autogestion 121
autonomist-Marxism 11, 133, 134
autopsies 96

Bachelard, Gaston 120
Baetens, Jan 26
Baldus 46
Barr, Olivia 8, 12
Barsdorff-Liebchen, Nicolette 25
Barthes, Roland 78, 80n10
Bataille, Georges 162
Baudelaire, C. 150
Bayley, Adrian 73, 76, 77, 81
Bayley v Nixon 73n1

Bayley v R 73n1, 77
Begg, Zanny 9, 11
Bell, Vaughan 157, 161
Benjamin, Walter 14, 26, 43, 115-6, 125–7, 150, 163
Bergson, Henri 119, 123
Bidwill 64
Black Power Movement 57
Blackstone, William 84
bodily inhabitance 13, 115–21
body: and violence 31, 33; as deployment of energy 120; deployment in space 120; disembodiment 80; dislocated 81; distribution in space 22–3; female 80; unjust emplacements of 26; *see also* bodily inhabitance
Böhme, Gernot 28
Bolton, Matt 56, 67
borders, 7, 34
bourgeois culture 63
bourgeois home 120
Braverman, Irus 7n8
Brennan, Teresa 33, 160
Brenner, Neil 121
Brighenti, Andrea 160–1
Brown, Alexandra 9, 14
Brunswick 73–6, 82–4, 90
Buckley, Craig 144
buildings: architecture without 133–4, 140–2, 144, 147; distinguished from dwelling 103; for court sittings 104; public 100, 104
Bulger, Jamie 77–9
burial 86; and transforming space into place 98; rituals 96–8
Butler, Chris 9, 13–14, 63, 65

C3West 55
Camera Lucida 78, 80n10
Canetti, Elias 151, 158–61
capital accumulation 4, 5
capitalism: and architecture 134–6; and atmospheric engineering 30; industrial 56; structural injustices 3
care: ceremonial 86; for place 86–7, 90; for the dead 86, 87; practices of 86
Carter, Paul 103

casual work 61
cemeteries: garden 96; as heterotopia 97, 98; as marketplace 97
ceremonial care 86
Certeau, M. 63, 64
Chippendale 58, 62
city, the: and industrial capitalism 56; and the crowd 150; and the unburied dead 97–8; as expression of capitalist production and consumption 135; as spatial phenomenon 7; attitudes to the dead 95–6; public space within 14, 67, 132, 133, 135–7, 143, 147; right to 5, 121–2; social justice in 5
Clarke, Samuel 117
class-exclusions 63
collaboration 62
collective unconscious 152–3, 155n4
colonisation 1–2; and buildings for court sittings 104; role of coroner 95, 98
common law 75, 84, 95
community engagement 55
community gardens 54
conflict 22, 24, 32; future of 25–26
consumerism 65; elite 58; global 5; radical 64–5
consumption: and art 11, 63, 65; ideological environment of 62; post-Fordist 59; the city as an expression of 135

contiguous, the 40–1
Contre-Attaque 162
cooperation 62
coroner 12–13: and techniques of place-making 104; duties of 99, 106; itinerant 99–102; role in the colonisation 95, 98; the office of 99, 100, 102–5
Coroners Statute 1865 (Vic) 100, 101n12
coronial law 94–107
courthouses 99, 104–5, 134
creative class 11, 60
creative consumers 63–7
creative industries 60–1
Creative Industries Action Plan (IAP) 60–1
creativity 60–1, 63
criminal justice system 89

168 Index

critical geography 13, 14, 115, 119
cross-cultural dialogue 65
crowd, the 8, 14–15, 150–64; and
atmosphere 161–2; and boundaries
158–9; and identity formation 14;
and irrationality 152, 153; and
leaders 153, 154; and shared mind
152–3; and social identity 156–7;
and suppression of individuality
153–4, 156; and temporality 159; and
transmission of affects 160; as a mode
160–1; denigration of 151–6; occupation
163; political 14, 162–3; taxonomy of
158
Crowds and Power 158
cultivation 103
culture 56; bourgeois 63; critique of 63;
distribution of 64
Culture in Action 55

daily rhythms 118
dead, the 86; and the political life of
the city 95; and the coroner 94–107;
attitude to 95–6; care for 86, 87; cult of
96; place of 95–9; storing bodies 100–2,
105; unburied 97–8
death investigation process 96; holding
an inquest 101–2, 105; storing bodies
100–2, 105
death taxes 99
Debord, Guy 144–5
Deicorp 57
'deindividuation' 14
Delaney v Old 2
Deleuze, G. 27, 34, 40–2, 114, 123–4; *The
Fold* 124
deodands 99–100
De Republica Anglorum 99
dérive 14, 144–5
Derrida, Jacques 126–7, 133, 139, 147
deterritorialisation 25
Deutsche, Rosalyn 56–8, 60
difference 5
Dikeç, Mustafa 5–6
discrimination 6
disease 2, 96
dislocation 81

distribution: of bodies in space 22–3; of
culture and agency 64; of goods 136; of
power 26, 28; of resources 1, 3–4, 163;
of space 163
distributive justice 3–4, 6, 14, 114
diversionary space 42–4
divine violence 125, 126, 163
domination 4, 5, 119; of space 13; social 5
Dominion of the Dead, The 97–8
Dorsett, Shaunnagh 95
Durkheim, E. 160
dwelling 103

ecological reclamation projects 55
égaliberté 6
Elaborated Social Identity Model (ESIM)
156, 158, 159, 161
Engels, Friedrich 58
England 99, 100
ESIM *see* Elaborated Social Identity
Model
everyday life 63, 122–3; and theory of
moments 124
'everydayness' 65
evictions 113
exploitation 11, 62, 63

factories 56, 58, 63
Fairfield 65–7
fairness 3, 9, 37
faraway, the 40–1
fascism 162
female body: disembodiment of 80;
violence to 81
Fictio legis 44
First Peoples 1–2
Florida, Richard 11, 60
Foley, Gary 57
formulary process 46
Foucault, Michel 97
France 113
freedom 163; and choice 137; of the self-
build process 141; within public spaces
132, 135; within the city 136
Freud, Sigmund 85, 86, 153
funerary rituals 96; *see also* burial
Fun Park project 64

future: of conflict 25–26; photography capturing 26

garden cemeteries 96
Gardiner, Michael 122–4, 127
Gatens, Moira 33
Gathering the Ashes of Phocion 88
Genoa 140
gentrification 54–67; and artists 56, 58–60, 67; and racism 58
geography: critical 13, 114, 115, 119; human 3, 5, 116, 118; Marxist 3–5, 114
Glass, Ruth 56
global consumerism 25
globalisation 128
Global Tools initiative 143
Gorenpul people 1, 2
Gottdiener, Mark 56, 58, 59, 62, 64
government planning 60
Gran, Jill 67
Greece 113, 150
Guattari, F. 27, 40–2, 114

Haldar, Piyel 47
Hamacher, Werner 126–7
Hardt, Michael 11, 61–2
Harrison, Robert Pogue 97–8, 103
Harvey, David 3–5, 54, 55, 67, 114, 118–19, 163
hawking 95, 100, 101, 106, 107
Heidegger, Martin 103, 120
heterotopia 97, 98
high-speed broadband 61
Hirvonen, Ari 128
historical-geographical materialism 118
Hoddle, Robert 100
Hogg, Russell 104
Hollein, Hans 143, 144
housing problems 58
housing stress 59
human geography 3, 5, 116, 118
humanity 13
human rights 122

identity 16, 134; cultural 1; formation of 14; political 77; social 155n4, 156–8
Il commutatore 140

illusions 33–4
il sistema disequilibrante 135, 143, 144
immaterial labour 61–2
immersioni 136–9
Indigenous communities 57
indigenous lands 98
Indigenous Land Use Agreements 2
Indignados movement 113, 150
industrial capitalism 56
industrial labour 61–2
industrial modernity 152
informal economy 61
inhabitance 1; bodily 13, 115–21; of space 13, 113, 121, 128; politics of 9, 13, 116, 120–2, 128
injustice: and capitalist social relations 3; sources of 4; spatial dialectics of 5; urban 4, 64
intellectual labour 61
Iraqi refugees 65
Italy 134–5
iustitia 37, 38

Jacobs, Mary Jane 55
job mobility 61
Jones, Jonathan 55
judgment 34, 44, 48, 51
jurisdiction 12, 13, 38, 84, 95, 106; territorial aspect 39
jurisprudence 37–40, 46, 48, 51–2; feminist 81n12; Roman 45, 46n6, 47–9; Western 10, 39, 44
'just city', 3
justice: and politics of pure mediacy 126–7; *aporias* of 11; as a form of pure means 126; as 'experience of the impossible' 126–7; as an 'enabling' concept 4–5; as fairness 3; distributive 3–4, 6, 14, 114; 'foreclosure' of 125; moments of 124–5, 127; relation to law 37–9, 139, 147; walking as call for 86, 90; *see also* social justice; spatial justice
Justice, Nature and the Geography of Difference 4

Kafka, Franz: on photography 24n5; *The Trial* 10, 39–44
Kaldor Public Art Project 55

Kant, Immanuel 118
Kantorowicz, Ernst 46
Kennedy, Joe 56
King's Two Bodies, The 46
knowledge 52; and immaterial labour 61; and space 51–2
Kwon, Miwon 54–5

labour, 61; immaterial 61–2; industrial 61–2
Laclau, Ernesto 119
language: and inhabitation of place 103–4; as expression of dwelling 103; of spatial justice 9
La Pietra, Ugo 14, 132–47
La riappropriazione della città 14, 132–3, 141, 143–4, 147
La Trobe, Charles 104
law: and mourning 88–90; ceremonial 12, 90; common 75, 84, 95; coronial 94–107; medieval 45–6; relation to justice 37–9, 139, 147; Roman 45, 48–50; 'spatial turn' 7
lawful place 74–5, 85–6, 88–90; for the dead 94–5, 98, 106; loss of 87, 90
Law, Text, Culture 8
Lazzarato, Maurizio 11, 62
leaders 153, 154
Le Bon, G. 152–6
Lefebvre, Henri 5, 6, 115–16, 163; *Critique of Everyday Life* 122; *La Somme et le Reste* 122, 125; on appropriation of space 13, 115, 120–1; on 'right to the city' 5, 121–2; on everyday life 63; on inhabitance 13; theory of moments 13–14, 116, 122–5, 127; theory of space 117–21; *The Production of Space* 13, 115, 117, 118
legal fiction 44–7
legal movement 84
legal ordering 86, 95
legal pluralism 8
legal procedure 44, 46–50
legal spaces 8
Leibniz, G.W.: monadology 116, 123; relational conception of space 117, 120
Lesdema, Eric 21–35
liberal democracies 3

Life Day–Fortunes of War 21, 24, 26–8
Little Baghdad project 65
Lloyd, Genevieve 33
logos 103
Lonsdale, William 96–8
Look, Brandon 123
loss: and mourning 85; of an abstraction 85–7, 90; of lawful place 87, 90
Lydon, Mike 55–6

Manderson, Desmond 8
mapping 14, 142, 145, 147; psychogeographic 145
Martel, James 127
Marx, Karl 61
Marxist geography 3, 4, 5, 114
Massey, Doreen 119
mass intellectuality 62
materiality 81; of movement 83; of spatial justice 75; of the ground 82; of time 79
McClelland, J.S. 153–5
McVeigh, Shaun 95
Meagher, Gillian 12, 73–86, 89, 90
medieval law 45–6
melancholia 85
Melbourne 12, 73, 77, 82n14; coronial law 95–102, 104, 107; courthouses 99, 104; *see also* Brunswick
Middle Ages 97
middle class 56, 58, 60, 64
Milan 132–4, 137, 139–42, 144, 145, 147
Minjerribah 1–2
modeli di comprehensione 136, 139–40
modernism 63, 134
modernity 79, 81; industrial 152
moments: defined 122; theory of 13–14, 116, 122–5, 127
Moore, Gerald 30
Moreton Bay 1, 2
morgues 100, 103, 104, 105
Morgue Site Act 1886 (Vic) 105
Morton, Timothy 33
mourning: and loss 85; and melancholia 85; becoming the law 88–90; movement of 84; public 12, 73, 85, 89, 90; work of 85; *see also* mourning place

Mourning Becomes the Law 74, 87
mourning place 12, 75, 90
multinational corporations 56
Mussawir, Edward 9, 10
mythical violence 125

native title rights 2
nature 46; and fiction 44–6; and humanity 13; unconscious 153
necropolises 96, 98; *see also* cemeteries
Negri, Antonio 11, 61–2
Nell'acqua 137
Nel turbine 137
Nel vento 137
New Genre Public Art 55
new urbanism 55, 67
Newton, Isaac 9, 117
New York 56
non-representational theory 115, 119
North America 55
Nughi people, 2
Nuit Debout movement 113
Nunukul people 1, 2

obliqueness 25
ocularcentrism 81
Occupy movement 113
Occupy Wall Street 150
Ollman, Bertell 13
operaismo 62
Operaista theory 134–5, 145

Packer, Jamie 55
part-time work 61
Paulus 49
Per oggi basta! 140
Philippopoulos-Mihalopoulos, Andreas 6, 9, 10, 75, 114–16, 160
Philosophizing the Everyday 63
Phocion 87–9
photography: captured atmosphere 28–32; future-capturing 26; Kafka on 24n5; *Life Day–Fortunes of War* series 21–35; spatiality in 22
Pirie, Gordon 4, 116
place: care for 86–7, 90; inhabitation of 103–4; loss of 90; of the dead 95–9

place-making 95; as an activity of dwelling 103; techniques 104
place-naming 103–4
Plato 3
Platonism 152
Plutarch 87
Poetics of Space, The 120
polis 3
political crowd 14, 162–3
political corruption 128
political critique 139
political defiance 88–9
political liberties 3
political withdrawal 34

politics of inhabitance 9, 13, 116, 120–2, 128

possibility: of spatial justice 13, 115, 125–8; of the impossible 14, 116, 125, 127; realisation of 123
post-Fordism 14, 59, 62, 150, 151, 163
post liminium 45
post mortem examinations 96
Poussin, Nicholas 87–9
poverty 60, 64, 152; and spatial segregation 58
power distribution 26, 28, 163
Powerhouse Youth Theatre, Fairfield 65
procedural space: frames of analysis for 51–2; in Kafka's Trial 39, 40, 44, 48, 50–2
production process 62
public art 11; and urban planning 55; forms of 54–5, 62; globally recognisable 55; policy 55
public ceremonial law 12, 90
public ceremony 83–4; of collective walking 86; of law 74, 82, 89; of mourning 73–5, 82n14, 85–90; *see also* public ceremonial law
public houses 95, 99, 101–2, 105, 106
public interest 54–7
public mourning 12, 73, 85–7, 89, 90
public places 54

public space 54; and 'occupying' movements 113; freedom and agency within 132, 135–6, 143; within the city 14, 67, 132, 133, 135–7, 143, 147
public suffering 89
punctum 80

Queensland State Government 2

racism 58
radical politics 5, 113, 122
Rancière, J. 151–2
Rawls, John 3, 4
reality 45
recycling 55
Redfern 57–9, 62
reformism 134
refugees 26, 65
repression 6
res 48–51
responsibility 10, 22; civic 54; displacement of 23; for the less advantaged 58; spatial 10
res publicae 48
res religiosae 48
res sacrae 48
res sanctae 48
resources, distribution of 1, 3–4, 115, 163
rights 5, 121–2
rituals: as spatial practices 118; burial 96–8; Durkheim's theory of 160; funerary 96
Road to Botany Bay, The 103
Roberts, John 63
Roman fiction 45–6
Roman jurisprudence 45, 46n6, 47–9
Roman law 45, 48–50
Rome 45, 47
Rose, Gillian 74, 87–90
Ross, Alison 126
routines 118, 120
ruptures 33–4, 116, 122, 124, 128, 135
Russian Revolution 63
R v Bayley 73n1, 77

SBS Television 64
scenography 41–2

Schiavone, Aldo 37–8
Seeking Spatial Justice 114, 122
self-determination 4
self-development 4
sexual violence 2
shack dwellers' movement 113
Sidis, Boris 151
Situationists 143–5
slum settlements 141
Smith, Sir Thomas 99
social cleansing 57–8
social communion 62
social contract 3
'social factory' 61
social harmony 3
social identity 155n4, 156–8
social justice 4, 122; in space 4; in the city 5; territorial 4
Social Justice and the City 3–4
social ordering 86
Social Production of Urban Space, The 56
social relations: and space 52, 119; capitalist 3
social relationship 62
Social Revolutionaries Press Conference 64
Soja, Edward 5, 114, 122, 163
Sokoloff, William 139
Sophocles, *Antigone* 88, 89
South Africa 113
sovereign power 113
space 7–8; absolute 9, 117; and bodies 22–3; and judgment 24; and knowledge 51–2; and politics 113, 128; and social justice 4; and social relations 52, 119; appropriation of 13, 115, 120–1; as product of interrelations 119; deployment of body in 120; dimensions of 118; distribution of 163; domination of 13; inhabitance of 13, 113, 121, 128; legal 8; of spatial justice 9, 35; political uses 113–14; relational conception of 117, 120; representations of 118; self-management of 121; simultaneity 119; social use 118; transforming into place 98; *see also* public space; procedural space; spaces of representation

spaces of representation 118
Spain 113, 150
spatial justice 7, 9, 13, 14, 35, 116–17, 122; and architecture 133, 147; and art 11, 54; and the crowd 150–1, 156, 162–4; contours of 113–16; emergence of 35, 115; for the dead 107; history 3–6; language of 9; materiality of 75; possibility of 115, 125–8
spatial politics 115, 121, 163
spatial practices 95, 103, 118, 121
spatial segregation 58
Spinoza, Baruch 27
state power 113
status-symbol objects 143
story-telling 95, 103, 104
Struggle Street 64
studium 80
Superstudio 14
surveillance 81
Sydney 54–61, 64; *see also* Bidwill; Chippendale; Redfern
Sydney Festival 2014 64

tactical urbanism 55
Tactical Urbanism Manuals 55
Tafuri, Manfredo 134
Tarde, G. 152–3
Tayne, Hippolyte 151
temporality 79, 163; and the crowd 159
terra nullius 98
'territorial encroachment' 2
Theory of Justice, A 3, 4
Therese, Karen 64, 65
Thomas, Yan 44–9, 52
Thompson, Robert 77
time: concept of 25, 79, 117–19, 123–4; dislocated 81; materiality of 79
Tomba, Massimiliano 125
tombs 48, 96
Tormey, Jane 25, 26
Trabsky, Marc 9, 12–13
travelling 104
treasure troves 99–100
Tronti, Mario 134–5
truth 9, 10, 38, 44–8, 147n17

Ulpian 37–8
urban activism 55
urban development 54, 59–60
urban gardens 55
urban injustice 4, 64
urbanisation 4, 121
urban life 3, 56, 121
urban planning: and public art 55; models 61
urban uprisings 128

Venables, Jon 77
Venice Biennale of Architecture 2012 55
Vico, Giambattista 46n6, 86
vinculum substantiale 123–4
violence 10, 22–35; against women 82; and bodies 31, 33; and judgment 34; and meaning 32; and space 24; continuum of 26–8, 32; divine 125, 126, 163; inescapability of 32; law-preserving 125; law's relation to 81; mythical 125; of surveillance 81; ontological atmosphere of 31; to the female body 81

waiting rooms 161–2
walking 73, 83–4, 90–1; as act of justice 89; as call for justice 86, 90; as call for lawful place 90
Wall, Illan rua 8, 14
Werner, Philip 82, 90
Westbury, Marcus 56
Western jurisprudence 10, 39, 44
Wilmot, William Byam 95, 96, 100–2, 104, 105, 107
withdrawal 6, 31, 33–5, 114; from the atmosphere 35; space of 11, 33
Wolff, Robert Paul 3
working class 61–3; neighbourhoods 56, 57, 59, 62, 63
World War I 154
World War II 63, 155

Youl, Richard 104–5, 107
Young, Alison 77–8
Young, Iris Marion 4–5